Contested Terrain

CONTESTED TERRAIN

The Transformation of the Workplace in the Twentieth Century

RICHARD EDWARDS

Basic Books, Inc., Publishers

NEW YORK

Library of Congress Cataloging in Publication Data

Edwards, Richard C
Contested terrain.

Bibliography: p. 244
Includes index.
1. Labor and laboring classes—United States.
2. Industrial organization—United States.
3. Industrial sociology—Case studies. I. Title.
HD6957.U6E35 301.5′5 78-19942
ISBN 0-465-01412-7

Printed in the United States of America
DESIGNED BY VINCENT TORRE
10 9 8 7 6 5 4 3 2 1

CONTENTS

PREFACE

THE WORKPLACE TODAY is a vastly changed place from the shops and offices of seventy-five or a hundred years ago. Then nearly all employees worked for small firms, while today large numbers toil for the giant corporations. Here especially we see the results of the twentieth-century transformation of work. Where once foremen ruled with unconstrained power, there now stands the impersonality (and seeming invincibility) of the organization. Where once workers had few rights and no protections, there now exists a whole set of claims from job bidding rights to grievance appeals to the possibility of a career within the firm. Where once the distinction between workers and bosses was sharp and clear there now are the blurred lines of a more stratified and less class-conscious workforce.

Yet one feature endures: the workplace remains hierarchical, ruled from the top down. Why does this authoritarian rule exist? What forces have changed the form of hierarchy at work? What prevents producers—the workers—from managing the workplace themselves? And how has the changing organization of work shaped the working class as a whole? These are the questions that I investigate in this book.

These are not new questions, but they deserve reexamination because the conventional answers to them are so unsatisfactory. If you asked most social scientists why work is run by bosses and managers and not by the workers, they would likely tell you that such organization is "necessary" or "inevitable" or perhaps "efficient." Some proclaim, for example, that the hierarchical organization of work is a necessary corollary of modern production technology. Others assert that while hierarchy may not be necessary, it is efficient, making possible more profits for the employer, higher wages for the workers, and greater production for society than alternate arrangements can provide. Even the critics of capitalism, although their work has opened new avenues of investigation that have benefited my work, have not provided satisfactory answers. Some have implicitly accepted the efficiency theory, arguing—and bemoaning—the "fact" that the more modern and allegedly degraded ways of organizing work are more efficient. Other critics have rejected the efficiency argument, seeing instead a desire or a "need" on the part of employers to control workers.

All of these explanations beg serious questions. If hierarchy is technologically required, what accounts for technology's inflexibility in this regard? (This is particularly surprising since, as social and economic circumstances have changed, technology has seemed to be quite flexible in other respects, especially after sufficient time has elapsed to permit the development of new technologies.) If hierarchy is efficient, why has the experimental evidence indicated that self-management contains great potential for raising productivity? (This potential has already attracted much employer interest, though tapping the potential for profit has not been easy.) If some capitalists desire control, why do not other, more single-mindedly–profit-maximizing capitalists drive them out of business?

The explanation I advance is straightforward: hierarchy at work exists and persists because it is *profitable*. Employers are able to increase their profits when they have greater control over the labor process. However, this profitability does not in general result from greater efficiency (as that term is usually understood), and it certainly cannot be easily identified with the greater good of society. Moreover, while hierarchy is consistent with today's technology, that consistency must be understood as arising as much from the shaping of technology to provide greater control for employers as from an "imperative" operating in the other direction. Finally, employers understandably do desire control, but such control is instrumental, a means toward achieving greater profits. Thus, to understand the reason for workplace hierarchy and to comprehend the twentieth-century transformation of the labor process we need to focus on the profit system—that is, on capitalism.

Of course hierarchy has changed as well as persisted, and in searching for what has caused this transformation I have come to realize that the primary catalyst for change is the continuing contention of classes, the struggle of capitalists, workers, and others to protect and advance their interests. And since the strength or weakness, the success or failure, of any class has depended upon its (changing) position within society, we must investigate the larger dynamics of capitalism. In what follows, then, I pay considerable attention to the rise of the large corporation, the transition from predominately competitive to shared-monopoly industries, the growth of unions, and other features of capitalist development seemingly far removed from changes within the workplace itself. Yet these are important elements of the context that determines the possibilities for and constraints on workplace struggles.

This approach emphasizes the social relations of the workplace (rather than, for example, the change from craft-based to mass-production technology) for, I would argue, what is revolutionary about the modern corporation is its ability to restructure the social organization of the labor process. It is only within the context of class relations that the roles of technology and efficiency can be interpreted.

The method I have chosen to use in arguing my thesis is historical. I attempt to trace the various changes in workplace organization that have occurred and to assess the reasons for them. In this endeavor I draw repeatedly on the history and operations of a "panel" of large companies: American Telephone and Telegraph (AT&T), International Business Machines (IBM), Ford Motors, General Electric (GE), Polaroid, Pabst Brewing, Pullman, United States Steel, and International Harvester. The approach taken is not one of case studies per se, but rather repeated appeal to these companies for examples, illustrations, and evidence. My intention is to use these corporations to show how over time the processes of conflict and control have transformed the way work is organized.

I have benefited enormously from the criticism, ideas, and support of several of my friends. Many of the ideas have been developed collectively with Michael Reich. Samuel Bowles has been unendingly generous with his time and help since I began working on this topic several years ago. Joint work with Michael Reich and David Gordon has provided still another source of ideas and refinements. (While I suppose I must accept final responsibility for any mistakes in what follows, these friends have pored over enough of my drafts that they cannot escape completely blameless.) Joseph Bowring undertook several research tasks at little or no pay, and his diligence and intelligence have greatly helped the book. Ann Bookman unselfishly let me use material from her excellent thesis. Albert Hirschman made it possible for me to spend a year at Princeton, during which much of this book was written. Herbert Gintis, Michael Piore, Martin Kessler, Stephen Marglin, Charles Kindleberger, and many of my graduate students and faculty colleagues have read the manuscript and made useful criticisms of it. For all of this help, I am grateful.

Contested Terrain

CHAPTER 1

Three Faces from the Hidden Abode

ROUGHLY one hundred million Americans must work for a living. About ninety-five million of them, when they can find jobs, work for someone else. Three of those workers, who reflect both the unity and the diversity of the American working class, are Maureen Agnati, Fred Doyal, and Stanley Miller. These three share a condition common to all workers, past and present: they must sell their labor time to support themselves. Yet they also lead very different work lives, and the differences contain in kernel form the evolving history of work in twentieth-century America. Indeed, the study of how their jobs came to be so different goes far toward explaining the present weakness and future potential of the American working class.

Maureen Agnati assembles coils at Digitex, Incorporated, a small Boston-area manufacturer of electronics components.[1] Digitex's founder established the firm in the 1930s and continues to manage it today. The company employs about 450 people, four-fifths of whom are production workers. The labor force is mainly female and Portuguese, with a sprinkling of other ethnic workers—Italian, Haitian, Greek, Polish, and Asian.

Maureen is a white, twenty-six-year-old mother of two girls. Her husband Tom works in a warehouse at a nearby sheet-metal company. Maureen has worked for Digitex off and on for a number of years; she started after her junior year in high school, quit at nineteen when her first child was born, returned for one month to get Christmas money, quit again, and then returned again to work the spring months until the end of her older daughter's school term. Frequent job changes do not seem to be any problem at Digitex, and indeed, in some ways the company appears to encourage high turnover.

Maureen's work involves winding coil forms with copper wire. To do this, Maureen operates a machine that counts and controls the number of wraps put on each collar. She does the same task all day.

Nearly half of Digitex's workers are on the piece-rate system, which means that their wages partly depend on how fast they work. The company pays both a guaranteed base wage and a piece-rate bonus on top of the base. But the guaranteed wage is always low—roughly equal to the legal minimum wage—so the worker's attention turns to making the bonus. To be eligible for extra pay, a worker must exceed the particular job's "rate"; that is, the assigned minimum level of output needed to trigger the incentive system. The worker then earns a bonus depending on how many units she produces above the rate. The problem is that the rates are high and are often changed. For example, when Maureen returned to work this last time, she found that the rates were so "tight" that she frequently did not make any incentive pay at all. It seems to be common that when workers begin to make large premiums, the time-study man appears to "restudy" the job, and the rates cause a great deal of resentment.

The pay system causes resentment among the hourly workers too. The company keeps most of the information about wages secret; a worker cannot learn, for example, what her job's top pay is, how the job is classified, or even what the wage schedule is. Often two workers will discover that, while they are doing nearly the same work, their pay differs greatly.

As for the conditions of work, employees are watched constantly, like children in a classroom. The design of the machinery pretty much dictates what tasks have to be done at each work station, but in other ways the foreman actively directs the work. One way he does this is by assigning workers to particular stations. For example, Maureen was not hired specifically for "winding" and when she returned to work her foreman simply put her at the station. But he can change job assignments whenever he wishes, and he often moves people around. Since some jobs have easy rates and others have tight ones, the job he assigns Maureen to will determine both how much she makes and how hard she has to work.

The foreman and supervisors at Digitex have other ways of directing the work, too. They watch closely over the hours and pace of work, and they ring a bell to signal the beginning and end of work breaks. Workers must get permission to make phone calls or leave the work area. And despite the piece-rate system (which might seem to leave it up to the individual worker to determine how fast to work and hence how much pay she would receive), the bosses take a direct hand in speeding up production; workers who talk to nearby workers, who fail to make the rates, or who return late from breaks or lunch are likely to be targets for reprimands and threats. The various bosses (foremen, general foreman, and other officials) spend their days walking among the workers, noting and correcting any laggard performance.

The supervisors' immediate role in directing production gives them considerable power, of course, yet their full power springs from other sources as well. No real grievance process exists at Digitex, and supervisors can dismiss workers on the spot. Less drastically, foremen maintain a certain degree of control because they must approve any "benefits" the workers receive. They must approve in advance any requests for time off to attend a funeral, see a doctor, and so on. For hourly workers, the supervisors determine any pay raises; since the wage schedules are secret, supervisors can choose when and whom to reward, and in what amount. For piece-rate workers, who are not eligible for raises, the supervisors' decisions on rejects—what to count as faulty output and whether to penalize the workers for it—weigh heavily in bonus calculations. Foremen also choose favored workers for the opportunity to earn overtime pay. And when business falls off and the company needs to reduce its workforce, no seniority or other considerations intervene; the foremen decide which workers to lay off. Through these powers, supervisors effectively rule over all aspects of factory life. Getting on the foreman's good side means much; being on his bad side tends to make life miserable.

Maureen, like other production workers at Digitex, has few prospects for advancing beyond her current position. All people working under the piece-rate system, regardless of seniority, earn the same base pay. There are a few supervisory slots, but these jobs are necessarily limited in number and are currently filled. There simply is no place for them to grow. This fact perhaps accounts for the high turnover at Digitex: over half the employees have worked for the company for less than three years, and Maureen's pattern of frequently quitting her job does not seem to be unusual.

There has recently been a bitter struggle to build a union at Digitex. Maureen's attitude—"We could sure use one around here, I'll tell you that"—was perhaps typical, but the real issue was whether the company's powers of intimidation would prove stronger than the workers' desire for better conditions. Initially, the union won a federally monitored election to be the workers' bargaining agent. The company's hostility toward the union persisted, however; after signing an initial contract with the union it launched a vicious campaign to decertify the union. The second time around, the union lost. No union exists at Digitex today.

Fred Doyal works as process control inspector at General Electric's

Ashland (Massachusetts) assembly plant. The plant used to be run by Telechron Clock Company, a small independent firm, but GE bought it out. Today, the plant's thousand or so workers manufacture small electrical motors, the kind used in clocks, kitchen timers, and other very small appliances. The plant is highly automated, and slightly over half of its workers are women.

Fred operates sound-testing machinery to check the motors' noise levels. He monitors two hundred or so motors a day. The procedure is routine—he picks up the motors from the assembly area, returns to the "silent room," mounts them on the decibel counter, and records the result—and he performs virtually the same sequence every day. GE pays Fred about $13,000 a year.

There is little need for the supervisor to direct the work pace; the machinery does that, and when "you come on the job, you learn that routine; unless there is some change in that routine, the foreman would not be coming to you and telling you what to do; he just expects you (and you do) to know your daily routine, when you do repetitious work." In fact, the foreman generally appears only when a special situation arises, such as defective materials or machine breakdown. Other than that, workers mainly have contact with their bosses on disciplinary problems.

Evaluation and discipline do bring in the supervisors, but the union's presence tends to restrict their power. In a sense, the company evaluates Fred's work daily: "Everything I do, I record, and I turn in daily reports." The reports provide information not only about the decibel level of the motors but also coincidentally about Fred's output. Yet he is very confident that if he does a reasonable amount of work, his job will be secure. If the company tried to fire him, it would have to demonstrate to an outside arbitrator that its action is justified. In fact, any time the company takes disciplinary action, the union contract says that arbitration is automatic. In arbitration, Fred notes, the union has found that "discharge on a long-service employee, unless there's a horrendous record on this person, or if it was for something like striking a supervisor or stealing, discharge would be considered too severe by an arbitrator. Usually, you know? Don't bet on it, but that's the usual case."

There are, of course, lesser penalties. The disciplinary procedure begins with the written warning, and when the worker gets three written warnings, he or she can be suspended. Fred himself has been suspended for two days for "refusing to do a certain type of work." Suspension means the loss of pay, and it is probably the most common discipline at Ashland. Fred has known people who were suspended for up to a week because of absenteeism, and for lesser periods because of tardiness and insubordination.

Fred is in his mid-fifties, and he has worked for GE for thirty years. He started as a stock handler in the Worcester (Massachusetts) plant, moved up to be a group leader in the packing department, then transferred to shipping. At one point he had several employees under him, but he was "knocked off that job in a cutback." When they consolidated the plants he moved to Ashland to work in quality control. Presently he does not supervise anyone.

While Fred was moving up, the company had no formal procedure for filling vacancies. Switching from one job to another depended on "merit and so forth . . . some of it was ass-kissing." Now, however, in a change that Fred traces directly to the coming of the union, a new system prevails. If any job opens up, it must be posted, and everyone can apply for it. Qualifications and seniority are supposed to be taken into account in determining who gets the job. The company usually wants to decide unilaterally who is qualified, but "the union fights the company on this all the way." In fact, in Fred's experience the union is usually successful: "The company, rather than get in a hassle, and if they have no particular bitch against this individual who has the most seniority, the company will give that person the job."

Men do a lot better at Ashland than women. The plant jobs seems quite rigidly stereotyped. Women fill most of the lower-paying positions on the clock-assembly conveyors, while the men tend to get the more skilled jobs elsewhere in the plant. Men's jobs are also more secure. In the event of a partial layoff, any worker in a higher-classified job can bump any other worker of equal or lesser seniority in a lower-classified job; but of course one cannot bump upwards. Women, since they tend to be in the lower classifications, have few others (mainly women) whom they can bump. Men have most of the women to bump.

Fred believes that General Electric has not overlooked the benefits of this system.

> "Where that company has made all its money is on the conveyors; that's where they really build the clocks, see—a long assembly conveyor, thirty-five, forty women working on it. Those women are working every minute of the day; those women *really* make money for the company! The company didn't get rich on me, and the older I get, the less rich it's gonna get on me. But they got rich on those women. Those women are there every second, every second of their time is taken up. Now, they have on each of these conveyors what they call a group leader, and it's a woman, right? . . . These women are *highly* qualified, *highly* skilled, these group leaders. Way underpaid. There's a man that stock-handles the conveyor—man or a boy, whichever you want—he's just a 'hunky,' picks up boxes and puts them on the conveyor for the girls or moves heavy stuff. That man makes ten to fifteen dollars a week more than a woman who's a group leader."

In the supervisory staff, the sexual stereotyping is even more apparent.

There are quite a few bosses, counting all the foremen, general foremen, and higher managers. Yet there are only two women. "There have always been two; not always the same two, but two."

Recently, the rigid sexual division seems to have lessened somewhat, and women have applied for jobs that formerly were off limits. According to Fred, the company is wary of turning them down, because it is worried about a government antidiscrimination suit. (GE subsequently settled the suit, agreeing to pay damages.) The union has made some attempt to change the ratio of women's to men's wages, but Fred acknowledges that it has been "unsuccessful."

At the plant, men and women alike are very concerned about the possibilities of a general layoff. As Fred puts it,

> I'll give it to the company; they're great with the public relations bit. GE puts out two, three bulletins a week, and they're always telling those people [the plant's workers] about the foreign competition. What they're trying to do, and they're successful, is getting the idea across that if they don't work harder, if they don't stop taking off days off, and quit taking so much time on their coffee break, and so forth, that they're gonna have to take the plant and move it to Singapore, which, by the way, they have a plant in Singapore that makes clocks. . . . They've been very successful at this productivity thing, you know. They've scared people with it. This company, like a lot of companies, runs the thing by fear.

Fred is a strong supporter of the union (the United Electrical Workers), and he has from time to time held various official positions in the local. He is completely disillusioned about the AFL-CIO ("They sold out a long time ago"). For him, just following the Democratic Party is not enough: "Any union movement that doesn't have a political philosophy in this country is doomed."

Stanley Harris works as a research chemist at the Polaroid Corporation. "Research chemist" may sound like a high-powered position, and indeed the pay is quite good: Stanley makes about $18,000. But in terms of the actual work involved, the position is more mundane. Stanley's bachelor degree equips him to do only relatively routine laboratory procedures. He cannot choose his own research, and he does not have a special area of expertise. He supervises no one, and instead his own work is done under supervision. Stanley is, in effect, a technical worker.

On first meeting Stanley, one is not surprised to learn of his middle-level occupation. He is white, roughly fifty years old, and seems well educated. Despite the fact that it is the middle of the workday, his proffered hand is clean (and soft). He wears no special work clothes, spurning both the heavy fabrics necessary in production jobs and the suit and tie affected by the managers. In the lab, of course, he wears a white protective smock, but beneath is an unstylish, small-collar Dacron sports shirt and chino pants.

Here and there, traces of a blue-collar background appear. Stanley has a few teeth missing. His speech retains a slight working-class accent, and occasionally his grammar betrays him. He mentions that he lives in Lynn (Massachusetts), an old working-class city outside of Boston.

Stanley's career tells much about the employment system at Polaroid. He joined the company nineteen years ago as a production worker, when he "ran out of money going through college." Having already completed the science curriculum, he went to night school to fulfill his liberal arts requirements while continuing to work at Polaroid. After obtaining his BS degree, he began applying for the research openings advertised on the company's bulletin boards, and since Polaroid's hiring policies give preference to those who are already employees, the company eventually promoted Stanley into one of the lab jobs. These jobs encompass many ranks, from assistant scientist all the way up to senior scientist. Stanley started at the bottom, and his current position, research scientist, appears in the middle of the hierarchy.

In most of the research jobs, the specific work to be done combines a particular product assignment with the general skills and work behavior expected of a research chemist. Stanley's supervisor assigns him a project within the "general sweep of problems, anything having to do with a company product." Stanley then methodically applies standard tests ("the state of the art"), one after the other, until he finds the answer or his supervisor redirects his efforts. Rather than having his workday closely supervised by his boss or directed by a machine, Stanley follows professional work patterns, habits that are, in fact, common to the eight hundred or so other research workers at Polaroid's Tech Square facility.

Stanley's supervisor formally evaluates his work performance in the annual review. Although the evaluation format seems to change frequently—"Right now it is very curt, either 'good,' 'bad,' or 'indifferent'; but in previous years it was something like four pages"—the purpose and importance of the review have not changed. Stanley believes that the evaluation is crucial to his chances for promotion. "It goes to someone who has to okay it, and if he doesn't know you and he sees on a piece of paper 'poor worker,' it hurts you."

The formal evaluations are especially important because, while Stanley's boss assigns him projects and evaluates his work, he has little say in Stanley's promotions or pay raises or discipline. Those decisions are made higher up, by applying the company's rules to the individual's case. As Stanley explains it, the company contributes the formula while the individual provides the numbers, and then somebody "upstairs" just has to do the calculation. The rules for advancement seem pretty clear.

An important illustration of Stanley's point is the company's layoff policy. When demand for Polaroid's cameras fell off during the 1974–1975 recession, the company laid off sixteen hundred workers, about 15 percent of its entire workforce. Such a deep cut could be expected to create lasting insecurity among Polaroid's workers, and it undoubtedly did among the younger workers. But not for Stanley; the company's seniority-based bumping system protects him. If Polaroid eliminates Stanley's current job, he can displace any worker with less seniority in any of the jobs that he has previously held. "I'm not worried because of the fact that I started at the bottom, and so in theory I could bump my way all the way back to the bottom." In Stanley's view, such an enormous economic disaster would be required before layoffs reached him that, "I figure we'll all be out of work."

Stanley summed up his attitude toward unions in one word: "antagonistic." But the reason for his hostility is, perhaps, surprising. "Like all the movements that are idealistic at the beginning, they [unions] have degenerated to where they benefit a select group. . . . I'm not saying the idea is bad, but they have been corrupted." Stanley sees no use for a union in his own job, since, "if I put out, I'll get the rewards; at least, that's what I've found."

Maureen Agnati, Fred Doyal, Stanley Miller. Three different workers, three different ways of organizing work. Today we observe their situations as simply different arrangements in production, but they are in fact endpoints in a long process of capitalist development that has transformed (and continues to transform) the American workplace. The change does not reflect inevitable consequences of modern technology or of industrial society, but rather (as later chapters will argue) the transformation occurred because continuing capital accumulation has propelled workers and their employers into virtually perpetual conflict. And while both technology and the requirements of modern social production play a part in the story to come, the roots of this conflict lie in the basic arrangements of capitalist production.

Conflict and Control in the Workplace

Capitalism itself came into being when labor power (as opposed to merely labor's products) became a commodity, that is, a thing bought and sold in the market. Employers, in business to make profits, begin by investing their funds (money capital) in the raw materials, labor power, machinery, and other commodities needed for production; they then organize the labor process itself, whereby the constituents of production are set in motion to produce useful products or services; and finally, by selling the products of labor, capitalists reconvert their property back to money. If the money capital obtained at the end of this cycle exceeds that invested initially, the capitalists have earned a profit.

Focusing on the central role of the labor process in this sequence, Karl Marx noted that:

> The money-owner buys everything necessary for [production], such as raw material [and labor power], in the market, and pays for it at its full value . . . . The consumption of labor power is completed, as in the case of every other commodity, outside the limits of the market. . . . Accompanied by Mr. Moneybags and by the possessor of labor power, we therefore take leave for a time of this noisy sphere, where everything takes place on the surface and in view of all men, and follow them both into the hidden abode of production, on whose threshold there stares us in the face, "No admittance except on business." Here we shall see, not only how capital produces, but how capital is produced. We shall at last force the secret of profit making.
>
> On leaving this sphere of [the market], . . . we think we can perceive a change in the physiognomy of our dramatis personae. He, who before was the money-owner, now strides in front as capitalist; the possessor of labor power follows as his laborer. The one with an air of importance, smirking, intent on business; the other, timid and holding back, like one who is bringing his own hide to market and has nothing to expect but—a hiding.[2]

The market equality between buyer and seller of the commodity labor power disappears in this "hidden abode," and the capitalist takes charge. No wonder the capitalist strides ahead, "intent on business," for it turns out that the commodity he has purchased is not what is useful to him. What the capitalist buys in the labor market is the right to a certain quantity of what Marx has called *labor power*, that is, the worker's capacity to do work.[3] Labor power can be thought of as being measured in time units (hours, days) and it may be improved or expanded by any skills, education, or other attributes that make it more productive than "simple" labor power. Thus, the capitalist, in hiring a carpenter for a day, buys one day's quantity of carpenter labor power.

But the capacity to do work is useful to the capitalist only if the work actually gets done. Work, or what Marx called *labor,* is the actual human effort in the process of production. If labor power remains merely a potentiality or capacity, no goods get produced and the capitalist has no products to sell for profit. Once the wages-for-time exchange has been made, the capitalist cannot rest content. He has purchased a given quantity of labor power, but he must now "stride ahead" and strive to extract actual labor from the labor power he now legally owns.

Workers must provide labor power in order to receive their wages, that is, they must show up for work; but they need not necessarily provide *labor*, much less the amount of labor that the capitalist desires to extract from the labor power they have sold. In a situation where workers do not control their own labor process and cannot make their work a creative experience, any exertion beyond the minimum needed to avert boredom will not be in the workers' interest. On the other side, for the capitalist it is true *without limit* that the more work he can wring out of the labor power he has purchased, the more goods will be produced; and they will be produced without any increased wage costs. It is this discrepancy between what the capitalist can buy in the market and what he needs for production that makes it imperative for him to control the labor process and the workers' activities. The capitalist need not be motivated to control things by an obsession for power; a simple desire for profit will do.

These basic relationships in production reveal both the basis for conflict and the problem of control at the workplace.* Conflict exists because the interests of workers and those of employers collide, and what is good for one is frequently costly for the other. Control is rendered problematic because, unlike the other commodities involved in production, labor power is always embodied in people, who have their own interests and needs and who retain their power to resist being treated like a commodity. Indeed, today's most important employers, the large corporations, have so many employees that to keep them working diligently is itself a major task, employing a vast workforce of its own. From the capitalist's perspective, this is seen as the

*Of course, this conflict is only superficially confronted with regard to an individual worker. Any worker who, once on the job, refuses to work or who even works less than the most eager job-seeking unemployed person will simply be fired. Individual resistance by a worker, if it is detected, is easily dealt with, so long as a replacement is standing by in the unemployment line. Meaningful conflict arises, then, with regard to groups of workers or an employer's or an entire industry's workforce. The amount of labor that can be extracted from the purchased labor power depends on the workforce's willingness to perform useful work and the enterprise's ability to compel or evoke such work.

problem of management, and it is often analyzed simply in terms of the techniques of administration and business "leadership." But employment creates a two-sided relationship, with workers contributing as much to its final form as managers or capitalists.

In some cases, the management task may be trivial. Employers may, for example, contract for particular labor services when workers are hired; if the exact nature of the duties can be spelled out beforehand, competition among job applicants—i.e., the labor market—effectively enforces the contract. Similarly, employers may pay only for work actually done; if each worker's output is independent, piece-rate pay compels adequate production. Other workplace schemes may be directed toward the same end.

In general, however, capitalists have found it neither practical nor profitable to rely on such devices. Complete market contracting (by exhaustively specifying the worker's duties before hire) is usually impossible and almost always too expensive. Piece-rate pay has limited application and frequently engenders conflict over the rates themselves. In both cases, evaluation of the contracted work raises further problems. Other schemes—profit sharing, the distributing of company stock to workers, and more elaborate incentive schemes—also fail. Most importantly, all these devices founder because their targets, the workers, retain their ability to resist. Typically, then, the task of extracting labor from workers who have no direct stake in profits remains to be carried out in the workplace itself. Conflict arises over how work shall be organized, what work pace shall be established, what conditions producers must labor under, what rights workers shall enjoy, and how the various employees of the enterprise shall relate to each other. The workplace becomes a battleground, as employers attempt to extract the maximum effort from workers and workers necessarily resist their bosses' impositions.

An academic observer at the beginning of the 1930s gives us a glimpse of this workplace conflict in his account of one worker's experience:

> "Red," a beginner in industry, was working on an assembly line in a phonograph factory, producing small motors, on hourly rate. The line was turning out an average of only 30 motors a day. "Red" found it so easy to keep up his part of the work that he would pile up parts ahead of the next worker in the line. He would then move over and help perform the next operation until the other worker caught up. This went on until "Red" was shifted by the foreman to the final operation in the assembly line. Here he was in a position to work as fast as he liked so far as passing on his completed work was concerned, but he was constantly waiting for the man behind. In order not to appear slow this man had to put through a few more parts, which had its effect all along the assembly line. The process of speeding up developed slowly until the gang, which formerly put through about 30 motors a day, was turning out an average of 120 a day. To "Red's" surprise, the men objected strenuously to this increase, argued with

him and even threatened to "meet him in the alley" unless he slowed down his production. "Red" said that when production got up above 100 motors a day the threats became so insistent he began to fear "they might really mean something."[4]

When he placed "Red" at the end of the line, the foreman initiated the conflict by forcing a speed-up on all workers, and in self-defense they responded. In this case, our observer tells us, the workers won and " 'Red's' problem was 'solved' by his transfer to another department."

A similar situation, more recent, concerns a General Motors plant in 1971:

> At Lordstown, efficiency became the watchword. At 60 cars an hour, the pace of work had not been exactly leisurely, but after [new managers] came in the number of cars produced almost doubled. Making one car a minute had been no picnic, especially on a constantly moving line. Assembly work fits the worker to the pace of the machine. Each work station is no more than 6 to 8 feet long. For example, within a minute on the line, a worker in the trim department had to walk about 20 feet to a conveyor belt transporting parts to the line, pick up a front seat weighing 30 pounds, carry it back to his work station, place the seat on the chassis, and put in four bolts to fasten it down by first hand-starting the bolts and then using an air gun to tighten them according to standard. It was steady work when the line moved at 60 cars an hour. When it increased to more than 100 cars an hour, the number of operations on this job were not reduced and the pace became almost maddening. In 36 seconds the worker had to perform at least eight different operations, including walking, lifting, hauling, lifting the carpet, bending to fasten the bolts by hand, fastening them by air gun, replacing the carpet, and putting a sticker on the hood. Sometimes the bolts fail to fit into the holes; the gun refuses to function at the required torque; the seats are defective or the threads are bare on the bolt. But the line does not stop.[5]

These illustrations involve assembly-line production, but the basic relations exist in all workplaces; indeed, the shopfloor, the office, the drafting room, the warehouse, the hospital ward, the construction site, and the hotel kitchen all become places of continuing conflict. Workers resist the discipline and the pace that employers try to impose. At most times the workers' efforts are solitary and hidden; individual workers find relief from oppressive work schedules by doing what their bosses perceive as slacking off or intentionally sabotaging work. At other times resistance is more conspiratorial; informal work groups agree on how fast they will work and combine to discipline rate-busters; or technicians work to rules, sticking to the letter of the production manual and thereby slowing work to a fraction of normal efficiency. More openly, workers or even union locals (often against the commands of their leaders) walk off the job to protest firings, arbitrary discipline, unsafe working conditions, or other grievances. More public still, established unions or groups seeking to achieve bargaining rights strike in order to shut down production entirely.

The struggle in the workplace has a closely intertwined parallel in the bargaining that goes on in the marketplace. Here conflict concerns wages, as labor and capital contend over the reward for the laborer's time. Sometimes this bargaining occurs collectively; sometimes it takes an individual form. At times wage bargaining creates a crisis; at other times it assumes an entirely pacific form. But here, too, the clash of interests persists.

Thus, in the slogan, "A fair day's work for a fair day's pay," *both* elements become matters of conflict. "A fair day's work" is as much an issue for bargaining, resistance, and struggle as is the "fair day's pay." The old Wobbly* demand—"Good Pay or Bum Work!"—expressed one connection. But especially in times (such as the 1910s and 1930s) when self-consciously anticapitalist groups have appeared, these two conflicts merge to challenge the very basis of capitalist production itself.

Conflict in the labor process occurs under definite historical circumstances, or, what is the same, within a specific economic and social context. Most importantly, production is part of the larger process of capital accumulation, that is, the cycle of investment of prior profits, organization of production, sale of produced commodities, realization of profits (or loss), and reinvestment of new profits. This process constitutes the fundamental dynamic of a capitalist economy. But capital accumulation, while it remains the basic theme, is played out with substantial variations, and a whole set of factors—the degree of competition among capitalists, the size of corporations, the extent of trade union organization, the level of class consciousness among workers, the impact of governmental policies, the speed of technological change, and so on—influence the nature and shape and pace of accumulation. Taken together, these various forces provide both possibilities for and constraints on what can occur within the workplace. What was possible or successful in one era may be impossible or disastrous in another. Conflict at work, then, must be understood as a product of both the strategies or wills of the combatants and definite conditions not wholly within the grasp of either workers or capitalists. As Marx put it,

> People make their own history, but they do not make it just as they please; they do not make it under circumstances chosen by themselves, but under circumstances directly found, given, and transmitted from the past.[6]

Conflict occurs within definite limits imposed by a social and historical context, yet this context rarely determines everything about work organization. After technological constraints, the discipline of the market, and other forces have been taken into account, there remains a certain indeterminacy to the labor process. This space for the working out of workplace conflict is particularly evident within the large corporation, where external constraints

*A member of the radical Industrial Workers of the World (IWW), a labor organization that was a strong force between 1905 and 1920.

have been reduced to a minimum. Here especially, the essential question remains: how shall work be organized?

The labor process becomes an arena of class conflict, and the workplace becomes a contested terrain. Faced with chronic resistance to their effort to compel production, employers over the years have attempted to resolve the matter by reorganizing, indeed revolutionizing, the labor process itself. Their goal remains profits; their strategies aim at establishing structures of control at work. That is, capitalists have attempted to organize production in such a way as to minimize workers' opportunities for resistance and even alter workers' perceptions of the desirability of opposition. Work has been organized, then, to contain conflict. In this endeavor employers have sometimes been successful.

The Dimensions of Control

How much work gets done every hour or every day emerges as a result of the struggle between workers and capitalists. As later chapters will describe, each side seeks to tip the balance and influence or determine the outcome with the weapons at its disposal. On one side, the workers use hidden or open resistance to protect themselves against the constant pressure for speed-up; on the other side, capitalists employ a variety of sophisticated or brutal devices for tipping the balance their way. But this is not exactly an equal fight, for employers retain their power to hire and fire, and on this foundation they have developed various methods of control by which to organize, shape, and affect the workers' exertions.

Control in this sense differs from coordination, a term that appears more frequently in popular literature describing what managers do, and it may be useful at the outset to distinguish the two. Coordination is required, of course, in all social production, since the product of such production is by definition the result of labor by many persons. Hence, whether a pair of shoes is produced in a Moroccan cobbler's shop, a Chinese commune, or an American factory, it is an inherent technical characteristic of the production process that the persons cutting and tanning the leather must mesh their efforts with those who sew the leather, those who attach the heels, and others. Without such coordination, production would be haphazard, wasteful, and—where products more complex than shoes are involved—probably impossible as well. Hence, coordination of social production is essential.[7]

Coordination may be achieved in a variety of ways, however, and the differences are crucial. Coordination may be achieved by tradition—through long-established ways of doing the work and the passing on of these trade secrets from master to apprentices. Or it may be achieved directly by the producers themselves, as occurs when the members of a cooperative or commune discuss their parts in the production process to ensure that their tasks are harmonized. As the scale of production increases, workers may designate one member (or even choose someone from the outside) to act as a full-time coordinator of their interests, thus establishing a manager. As long as the managerial staff, no matter how large, remains accountable to the producers themselves, we may properly speak of their efforts as "coordination" or "administration."

A different type of coordination characterizes capitalist workplaces, however; in capitalist production, labor power is purchased, and with that purchase—as with the purchase of every commodity in a capitalist economy—goes the right to designate the use (consumption) of the object bought. Hence there is a presumption, indeed a contractual right backed by legal force, for the capitalist, as owner of the purchased labor power, to direct its use. A corollary presumption (again backed by legal force) follows: that the workers whose labor power has been purchased have no right to participate in the conception and planning of production. Coordination occurs in capitalist production as it must inevitably occur in all social production, but it necessarily takes the specific form of top-down coordination, for the exercise of which the top (capitalists) must be able to control the bottom (workers). In analyzing capitalist production, then, it is more appropriate to speak of control than of coordination, although of course, control is a means of coordination.*

"Control" is here defined as the ability of capitalists and/or managers to obtain desired work behavior from workers. Such ability exists in greater or lesser degrees, depending upon the relative strength of workers and their bosses. As long as capitalist production continues, control exists to some

*As this implies, control is thus not a form of coordination unique to capitalism, since it obtains, for example, in slave societies and in socialist societies like the U.S.S.R., where democratic coordination over the labor process has not been established. Coercive coordination is required in all class-based social systems.

Even where workers and capitalists enjoyed precisely the same objective interests in the efficiency or productivity of production—as would be true, for example, where each worker's wage was simply a fixed percentage of the firm's "profits"—coordination would take the form of control. Imagine that the capitalist and workers of a firm disagreed on how best to pursue maximum profits; as long as the capitalist has the final say, rather than being accountable to the workers, management must be able to force the workers to follow the capitalist's program rather than the workers'. As this example illustrates, coordination need not involve coercion, but control does.

degree, and the crucial questions are: to what degree? how is control obtained? and how does control lead to or inhibit resistance on a wider scale? At one extreme, capitalists try to avoid strikes, sit-downs, and other militant actions that stop production; but equally important to their success, they attempt to extract, day by day, greater amounts of labor for a given amount of labor power.

In what follows, the *system of control* (in other words, the social relations of production within the firm) are thought of as a way in which three elements are coordinated:

1. Direction, or a mechanism or method by which the employer directs work tasks, specifying what needs to be done, in what order, with what degree of precision or accuracy, and in what period of time.
2. Evaluation, or a procedure whereby the employer supervises and evaluates to correct mistakes or other failures in production, to assess each worker's performance, and to identify individual workers or groups of workers who are not performing work tasks adequately.
3. Discipline, or an apparatus that the employer uses to discipline and reward workers, in order to elicit cooperation and enforce compliance with the capitalist's direction of the labor process.

The Types of Control

Systems of control in the firm have undergone dramatic changes in response to changes in the firm's size, operations, and environment and in the workers' success in imposing their own goals at the workplace. The new forms did not emerge as sharp, discrete discontinuities in historical evolution, but neither were they simply points in a smooth and inevitable evolution. Rather, each transformation occurred as a resolution of intensifying conflict and contradiction in the firm's operations. Pressures built up, making the old forms of control untenable. The period of increasing tension was followed by a relatively rapid process of discovery, experimentation, and implementation, in which new systems of control were substituted for the older, more primitive ones. Once instituted, these new relations tend to persist until they no longer effectively contain worker resistance or until further changes occur in the firm's operations.

In the nineteenth century, most businesses were small and were subject to the relatively tight discipline of substantial competition in product markets. The typical firm had few resources and little energy to invest in creating more sophisticated management structures. A single entrepreneur, usually flanked by a small coterie of foremen and managers, ruled the firm. These bosses exercised power personally, intervening in the labor process often to exhort workers, bully and threaten them, reward good performance, hire and fire on the spot, favor loyal workers, and generally act as despots, benevolent or otherwise. They had a direct stake in translating labor power into labor, and they combined both incentives and sanctions in an idiosyncratic and unsystematic mix. There was little structure to the way power was exercised, and workers were often treated arbitrarily. Since workforces were small and the boss was both close and powerful, workers had limited success when they tried to oppose his rule. This system of "simple" control survives today in the small-business sector of the American economy, where it has necessarily been amended by the passage of time and by the borrowings of management practices from the more advanced corporate sector, but it retains its essential principles and mode of operation. It is the system of simple control that governs Maureen Agnati's job at Digitex.

Near the end of the nineteenth century, the tendencies toward concentration of economic resources undermined simple control; while firms' needs for control increased, the efficacy of simple control declined. The need for coordination appeared to increase not only with the complexity of the product but also with the scale of production. By bringing under one corporate roof what were formerly small independent groups linked through the market, the corporation more than proportionately raised the degree of coordination needed. Production assumed an increasingly social character, requiring greater "social" planning and implying an increased need for control. But as firms began to employ thousands of workers, the distance between capitalists and workers expanded, and the intervening space was filled by growing numbers of foremen, general foremen, supervisors, superintendents, and other minor officials. Whereas petty tyranny had been more or less successful when conducted by entrepreneurs (or foremen close to them), the system did not work well when staffed by hired bosses. The foremen came into increasingly severe conflict with both their bosses and their workers.

The workers themselves resisted speed-up and arbitrary rule more successfully, since they were now concentrated by the very growth of the enterprise.[8] From the Homestead and Pullman strikes to the great 1919–1920 steel strike, workers fought with their bosses over control of the actual process of production. The maturing labor movement and an emergent Socialist Party organized the first serious challenge to capitalist rule. Intensifying conflict in society at large and the specific contradictions of simple control in the workplace combined to produce an acute crisis of control on the shop floor.

The large corporations fashioned the most far-reaching response to this crisis. During the conflict, big employers joined small ones in supporting direct repression of their adversaries. But the large corporations also began to move in systematic ways to reorganize work. They confronted the most serious problems of control, but they also commanded the greatest resources with which to attack the problems. Their size and their substantial market power released them from the tight grip of short-run market discipline and made possible for the first time planning in the service of long-term profits. The initial steps taken by large companies—welfare capitalism, scientific management, and company unions—constituted experiments, trials with serious inherent errors, but useful learning experiences nonetheless. In retrospect, these efforts appear as beginnings in the corporations' larger project of establishing more secure control over the labor process.

Large firms developed methods of organization that are more formalized and more consciously contrived than simple control; they are "structural" forms of control. Two possibilities existed: more formal, consciously contrived controls could be embedded in either the physical structure of the labor process (producing "technical" control) or in its social structure (producing "bureaucratic" control). In time, employers used both, for they found that the new systems made control more institutional and hence less visible to workers, and they also provided a means for capitalists to control the "intermediate layers," those extended lines of supervision and power.

Technical control emerged from employers' experiences in attempting to control the production (or blue-collar) operations of the firm. The assembly line came to be the classic image, but the actual application of technical control was much broader. Machinery itself directed the labor process and set the pace. For a time, employers had the best of two worlds. Inside the firm, technical control turned the tide of conflict in their favor, reducing workers to attendants of prepaced machinery; externally, the system strengthened the employer's hands by expanding the number of potential substitute workers. But as factory workers in the late 1930s struck back with sit-downs, their action exposed the deep dangers to employers in thus linking all workers' labor together in one technical apparatus. The conflict at the workplace propelled labor into its "giant step," the CIO.

These forces have produced today a second type of work organization. Whereas simple control persists in the small firms of the industrial periphery, in large firms, especially those in the mass-production industries, work is subject to technical control. The system is mutually administered by management and (as a junior partner) unions. Jobs in the GE plant where Fred Doyal works fit this pattern.

There exists a third method for organizing work, and it too appeared in the large firms. This system, bureaucratic control, rests on the principle of embedding control in the social structure or the social relations of the workplace. The defining feature of bureaucratic control is the institutionalization of hierarchical power. "Rule of law"—the firm's law—replaces "rule by supervisor command" in the direction of work, the procedures for evaluating workers' performance, and the exercise of the firm's sanctions and rewards; supervisors and workers alike become subject to the dictates of "company policy." Work becomes highly stratified; each job is given its distinct title and description; and impersonal rules govern promotion. "Stick with the corporation," the worker is told, "and you can ascend up the ladder." The company promises the workers a *career*.

Bureaucratic control originated in employers' attempts to subject nonproduction workers to more strict control, but its success impelled firms to apply the system more broadly than just to the white-collar staff. Especially in the last three decades, bureaucratic control has appeared as the organizing principle in both production and nonproduction jobs in many large firms, and not the least of its attractions is that the system has proven especially effective in forestalling unionism. Stanley Miller's job at Polaroid is subject to bureaucratic control.

Continuing conflict in the workplace and employers' attempts to contain it have thus brought the modern American working class under the sway of three quite different systems for organizing and controlling their work: simple control, technical control (with union participation), and bureaucratic control. Of course, the specific labor processes vary greatly: Maureen Agnati's coil wrapper might have been a typewriter or a cash register, Fred Doyal's job might have been in a tire plant or a tractor factory, and Stanley Miller's work might have involved being a supervisor or skilled craftsman. Yet within this variety of concrete labors, the three patterns for organizing work prevail.

The typology of control embodies both the pattern of historical evolution and the array of contemporary methods of organizing work. On the one hand, each form of control corresponds to a definite stage in the development of the representative or most important firms; in this sense structural control succeeded simple control and bureaucratic control succeeded technical control, and the systems of control correspond to or characterize stages of capitalism. On the other hand, capitalist production has developed unevenly, with some sectors pushing far in advance of other sectors, and so each type of control represents an alternate method of organizing work; so long as uneven development produces disparate circumstances, alternate methods will coexist.

The following chapters explore the dynamic of class conflict within the labor process; but the impact of this dynamic extends far beyond the workplace. The redivision of labor splintered the working class; rather than creating new "classes," it has established enduring *fractions* of the same class, and, as the last chapter will suggest, by changing the constellation of class forces in society it has reconstituted the basis of American politics.

Class-fraction politics may well have created a situation in which American society is stuck between capitalism and its future. On the one hand, the fractionalizing of the working class in the economic sphere has probably made class confrontation unlikely; in the foreseeable future, it has certainly left the working class too weak and too seriously divided to challenge capitalist hegemony. On the other hand, the continuing class-rooted conflict (in the form of class-fraction politics) has steadily expanded the role of government and pushed it to impose increasingly costly (for capitalists) limitations on business. Within the context of the long post–World War II boom, and while the United States' international position went unchallenged, the contradictions in this process could be patched up by sharing the spoils of rapid growth. In the harsher times of the 1970s, no such easy solution seemed possible.

This impasse in the class struggle has momentous consequences for the future of democracy. As will be argued later, capitalists have sought over the past few decades to restrict the tendency toward deadlock by restricting democratic government itself. They have continued to defend the form of democratic rule, but they have lent their weight to the long-term erosion of its content. The rise of rule by the great state bureaucracies, the "imperial presidency," and government by executive or administrative order provides the undemocratic substance of modern democratic government.

On the other hand, it appears that working-class fractions will increasingly be pressed to defend and extend political democracy as a way of pushing for their more immediate economic and social needs. In this, concerns at the workplace intersect directly with larger-scale issues, for the great contradiction in bureaucratic control is its implicit tyranny. Workers are treated fairly within the rules, but they have no say in establishing the rules. The (perhaps inevitable) response, already apparent within the past few years, is the call for democracy at work. But if it is to be genuine and not merely the latest wrinkle in employer control, democracy at work requires socialism. Industrial democracy alongside political democracy—long a dream of socialists—thus appears as a unifying demand in the working class's disunity.

The present situation represents an historic conjuncture. Society once again faces the basic questions of capitalism, socialism, and democracy. How these questions will be answered is by no means certain.

CHAPTER 2

The Personal Touch: Competitive Capitalism and the Simple Forms of Control

BUSINESS in the nineteenth century was conducted by enterprises that, by today's standards, were very small. In the mid-1840s, when the Best brothers established the beer concern that eventually became the Pabst Brewing Company, family members provided almost all the needed labor. But even by 1870, when Best and Company had risen to the status of second largest brewery in the country, it still employed no more than a hundred workers, including those in the office. Similarly, in 1849 the McCormick Company began production at its Chicago harvester works with 123 employees. Despite sales and production that expanded so rapidly that McCormick boasted that its works were "the largest factory of its kind in the world," the company employed no more than three or four hundred workers on the eve of the Civil War. Initially, Pullman sleeping cars were constructed by a "small crew of carefully selected carpenters and mechanics," who worked under George Pullman's "watchful eye"; in 1870 the company employed about 200 workers.[1] Factories and workshops (or what the Census Bureau calls "establishments") in other industries were similarly small. Only the railroads and the New England textile mills, pioneers of large-scale industry, employed more than a thousand workers before the 1880s.

The small size of the firms in which most production took place is reflected as well in the available evidence of capitalization in nineteenth-century firms. For example, one study ranked firms in the 1880s as "very large" if they had net assets (invested capital plus reinvested profits) of $10 million or more.[2] Today such a firm would be called "middle-sized" at best, yet only a very few nineteenth-century manufacturing companies, and perhaps fifteen highly capitalized railroads, surpassed this mark. All other (nonfinancial) firms in the economy had net worths of less than $10 million.

The ownership and management of nineteenth-century firms also reflected a small-business character, for managerial control tended to be overwhelmingly concentrated within the families or partnerships of the founding entrepreneurs. Only the railroads, the textile companies, and a few other firms were more widely owned. Most—like Best and Company, the McCormick Company, and all the large iron companies—were family-held or organized as partnerships. With no real capital market, family-owned stocks, and no outside sources of managerial talent, both profits and management responsibility necessarily remained with the family.

Moreover, because they were small, firms tended to have a local outlook and to depend on a strictly limited market area. As Alfred Chandler has noted, companies

> bought their raw materials and sold their finished goods locally. Where they manufactured for a market more than a few miles away from the factory, they bought and sold through commissioned agents who handled the business of several other similar firms.[3]

Other constraints on business activities—prices that could not be higher than those of competitors and wage rates that were determined through area-wide labor markets—severely restricted what the individual capitalist could do in setting wages or prices. Thus with so little control over its environment, the small firm's success largely depended on the capitalist's ability to extract labor from labor power.[4]

Until the last one or two decades of the nineteenth century, entrepreneurial firms were representative of the economy. Such firms together organized the overwhelming bulk of the nation's nonagricultural production. But individually, each employed a small workforce, each used a relatively unsophisticated marketing and sales staff, and, in fact, each existed essentially as an extension of the capitalist (or, in the case of partnerships, a few capitalists), who acted as the organizing and motivating force. The "firm" as an entity separate from the activities of the entrepreneur hardly existed.*

*An interesting example of this is the early career of Richard Sears. Sears began as a railroad station agent and sold watches along the line as a sideline. He soon was so successful that he turned to peddling full-time and eventually sold out the R. W. Sears Watch Company along with the promise not to open up a new business that would compete with his old business. The old business didn't amount to much, and Sears again established a trading company that was the true predecessor to Sears, Roebuck. (Boris Emmet and John Jeuck, 1950, pp. 32–33.)

The Entrepreneurial Firm and Entrepreneurial Control

In the entrepreneurial firm, although the need for control was great, the mechanisms for achieving it were very unsophisticated, and the system of control tended to be informal and unstructured. The personal power and authority of the capitalist constituted the primary mechanism for control. In Stephen Hymer's words, the entrepreneur "saw everything, knew everything, and decided everything."[5] Alone or perhaps in concert with a few managers, he watched over the entire operations of the firm. He supervised the work activities directly; he maintained a close watch on his foremen; and he interceded immediately with full power to solve any problems, overriding established procedures, firing recalcitrant workers, recruiting new ones, rearranging work schedules, reducing pay, handing out bonuses, and so forth.

The entire firm was, in a way, the capitalist's own workshop. His knowledge of and involvement with his employees was great. As a result, it was difficult for employees to avoid his scrutiny. For example, Leander McCormick, younger brother of Cyrus, was in charge of production at the McCormick Works for over thirty years. Aided by four foremen (one each for the wood, iron, casting, and repair departments), he actively oversaw the plant operations, evaluated the workers, fought against unionizing efforts, and recruited new workers. He and his foremen were the control apparatus. Similarly, the Best family, including sons-in-law Frederick Pabst and Emil Schandein, provided all of the managerial and supervisory personnel required in the brewery until nearly the end of the century. During the early 1880s, Thomas Edison personally directed the operations at his factories in Harrison (New Jersey) and New York City, relying on three "personal and loyal associate(s)" as factory managers.[6]

The capitalist's control was further enhanced by the geographical concentration of the firm's operations. Having everything in one place made it possible for an entrepreneur to involve himself personally in all aspects of production. His ability to direct workers' activities was especially great where the whole production process itself was simple, as for example, in manufacturing, where the operations and outputs were primarily physical. It was relatively easy for the manager to determine whether workers were performing their jobs properly, and this probably increased the pressure on foremen to keep their subordinates working hard. But even where production was more complicated, the capitalist was often technically as competent as the workers. Indeed, it appears that many entrepreneurs began as skilled workers and so knew enough about the production process to supervise it properly.

Furthermore, the personal leadership and appeal—the charisma, to use Max Weber's word—of the capitalist himself served to motivate workers. After all, the capitalist-entrepreneur was responsible for more than technical coordination. His success depended on his ability to get work out of his workers, whether by harsh discipline or by inspiration; undoubtedly, most attempted to use both. Successful entrepreneurs understood the possibilities (and limits) of such personal motivation and to some extent realized its benefits. Workers undoubtedly were oppressed and exploited by such employers, but they also became enmeshed in a whole network of personal relations. They had someone with whom to identify.

The entrepreneurial form of control was not necessarily limited to firms so small that the only boss was the capitalist. The capitalist may, in fact, have been aided by a coterie of managers, straw bosses, and foremen. What was essential, however, was that the entrepreneurial firm was small enough for all, or nearly all, the workers to have some personal relationship with the capitalist, and that the group of managers was small enough for each to be effectively directed, motivated, and supervised by the capitalist. Thus, even though it was impossible for a capitalist to be the immediate supervisor of all the workers in a firm employing two or three hundred people, it was still possible for him to supervise all the bosses and to know all the workers.

Personal control by the capitalist inherently involved rather equal power relations among workers. While some workers held supervisory responsibility for others, nonetheless the actual exercise of power was concentrated in the capitalist's hands. Ultimately all workers were equal because all were quite powerless; the owner had all the power. Frequent contact with the firm's owner also reduced power differences among the workers. Since all workers developed direct relationships with the capitalist and could appeal to him, any foreman's commands were tentative, subject to the capitalist's evaluation. He could intercede directly whenever required, and so he depended on his own judgment and directives; he did not have to legitimize the foreman's position to ensure that his interests were being pursued. Moreover, the capitalist's intervention was typically erratic and arbitrary, since he only exercised his power as required. This use of power tended to undermine the exercise of routinized and formally organized power. Indeed, this was the advantage of entrepreneurial control in the small firm—the capitalist could intervene personally at all levels and in all activities to facilitate production.

Naturally, control exercised personally by the capitalist could be no more effective than the force of the individual capitalist's personality; not all would-be tycoons were successful. Although no statistics exist to measure the failure rate among small firms in the nineteenth century, small businesses have historically suffered from high mortality. The capitalist's leadership qualities and ability to intervene and use power forcefully by no means guaranteed successful control.

Yet in successful firms, entrepreneurial control, despite being informal, erratic, and subject to favoritism and arbitrariness, provided the basis for profitable control. The personal ties that owners of small businesses established with their workers in many cases tended to obscure the real class differences between them. Loyalty had a direct and personal meaning for workers, and many were reluctant to break the bonds it formed. At McCormick, for example, the company could count on some employees to side with it rather than with union organizers; this divided the workforce and prevented unionization. Only later, when the workforce had grown far beyond the size at which personal ties to the entrepreneur could be important, did workers organize successfully. And at Pabst, despite exceptionally long hours, no successful organizing drive was possible until the class differences—so long hidden by friendships, common German heritage, and other personal bonds—were at last exposed so clearly that they could not be ignored.[7]

The Expanded Firm and the Contradiction with Entrepreneurial Control

In every stage of capitalism, some small firms have been able to gain significant advantages over their competitors and thereby greatly expand their operations. This process was particularly prevalent during the middle and late nineteenth century, when successful firms moved beyond local and regional markets and began producing for a national market. The McCormick Harvesting Machine Company, for example, despite competition from half a dozen or more reaper and mower producers, began selling its machines in the East and in midwestern areas increasingly remote from its home in Chicago. In consequence, production in 1884 required 1,400 workers and in 1899 more than 4,000. The Pabst Brewing Company had moved into New York and even into foreign markets by the end of the century, and by the mid-1890s it was regularly employing over 700 workers. As their operations grew with the demand for steel rails, several iron and steel companies employed more than a thousand workers; at its Homestead Works alone, the Carnegie Steel Company employed nearly 4,000. Edison, the predecessor of General Electric, employed about 1,000 workers in its factories in the early 1880s but had grown to 2,400 workers by 1890 and, through merger, to 10,000 by 1892. Employment at the Pullman Palace Car Company grew rapidly as the demand for sleeping car accommodations expanded with the extension of the railroads. By 1875, the workforce at the Pullman works alone was up to 600 men, and it grew to 2,700 by 1885 and 5,500 by 1893; employees at all of the company's plants numbered over 14,500 by 1893.[8]

Even earlier, the trend to large workforces could be seen in the textile mills and the railroads. The Boston Manufacturing Company employed several hundred workers as early as the 1840s, and since virtually the same small group of capitalists owned all the mills at Lowell, Massachusetts, the entire group of mills in that town—employing some 5,000 to 8,000 people—could well be considered as a single enterprise. By the mid-1850s, the Erie Railroad was employing more than 4,000 workers, and the workforce of the Pennsylvania Railroad reached nearly 50,000 by the late 1880s.[9]

The general expansion of the firm can be seen in other ways. The Census Bureau provided some rather faulty but still useful statistics on the increase in average "establishment" size between 1860 and 1900. For example, iron and steel works increased on average from 65 workers in 1860 to 333 workers by 1900; agricultural implements manufactories jumped from 8 to 65 workers. Twelve out of the fourteen industries studied saw average establishment size more than double during these decades. Actually, these data are averages, and as such they disguise the emergence of the huge factories that were increasingly prevalent by the turn of the century. One historian has searched states' archives to produce a list of the factories in the Northeast and the Midwest that in 1900 employed 2000 or more employees; seventy plants qualified for the list.[10]

As these firms outgrew their entrepreneurial origins, direct personal control by the capitalist became increasingly difficult. At the New York Central in the 1850s, the general superintendent tried unsuccessfully to run the by then large railroad as an entrepreneurial firm. By the late 1880s, Edison had abandoned his attempt to supervise his factories personally; the firm's employment had soared as the company stretched to produce for the growing electrical market, and entrepreneurial direction was no longer possible.[11] In such expanded firms, the capitalist and his top managers could personally oversee only a small part of the business's activities, yet they were forced to direct the whole operation. More and more managers had to be employed, but soon not even all the managers could be supervised directly.

The increasing separation of the entrepreneur and his top managers from the daily activities of the workers made it impossible for them to direct production personally. A worker at Pullman in the 1890s stated it simply: "In a large establishment like the Pullman shops there must necessarily be a large force of foremen, under foremen, [and] sub-bosses, as well as heads of departments and higher officials." And as one historian noted, "Even if George Pullman remembered Charles Reade's advice—'put yourself in his [the worker's] place'—it could not have helped him to understand the needs and problems of his many employees. His company had grown too large for such a personal touch."[12]

Not only was it physically impossible for capitalists and highest-level managers to oversee all the activities in a large firm, but it also became increasingly difficult for them even to know what the correct work activities were. As tasks became more finely divided, as the interdependence among jobs grew, and as more and more types of production were incorporated in the firm's operations, the knowledge and familiarity required for supervision likewise increased. Bosses necessarily became managers, rather than "head workmen." Their attempts to intercede in organizing production became dysfunctional. Whereas in the small firm such intervention expedited production, in large firms the owners' efforts just as frequently caused disruption. Henry Ford, Sr. provided a classic illustration when, as late as the 1930s and 1940s, he refused to yield personal control over his firm, although the company had long since passed the point where it could be run as a one-boss workshop. Ford constantly interfered with engineering, production, and marketing decisions, and he even refused to permit his employees to maintain an organizational chart. Bankruptcy was narrowly averted only by the succession of Henry Ford II, who instituted modern management practices.[13]

Greater organizational distance and increasing differences in life situations between capitalist (or managers) and workers gradually weakened the extent of personal contact and identification. The capitalist's presence in the firm no longer had much personal impact for the workers. What was true for the worker-capitalist relationship applied to the capitalist-foreman relationship as well. As the firm grew, the capitalist's personal impact on his bosses declined correspondingly. In a small firm, the capitalist's personality could dominate a small group of managers, causing them to identify with him and be motivated by this identification. But this was no longer the case in the expanded firm. Railroad managers, for example, had to worry about the honesty (as well as the efficiency) of conductors, division superintendents, and others who handled freight and passenger revenues.[14] Just as workers who were removed from the capitalist's personal presence had less to identify with, so, too, did the managers. There was, however, a difference. Individual workers were responsible for particular tasks; managers and foremen were responsible for motivating or controlling whole shops or branches of production. The effect of unmotivated managers could extend to many workers and to large portions of the firm's operations.

Thus the expansion of formerly entrepreneurial firms undermined the personal sway that an individual capitalist could hold over his workers. The method of control came into conflict with the requirements of production. Pressure built up for more regularized and structured management practices, for methods that did not depend on the extensive personal intervention of the capitalist.

As Alfred Chandler has noted, capitalists realized that what was required was a much more systematic control mechanism, a more "rational" framework for the exercise of the enterprise's power. Daniel McCallum, general superintendent of the Erie Railroad, wrote that the cause of the railroad's failure to be more profitable lay in "the want of a system [of management] perfect in its details, properly adapted and vigilantly enforced.[15] Organization manuals that several railroads prepared—complete with "principles" of management, organizational charts, separation of the firm into divisions, and so on—indicated the distance these firms had come from the entrepreneurial firm. The first (and lesser) of the transformations in the organization of work was about to occur.

The Expanded Firm and Hierarchical Control

The new system, hierarchical control, marked the firm's first accommodation to its growth. While it did not change the nature of the firm's power relationships, hierarchical control did change who exercised power and the way it was exercised. In the large firm, it was no longer possible for the capitalist to exercise all the power required to direct production, and the right to exercise some power had to be delegated to hired bosses.

The iron and steel industry led the way. In this industry, and in a few others, skilled workers—and not capitalist-entrepreneurs—had long ruled the workplace. In some respects these skilled workers acted as the foremen in hierarchical control; for example, they hired their own helpers and established the pace of work. The skilled steelworkers sold their product (iron and later steel) to the capitalist for a price known as the tonnage rate; they decided how much and when to produce; and because they had the essential "craft secrets" needed to make iron, they could largely determine how iron was to be made. Thus skilled workers retained a significant degree of control over production. For the capitalists, however, this system was entirely too inflexible for the growing national market. Skilled workers rigidly limited apprenticeships, they tended to oppose technical innovation, and most important, they refused to drive themselves as hard in pursuit of ever-greater output as the industry's capitalists desired. In a struggle that stretched over the last several decades of the nineteenth century and that was often punctuated by bloody battles, the capitalists broke the power of the craftsmen and opened the way for reorganization of the industry.[16] Their first step was to create hierarchical control.

In iron and steel, as well as in industries not delayed by struggles with craft workers, the new model was of an army. A hierarchical structure was instituted, with foremen and supervisors to watch over other employees, and the entire enterprise assumed the shape of a giant pyramid. A direct chain of command was created in which those who were delegated power were made responsible to successively higher and more concentrated echelons. One observer, struck by the "highly militarized" organization of the steel industry, found military terminology appropriate to describe its organization.

> The general staff of the Carnegie Company is one of the most efficient in the whole world of business. The superintendents, department managers and foremen are splendidly loyal efficient officers with high morale. Bound to them are the non-commissioned officers, such gang leaders as rollers, blowers, melters, and the other top-skilled Americans, who are part bosses, part workmen. Altogether this administrative group, almost a third of the force, has a real military efficiency.[17]

Hierarchical control was based on the concept that each boss—whether a foreman, supervisor, or manager—would re-create in his shop the situation of the capitalist under entrepreneurial control. Daniel Nelson has aptly termed this system "the foreman's empire."[18] Each boss would have full rights to fire and hire, intervene in production, direct workers as to what to do and what not to do, evaluate and promote or demote, discipline workers, arrange rewards, and so on; in short, each boss would be able to act in the same arbitrary, idiosyncratic, unencumbered way that entrepreneurs had acted. As Daniel McCallum of the Erie Railroad put it, "All subordinates should be accountable to and be directed by *their immediate superiors only;* as obedience cannot be enforced where the foreman in immediate charge is interfered with by a superior officer giving orders directly to his subordinates." Local supervisors on the Baltimore and Ohio Railroad "directed the work done on the maintenance and repair of all fixed structures in their area and had full responsibility for personnel, including appointing foremen in workshops, as well as bridge watchmen and water station and switch keepers." Similarly, the Erie Railroad delegated to each supervisor "the authority . . . to appoint all persons for whose acts he is held responsible, and [he] may dismiss any subordinate when, in his judgment, the interests of the company will be promoted thereby."[19]

The degree to which the intervening layers of supervisors actually acted as "subentrepreneurs" varied greatly. At the Pullman works, most workers were paid piece-rates. A foreman would be given an appropriation for a certain amount of work, and he in turn would set the prices for various jobs. Even though the appropriation was simply a bookkeeping device, the foreman did establish the structure of wages paid to his subordinates, and those foremen who did not spend the entire appropriation were rewarded. In more extreme form, some New England machinery shops turned to the "inside contract" system, where components of the work were actually subcontracted to employees who acted as gang bosses. The capitalist provided the machinery, plant, and raw materials necessary. The subentrepreneurs sometimes earned wages but more often survived on the profits (or losses) of the subcontract; they themselves hired employees and set them to work. Most capitalists did not go this far in treating supervisors as entrepreneurs, but nearly all provided foremen with almost absolute power over their subordinates.[20]

Of course, these subentrepreneurs could never really re-create entrepreneurial control because, unlike true entrepreneurs, foremen and supervisors under hierarchical control were not their own bosses. Hiring and firing decisions could always be countermanded by a higher-level supervisor, and the foreman himself could be fired. Supervisors were in some ways constrained by company-wide policies (such as wage rates for categories of workers) and were always subject to the same overall scrutiny as others in the organization. Most importantly, the profits went to the real owners, not to the subentrepreneurs. Nonetheless, the purpose of this type of management was to give each supervisor or foreman as much power over subordinates as was needed to get the work done, or, as the management literature put it, "authority was to be commensurate with responsibility." In this area, the system succeeded.

Hierarchical control incorporated the principle of vertical lines of communication and discouraged lateral contacts. The inability of capitalists and top-echelon managers to oversee all production operations meant that formal mechanisms for coordination (written reports, official lines of communication, and so on) were required to replace the informal and irregular coordination that had been conducted personally by the entrepreneur. Whom people "reported to" became firmly established.

While vertical information flows did not necessarily lead to greater coordination (coordination typically involves synchronizing the efforts of laterally related production units), they were necessary for establishing top-down control. In those instances where the workers' interests diverged from those of the managers, and where the honesty and diligence of even the intervening layers of supervisory staff were always in doubt, it was important to keep workers (or even foremen) in the different shops from undertaking direct and independent coordination. Thus, sales agents on the Pennsylvania Railroad did not pass data on freight and passengers directly to those responsible for carrying the trade; instead, the information made its way up the chain to the central office, where it was evaluated and, in part, transmitted to the Transportation Department. On the Erie, written reports were required of all the departments; the information was used, according to Chandler, to make efficiency comparisons between departments, to check on the honesty of agents, and "assist in the administration of the road."[21]

However irrational it was from the standpoint of efficiency, hierarchical control constituted a "rational" framework for the regular and permanent delegation of the capitalist's powers. Each supervisor was simply assigned the task of directing the work within his shop or division and making his subordinates work as hard as possible. And in enforcing his orders, the supervisor could call upon most of the powers exercised by the capitalist in an entrepreneurial firm.

Despite its other innovations, hierarchical control did not alter the form in which capitalist power was exercised. Foreman-worker relations in the expanded firm were based on the same type of power as were capitalist-worker relations in the entrepreneurial firm. The work tasks were organized and controlled by the continuous, direct, ad hoc, and arbitrary instructions of the foreman. They were enforced by positive rewards, by physical force, and/or by the dismissal of workers.

Indeed, the system increased the visibility and arbitrariness of unequal power relations, making it easier for a supervisor to direct work and enforce compliance. The result was arbitrary command rule by foremen and managers, who became company despots encumbered by few restrictions on their power over workers. The work motivation inherent in such control was simple: perform your task correctly or be docked in pay, fired, or, on occasion, beaten (as in Henry Ford's plants and probably elsewhere). Power was unmistakably vested in the person of the supervisor.

Hierarchical control thus became a giant framework for what has come to be known as "close" supervision. Orders were received from the level above and transmitted to the levels below. The foreman directed operations by giving instructions and commands and by checking on work. Compliance was achieved because foremen exercised the capitalist's power, especially the power to punish or fire workers.

Although scarcely adequate to deal with later problems of management, hierarchical control did provide an interim solution to the growing contradiction between the size of most firms and entrepreneurial control. The management experiments tried by the railroads and adopted elsewhere—especially in the iron industry, in coal mining, and in other heavy industries—seem obvious in hindsight, but they were often praised by contemporaries as important innovations. And indeed they were, though not in the way their adherents anticipated. Hierarchical control itself contained contradictions, and the system of production based on it soon came under militant attack.

The Persistence of Simple Control: The Modern-Day "Periphery"

Although entrepreneurial and hierarchical control were important in the historical development of the boss-worker relationship, these "simple" systems of control are not just historical curiosities. The American economy today is dominated by big business, but an important and substantial segment of production continues to be carried on by small businesses. Of the approximately 12 million enterprises in the United States, all but a few thousand fall into the categories of small and medium-sized business; in fact, well over 11 million can fairly be classified as "entrepreneurial" firms. These enterprises constitute what Robert Averitt has called the economy's "periphery." And for the peripheral economy, simple control remains the order of the day.

Found primarily in retail and wholesale trade, light manufacturing, and personal and business services, the small businessman or businesswoman of today operates much like his or her predecessors did a century ago. In small firms, family members often work long hours and provide much of the labor required. Hired workers labor alongside and assist the employer. The entrepreneur often plays the part of chief workman, setting the pace of work and acting as a highly motivated rate-buster, making it more difficult for other workers to protect themselves from exploitation. In slightly bigger firms, the owning family typically runs the firm, filling key managerial slots and keeping watch over the supervisory staff. In some ways—notably in the use of outside professional consultants, the incorporation of computerized cost analysis, and the dependence on personnel and job-design specialists—the small firm's management has profited from the general advances in the art of management. But in its fundamentals, simple control persists.

The peripheral economy has traditionally been difficult for unions to organize and, except in construction, it has remained largely free of them. It represents a reservoir of stagnant and backward technologies or, paradoxically, of firms built on recent innovations that have not yet been engulfed by some corporate giant. The periphery provides generally low wages, few forms of job protection, and high labor turnover. Although it continues to be important in aggregate production and especially in certain industries, it generally is a declining sector, as the large corporations continually encroach on its markets.

Ann Bookman's work at the Digitex Company—Maureen Agnati's employer—gives us a penetrating view of this world. Bookman worked at Digitex for two years, and she recorded her experiences. The company's workforce, less than five hundred strong, is small enough so that the company remains paternalistic and lacking in formal structure. The thirty or so supervisors wield enormous powers, and the workers have been able to impose only the most informal constraints on them. In relation to hiring and firing, leaves, absences, vacations, overtime and part-time work, and raises and promotions:

> The only generalization that can be made about company policy . . . is that the company has no single policy for any of them. There are some vague "rules," but basically each of these things is decided on an employee-by-employee basis through discussions between the individual worker and one of the higher-ups in management. This creates a climate in which paternalism flourishes.[22]

The wage rates for each job are kept secret, and workers are at the mercy of their bosses in matters of pay. Bookman notes that it is common practice at Digitex for the starting pay of two employees working at the same job to differ. Raises are handled equally arbitrarily, with no set timetable for evaluation and no established policy of who gets raises or why. All depends on the foreman's decision, and workers must maintain good relations with him if they hope to get a raise.

The petty tyranny of the bosses extends to nearly every aspect of factory life and colors all social relationships. Among the many instances Bookman cites, perhaps the most revealing shows the interaction of sexual and employment relations:

> In Winding, the young male foreman spends a lot of time with the women pieceworkers and encourages flirtatiousness in his relationship with the pieceworkers. For example, he would ask women in a very leading way what they did over the week-end or the preceding night, with the implication that he was really asking if they had had any sexual experiences. . . . He often played favorites, spending most of his time with one or two non-Portuguese workers, until he was warned by the General Foreman about the pitfalls of this kind of behavior. For several days after the warning he talked to none of the pieceworkers, and when finally questioned by one of us about his silence, he said, obviously quoting the General Foreman, "You girls are like an orchestra that must be properly conducted. It is bad to play one instrument too much!" Within a week after this incident he had returned to his old pattern of favoritism.[23]

Bookman notes, however, that this foreman's favoritism has important consequences: he determines which women are assigned to jobs with better rates (that is, higher pay), which women have to sit on benches that face the wall, which women get overtime, and so on. He does indeed rule a "foreman's empire."

Simple control thus survives in the economy's periphery. For the new industrial giants at the turn of the century, however, the system soon ran into problems. Its contradictions were exposed by two related developments—the continued growth in the size of the firm's workforce and the rising socialist challenge to capitalist hegemony.

CHAPTER 3

Running Full: The Breakdown of Competition

THE WORKPLACE in the twentieth century has continued to be a fiercely contested terrain, but the struggles between capitalists and workers have for the most part been of a quite different character from those of the nineteenth century. The whole context of the struggle changed, as continued accumulation pushed American capitalism from its competitive to its monopolistic phase.* For one thing, the new economic context meant that the large corporation became the primary locus of workplace struggles. More fundamentally, the new situation altered the prospects and possibilities confronting both classes.

The transition to monopoly capitalism occurred between 1890 and 1920. It was one of those changes that seemed to represent nothing more than a continuation of past trends but that, in retrospect, qualitatively changed the operation and dynamics of the system. In this transition we can see two rather different processes. The first is the process of monopolization that occurred within particular industries: competition drove small and inefficient producers out of business. With finance capital acting as the mobilizing force, giant firms began producing for significant shares of the national market—and sharing monopoly profits—in each of the major industries.

Second, there was also the broader triumph of the regime of monopoly capitalism. In order to establish their hegemony, monopoly capitalists had to resolve conflicts within the capitalist class, establish new relations between the

*Throughout this book, unless specific definition is given, "monopoly" refers to a situation in which producers have significant discretionary market power. This term thus covers the economist's cases of monopoly (single-seller markets) and oligopoly (few-sellers markets).

corporate economy and the state, and smash the growing labor and socialist opposition.

Neither the consolidation within each industry nor the establishment of the new regime occurred automatically or without opposition. That exemplar of the new giants, U.S. Steel, reported that in nine of the thirteen years before the war began, its profits were lower than those earned in 1902, the company's first full year of operation. The Steel Trust's chairman, Judge Gary, had in 1907 begun his famous "dinners" to head off threatened price competition from independent producers; but Gary was forced to abandon such blatant price-fixing under threat of conspiracy prosecution. While U.S. Steel had consolidated a majority of the industry under its banner, significant capacity remaned outside the trust. The Standard Oil model—direct control of prices through virtually complete control of industry capacity—could not be achieved in steel. Similar limitations prevailed in meatpacking, electrical products, and other industries.

The new corporate capitalists also faced considerable opposition beyond their immediate competitors. A loose multiclass coalition threatened to force government antitrust action to roll back the results of the consolidation movement. The threat was made more plausible by the successful prosecution in 1911 of Standard Oil and American Tobacco.

More ominously for the capitalists, the working class appeared to be gathering strength for a major challenge to capitalist political hegemony. By 1912, the Socialist Party—openly proclaiming the overthrow of capitalism as its goal—was able to attract nearly a million ballots in the presidential election, some 6 percent of the total. The Industrial Workers of the World, under the banner of "One Big Union of All the Workers," led the Lawrence (Massachusetts) strikers to victory over the American Woolen Company, a product of one of the huge, turn-of-the-century mergers. Elsewhere, the prestigious German Social Democracy, a main force in the Second International, constituted the leading party in the Reichstag, and all over Europe socialist and communist groups appeared ascendant. In 1912, monopoly capitalism did not hold a secure lock on the future.

Yet by the early 1920s the situation had been reversed. The big corporations were securely ensconced in their industries, practicing cooperative—or, in J. K. Galbraith's useful term, "co-respective"—price-setting and market-sharing behavior. Competition had been reduced to "competition among the few"; moreover, it had clear limits, the banning of price competition being the most significant. The anti-big business protests of farmers, small businessmen, labor, and consumers had become muted and meaningless. The Socialist Party, reeling from internal splits, the postwar red scare, and the Palmer Raids, broke apart. The Wobblies, like all significant labor opposition, were hounded from town to town, jailed, deported, and blacklisted, and their organization was smashed. Internationally, the inspiration of the Bolshevik victory was tempered by the total collapse of progressive movements elsewhere in Europe, including the totally discredited Second International and German Social Democracy. And the Soviet party began making the compromises necessary for its deformed life under the regime of "socialism in one country."

Everywhere, and especially in America, monopoly capitalists appeared triumphant. The new industrial captains prevailed; the size and market power of their corporations provided them with the necessary resources. The corporate capitalists' victory during this period created the foundation for the present stage of capitalism and established the context within which the relations of the labor process would again be revolutionized.[1]

This chapter investigates the consolidation process as it occurred within particular industries. The next analyzes the conflict that surrounded the installation of the new regime.

The Natural Limits of Competition

When there are many firms in an industry and each firm is small relative to the size of the market, the actions of any one firm will necessarily have only a small impact on the market. However, if all firms are subject to more or less the same circumstances, they will tend to respond similarly to those circumstances, and in that case their combined or aggregate effect will be significant. This is the case when competition within an industry—by reducing prices and shrinking profit margins—drives all producers to seek new markets, expand production, and reduce costs in order to survive. Individual survival strategies lead to mass demise.

Competition inexorably pushes firms to seek out new ways to gain an edge, to recapture old markets and conquer new ones. Not only are old technologies and practices stretched to their limits, but capitalists constantly search for new productive methods. In the economist's language, entrepreneurs expand production out along their cost curves, but competition robs them of their expected profits. The entrepreneurs are thus driven to reinvest profits or borrow more funds, hoping that innovation or expansion will lower their entire cost curves and thereby reclaim the lost margins. But soon their competitors will also adopt any innovations and prices will decline to reflect that event. Once again, the stage is set for a new competition, this time with fewer competitors surviving to fight the next battle, a battle to be waged on a much grander scale.

Pressure to expand frequently results in overproduction. If the market is growing, it would theoretically be possible for each firm to grow in step with the market. Yet nothing ensures this happy coincidence, and in general each survivor benefits partly from the market's growth and partly from the failure of less fortunate firms. At the beginning of the process, when there are many firms, the success of the few may not appear to be so directly tied to the misfortune of the many, though of course it is. But when the numbers dwindle, the life-and-death nature of the struggle becomes evident.

Take iron and steel as an example. In the 1870s the iron and steel industry was composed of many small producers, and no one firm was large relative to the national market. As the expanding railroad network broke down the barriers protecting local and regional markets, producers began facing increased competition from more distantly located rivals. This competition tended to drive prices down and erode profit margins. Most producers sought to recoup declining profits by expanding production and sales, but this only resulted in overproduction, an intensification of competition, and a tendency for prices and profit margins to fall even further. Some marginal or inefficient producers were forced out of the industry; others were acquired by more prosperous firms.

Firms such as the Carnegie Company that succeeded in achieving dramatic cost reductions were able to earn sizable profits and expand. But because there were hundreds of firms to begin with, the expansion of some—even at the cost of driving others out of existence—still left the industry with many competing firms. The continuing and increasingly fierce competition further eroded profit margins, forcing producers to intensify their efforts to cut costs and expand their volume and thus restore profits. Their success only exacerbated the problem and further intensified the competition.

This cycle—intensifying competition among firms whose production capacities were expanding much more rapidly than the market—seems, in most observers' opinions, to have characterized the iron and steel industry until the mid-1890s.[2] One contemporary who agreed with this observation was Andrew Carnegie himself. Presaging the theory of overhead costs, he noted:

> A demand exists for a certain article beyond the capacity of existing works to supply it. Prices are high and profits tempting. Every manufacturer of that article

immediately proceeds to enlarge his works and increase their producing power. . . . In a short time the supply becomes greater than the demand and there are a few tons or yards more in the market for sale than are required, and prices begin to fall. They continue falling until the article is sold at cost. . . .

Political economy says that here the trouble will end. Goods will not be produced at less than cost. This was true when Adam Smith wrote, but it is not quite true today. . . . As manufacturing is carried on today, in enormous establishments with five or ten millions of dollars of capital invested and with thousands of workers, it costs the manufacturer much less to run at a loss per ton or per yard than to check his production. Stoppage would be serious indeed.

The condition of cheap manufacture is running full. Twenty sources of expense are fixed charges, many of which stoppage would only increase. Therefore, the article is produced for months and, in some cases that I have known, for years, not only without profit or without interest on capital, but to the impairment of the capital invested. . . . [3]

For a while the successful expand at the expense of the inefficient, but this process cannot persist indefinitely. Eventually, the remaining firms become sufficiently large relative to the market that the actions of any one of them do affect the entire market. From the capitalists' perspective, the costs of continuing competition become clearer. More importantly, the number of firms sharing the market is sufficiently reduced so that collusion becomes possible.

In steel, the Illinois Steel Company, Carnegie, Jones and Laughlin, and a few other firms began to dominate the national market through their ability to produce basic products at lower cost. Throughout the 1890s, these surviving steel producers feverishly expanded their plant capacities, acquired failing or competing firms, and sought market advantages by undercutting their rivals' prices. Competition was quite clearly narrowing to a struggle among the few, with some (especially the Carnegie Company) reaping large profits while others were being driven to desperate efforts to survive. One result was widespread and for some firms (including the huge Morgan-promoted Federal Steel) repeated consolidations. But despite these efforts, the steel industry in 1900 still faced what appeared to be a new and violent round of competition. Merely to protect previous investments and markets, Carnegie, Federal, and others were driven to invading each others' established fields of specialty, and they planned capacity expansions "far beyond [the nation's] normal consuming power."[4]

Throughout the American economy firms emerged from the hectic race for national markets with industrial capacities that had outrun their own markets. Thus, for example, Best and Company/Pabst Brewing expanded its own (Milwaukee) plant as it increasingly broke out of its regional market to vie for national sales. But it also purchased the facilities of other, less successful brewers, notably the Empire and South Side works in Chicago, in order to extend its operations to new markets. Competition pushed the brewery industry towards domination by a few firms. Competition undermined the basis for future competition and thereby created the conditions for monopoly.

The impact of competition was felt in other ways as well at the end of the nineteenth century. The dramatic price declines, evident in industry after the 1870s and based no doubt on the introduction of cost-saving technologies as well as on the availability of masses of cheap immigrant labor, indicated that competition was forcing producers to pass their cost savings along to consumers.[5] Producers confronted unstable demand and declining prices. Certain firms emerged as most efficient, but all producers failed to gain the profits anticipated.

The pressures for firms to expand and the consequent erosion of competition thus produce a fundamental dynamic within the accumulation process: capital tends to become increasingly centralized.

Consolidation and the Rise of Big Business

At the turn of the century the economy was hit with an enormous merger wave, a dramatic cresting of the powerful centralizing current. As Marx noted:

> Commensurately with the development of capitalist production and accumulation there develop the two most powerful levers of centralization—competition and credit.[6]

In the 1880s and early 1890s, the force exerted by the first lever—competition—was making itself felt in the declining profit margins and the necessity to expand production in order to survive. Production was forced to a new and wider scale, and competition imparted a dynamic character to every industry. The time was ripe for consolidation.

For a time, institutional barriers inhibited further centralization. Lack of widespread credit markets hampered the financing of new acquisitions. Both the common law and antitrust legislation placed "combinations in restraint of trade" in some legal jeopardy. Industrial capitalists, accustomed to achieving profits by outdoing others, approached collusion as merely a short-term tactic. The depression of the middle 1890s further impeded the progress of consolidation.

The conflict between competitive forces pushing towards centralization and institutional barriers inhibiting it produced mixed results for a time. The railroads, for whose securities there already existed a fairly broad market, were consolidated under J. P. Morgan's influence between 1885 and 1895. The Rockefeller (Standard Oil) and Havermeyer (American Sugar) trusts had been established before 1890, and American Tobacco began consolidation in 1890. Still, these results, though important, were exceptional.

But when the depression ended in 1897, the institutional barriers to consolidation had largely disappeared, while the economic impetus gained force. The New Jersey law and strict judicial interpretations of the Sherman Antitrust Act eliminated all legal problems—or so it seemed. More importantly, the rapid capital accumulation of the 1870s and 1880s had led to the growth of investment banking, life insurance, and other financial intermediaries holding liquid capital that required investment outlets. Similarly, the continued infusion of European, especially British, capital reinforced the demand for investment mechanisms. In response, a market in industrial stocks had grown up that provided financiers with greater access to capital for promoting consolidations. The 1880s and 1890s witnessed a particularly dramatic growth in publicly traded industrial securities.[7] Marx's second lever—credit—was now brought to bear.

The great wave of mergers that followed, from 1898 to 1902—literally the expression of the dammed-up pressures for consolidation—drastically transformed the structure of large business in the United States.

For individual firms involved in the transition, like McCormick, the changes were clearly visible. The 1880s and 1890s had been years of intense price competition among harvester manufacturers. But in 1904 the McCormick Harvesting Machine Company was united with its four largest competitors—the Deering Company; Warder, Bushnell, and Glessner; the Plano Company; and the Milwaukee Company—to form the International Harvester Company. The new firm produced about 85 percent of the total output of harvesting machines in the country, and since its few remaining competitors were located in New York, I-H's control over the crucial midwestern markets was virtually complete.[8]

Similarly, the fledgling electrical industry quickly passed through its competitive phase and settled into a monopolistic structure with the consolidation of Edison, Thomson-Houston, and other firms into General Electric. By 1900, only GE and Westinghouse survived to share the market.[9]

The most dramatic consolidation occurred in the steel industry, where the competition had been so intense through the 1880s and 1890s. Beginning in 1898, financial promoters merged and remerged iron and steel firms to reduce competition. Finally, the Morgan interests created the United States

Steel Corporation, the largest though not the last combination in the industry (Bethlehem was consolidated soon after). U.S. Steel, agglomerating some 165 companies, controlled approximately 60 percent of the entire steel market, with much greater control over certain products such as seamless tubes and wire nails. Not surprisingly, the long-term decline in steel prices was halted.[10]

Ralph Nelson provides the most complete data on these mergers in manufacturing. His figures suggest that between a quarter and a third of the entire manufacturing capital stock of the nation underwent consolidation during these few years. The percentage is large but not surprising, given that John Moody had earlier reported that fully 236 of the 318 important consolidations ("trusts") active in 1904 were incorporated after January 1, 1898.[11]

Yet, while the years 1898–1902 appear most dramatically as a turning point in United States economic history, the merger wave was only the most visible part of an even broader consolidation movement. In addition to the peak-year mergers, the period from the 1890s through the First World War also produced Standard Oil, American Telephone and Telegraph, Alcoa, General Motors, and a host of other huge firms. Moreover, the movement was not restricted to heavy industry. Big, dominating companies were organized by the producers of products as diverse as biscuits (National Biscuit), bananas (United Fruit), chewing gum (Wrigley's), paper (International Paper), meat (Swift and Armour), bicycles (American Bicycle), photographic supplies (Eastman Kodak), typewriters (Union), and sewing machines (Singer).

From American Tobacco and the other pioneering consolidations before the great 1890s depression to the World War I-vintage combinations like General Motors, competition led almost invariably to centralization of capital. The intervention of finance capital—credit—speeded up the process. It was not necessarily a smooth movement. Huge firms appeared earlier in some industries than in others; sometimes they suffered setbacks; and on occasion they even reversed direction, as in trans-Atlantic commerce, where Morgan's great combine, International Mercantile Marine, failed to maintain its size. Nonetheless, the consolidation movement sooner or later encompassed an enormous range and diversity of industries, and the organization of production throughout the industrial core of the economy was forever altered.

The Fruits of Consolidation

The centralization process did not immediately produce profitable firms securely dominating their "own" industries. Serious obstacles confronted the new giants, as is evident from the indifferent success of many large corporations between the merger wave and the early 1920s. Thus, of the one hundred firms with the greatest assets in 1903, only forty-five remained large enough to be listed among the top one hundred in 1919. Moreover, nine of the top one hundred in 1903 had gone bankrupt and been liquidated by 1917; seven had been acquired by other firms; and fifty-seven others, while still in business in 1917, had assets worth less in real terms than they had been in 1903.[12] While some consolidated firms were quite successful from the start, many obviously were not.

The 1890–1920 consolidation has often been interpreted as historically necessary to capture the benefits of technical economies of scale. With economists' usual assumption of competition, the survival of many large firms is taken as *prima facie* evidence for their technical superiority. And indeed, figures as diverse as Karl Marx and Andrew Carnegie had stressed the role of technical economies in pushing producers towards ever-larger volume.[13] Moreover, there is ample evidence (for example, in the continuously declining industrial product prices after 1870 or in the technical innovations in specific industries such as meatpacking and steel) to suggest that economies of scale fueled the cut-throat and unstable competition that took place during the last decades of the nineteenth century.

Yet the economies of scale argument does not appear to be an adequate explanation for the mergers. The usual measurement difficulties surrounding the concept of economies of scale preclude anything but highly tentative answers, and, in some cases, efficiencies may indeed have been realized. But what little evidence does exist indicates that, in general, plant size had increased sufficiently *before* the turn-of-the-century mergers to realize all technological economies of scale. For example, U.S. Steel continued to operate nearly all the plants previously operated by independent companies. So, too, did General Electric, International Harvester, and most other big consolidations.[14]

Studies such as those by the economist Joe Bain tend to support the inferential data, though we must do some manipulation to make his results for 1947 apply to the turn of the century (see Appendix Table A-1). For the eleven industries that can be analyzed, only one—the manufacture of typewriters—was in the position of having its largest firm still too small to capture fully the economies of scale. The other ten industries all had firms *larger* than needed—ranging from 4.7 to 34 times larger than the size needed to realize the technical economies.

It appears that the new firms met with mixed success because centralization had pushed them beyond the scale needed to achieve technical efficiency. Larger firm size produced meager results in terms of technical economies. This is not to suggest that the new giants were not in some "survival" sense superior; clearly they were, but their later superiority derived from characteristics other than technical economies of scale. The most obvious of these new characteristics, apparent to contemporary observers even if studiously avoided by economists since, was the increased market power of the new firms. But this new advantage from scale was quite unlike the old economies of scale in one respect. If a firm achieves technical economies, it can gain an immediate advantage by reducing its prices and underselling its rivals; it needs no cooperation from other firms to realize the benefit. But such is not the case where increased scale produces benefits by means of enhanced market power. Here, unless the firm achieves complete mastery of the industry, it can only realize the benefits through some kind of cooperation with other producers—Galbraith's idea of "co-respective behavior."

There can be little question that the turn-of-the-century mergers increased the *potential* for market power: nearly all the mergers were horizontal.[15] And the consequences of market power are quite clear. Consolidations that controlled less than 50 percent of their markets failed nearly three times more often than those firms that did have extensive market control (see Appendix Table A-2). Evidence relating monopoly power to prices and hence inferentially to profits, as well as evidence directly available on the relation of market power to profits, suggests that the consolidated firms were able to parlay their increased market power into higher profits.[16] This coincides with evidence from later periods; as L. W. Weiss, in a careful review of the literature relating monopoly power (what he terms "concentration") to profits, notes:

> Almost all of the thirty-two concentration-profits studies except Stigler's have yielded significant positive relationships for years of prosperity or recession, though they have depended on a wide variety of data and methods. I think that practically all observers are now convinced [of this]. Like the expansion of mercury in the thermometer, we have good reason to expect profits to increase with market power and have observed it many times.[17]

These results, though indirect and imprecise, are suggestive: the big firm's market power was a central element in its survival. With market power a large firm could dictate prices and other market behavior and gain relief from the anarchy of competition. Firms with substantial discretionary power in their product markets did better than other large firms, even if monopoly power alone was not enough to guarantee success nor lack of it sufficient to consign a firm to that high expectation of turnover that characterized smaller firms.

Yet, as indicated earlier, advantages of size that accrue in the form of increased market power, rather than of technical economies, are not automatic; potential market power must be translated into *effective* market power. In the absence of control by one firm over an industry's capacity, capitalists had to create mechanisms for achieving "cooperation."

In most cases, cooperation called for a new strategy.[18] The biggest producers needed to cooperate in order to place boundaries and restrictions on competition. Limits had to be calculated to provide market stability and maximum profits. Finance capital, with investment in many industries and in multiple companies within each industry, had initially been the impetus for consolidation, and now it provided one force for cooperation. Morgan representatives—Judge Gary at U.S. Steel, George Perkins at International Harvester—pushed hard for "cooperative" policies. Elsewhere, producers themselves began to work out joint action. The "Big Four" meatpackers had established the jointly owned National Packing Company "for the harmonious determination of general policies and for the control of the trade."[19]

But as corporate capitalists began these efforts, they faced severe difficulties in getting competing producers to agree on market shares and in monitoring and enforcing the codes without incurring prosecution. A means of establishing communication and of coordinating policies was required so that the oligopolists could come to agree on the terms of corespective behavior.

The corporations also faced more serious opposition from outside their own ranks. The rising tide of working-class militance presented both a general challenge to capitalist rule and a much more specific threat to capitalist control over the immediate process of production. So, too, the growing opposition of middle-class reformers, in the form of an accelerating antitrust campaign, inhibited the big capitalists' ability to coordinate their efforts. In all these ways, both the centralization of capital and the new regime resulting from that centralization were placed in jeopardy.

CHAPTER 4

Until the Battle Is Fairly Won: The Crisis of Control in the Firm

TWO quite different forces opposed the new regime of monopoly capitalism. The first was the growing working-class movement. Working-class resistance encompassed both a countering industrial organization and a political challenge. The Industrial Workers of the World—organizing the masses of unskilled, low-wage workers and refusing to cooperate with employers even in the signing of contracts—symbolized the syndicalist strategy. The Socialist Party, running candidates for most public offices, electing dozens of mayors and other officials, and having a formidable national campaigner in Eugene Debs, embodied the political strategy. Despite their differences in outlook and program, these groups and others turned every major working-class community into a steaming cauldron, furiously bubbling with union organizers, "left-wing" AFLers, socialists, anarchists, syndicalists, Christian socialists, populists, and others whose only program was resistance to their capitalist overlords. The working class movement relied on organization, on its ability to disrupt production, and on the weight of numbers. Its dual lines of attack created a crisis of control within the firm and an intense political challenge throughout society.

The second opposing force, much less uniform and self-conscious, was a broad multiclass coalition of small capitalists, farmers, intellectuals, and middle-class and professional groups that banded together to form a loose and diverse reform movement. This alliance, rooted in thoroughly respectable elements in society, was usually able to draw upon the votes and sympathies, and occasionally the organizational support, of the working class. Its principal target was the increasing economic and political power of the trusts and combines. The reformers waged their campaign in the media, in special commissions and conferences, in govenmental bodies at all levels, and in the courts. Their weapons were political influence, professional expertise, and muckraking. Although some attention was given to regulatory efforts of various sorts, the chief line of attack was antitrust.

The challenge to corporate capitalists was serious and sustained, precisely because its dual character mobilized more of society against the new regime than would have been possible under a single banner. At other times big capitalists have enlisted working-class support to override opposition from small capitalists and other property holders; more frequently, big capitalists have organized small capitalists and other property holders to fight the workers. But during this period of transition, the corporations found themselves opposed by both their potential allies.

The corporations' opponents shared a common enemy but little else. Especially on the issue of unionism, workers and small capitalists were bitter enemies, and their diverging interests help explain the failure of the two groups to coalesce, a crucial factor in the corporations' ultimate victory. Yet the middle classes were pulled from both sides, opposing corporate encroachment as much as they fought for the open shop. Acting independently but having a combined impact, the opposition to the new regime ensured that for two or so decades, the outcome was by no means certain.

Triumph and defeat are not the only consequences of conflict. The future organization of the labor process would be shaped by the nature as well as by the outcome of the workers' struggles. The workers' militance created a crisis of control within the firm, a crisis that revealed the flaws in the existing organization of work. Even though the workers were defeated, the corporations took notice, for after the immediate crisis had passed, corporate capitalists had to deal with the chronic causes underlying the crisis.

The Rising Tide

The most powerful opposition to the new regime came from the workers. Their challenge was not new: starting as far back as the nationwide revolt among railroad workers in 1877, Labor had increasingly opposed Capital over the long hours, the constant efforts to speed up the pace of work, the abusive and dehumanizing conditions, and the low wages that prevailed in most industries. In 1886, strikes over local issues by the McCormick Works employees and the Milwaukee brewery workers (including those at Pabst) added to the impassioned national movement for the eight-hour day. In 1892, striking steelworkers fought a bitter and historic struggle with the Carnegie Company, which was aided by several hundred Pinkerton Agency troops and eventually by the Pennsylvania National Guard. In 1894, the Pullman strike quickly encompassed several hundred thousand workers who joined the boycott of Pullman cars, and federal troops were required to restore "law and order." The militant resistance and countering violence continued—near-open warfare in the Colorado mines in 1903 and 1904; the great IWW strikes at McKees Rocks (1909), Lawrence (1912), and Akron and Patterson (1913); the coal miners' struggle (1914), in which Rockfeller's troops, besides killing several strikers, burned eleven children and two women; the enormous wave of strikes and labor actions during the First World War, involving workers in almost every industry and including especially sharp strife at Harvester and General Electric; and the final "holocaust" of 1919, including the massive strike at U.S. Steel, the Boston policemen's strike, and the Seattle general strike. The monopoly phase of capitalism, like capitalism itself, was ushered in with "force as its midwife."

The list of strikes reads like a roster of the consolidations: the railroads, McCormick, Carnegie (Homestead), Pullman, General Electric, U.S. Steel, International Harvester. Since the centralization of capital increasingly placed production in the hands of the biggest capitalists, it was perhaps natural that the big corporations should be in the forefront of the struggle with labor. In each case, capital was more broadly organized than the workers, and the workers lost. At Pullman, for example, workers were able to shut down the Pullman works and later the Chicago rail yards, but coordination among railroad magnates was sufficient to keep most of the rail lines in operation, thereby forestalling a nationwide crisis. (Even so, it required the intervention of troops to break the strike.) In 1901, with the formation of U.S. Steel, a battle of "all-embracing importance" loomed in the steel industry. One of the biggest AFL unions, the Amalgamated Association of Iron, Steel, and Tin Workers, represented the skilled steel workers. Although formerly powerful, it had been defeated at Homestead and in 1901 faced extinction. As John Commons' authoritative *History of Labor in the United States* put it:

> The fight was to decide whether the newly constructed citadel of wealth, the United States Steel Corporation, was to remain union or non-union, and whether the large industrial and financial interests were to accept unionism. . . . The controversy, as such, did not involve any question of wages, hours, or working conditions. It turned wholly on the extension of unionism.[1]

After a long and bitter struggle, the ability of U.S. Steel to shift production from union to nonunion plants and thus to play one group of workers against the other eventually broke the strike. Once again, the more comprehensive organization of capital proved decisive. The strike marked the end of one phase of labor history and turned the AFL toward a more conservative and more economic strategy.[2]

Although they won almost every specific battle, the capitalists nonetheless found themselves faced with mounting opposition. After the 1901 steel strike, leadership in aggressive unionism passed from the craft to the industrial unions. With the formation of the Socialist Party in 1901 and the Industrial Workers of the World in 1905, working-class activists effected a level of organization potentially as comprehensive as that which it opposed, and in the period before the war this potentiality was brought much closer to realization. Particularly after the IWW's Lawrence victory and Eugene Debs' impressive tally in the Presidential election—both in 1912—the future shape of industrial control appeared to be much in question.

For the press of the day and for historians since, the transition to monopoly capitalism was defined by "public" events, most dramatically, by mergers and the creation of giant corporations. Similarly, the labor history of the transition period is typically interpreted as resulting from developments in the labor force at large: the population's continuing shift from agriculture to industry, the growing proletarianization of the workforce, the declining importance of workers' skills, the role of immigrant labor, and the rise of unions and other working-class organizations. Given this emphasis on events external to the sphere of production, later commentators have been able to uncover only the most general linkages between the increasing centralization of production and the growth of labor militance.[3]

Yet, important as public events were, they represent only part of the story. For bosses and workers, the transition brought an immediate change in daily life. That change occurred in capitalism's "hidden abode," in the private sphere behind the doors marked "employees only." Here, the centralization of capital created a general crisis of control within the firm.

This crisis emerged from the contradiction between the firm's increasing need for control on the one hand and its diminishing ability to maintain control on the other. The need for control was a concomitant of the firm's continuing growth. For the new giants, the more far-flung operations, the more minute division of labor, and the greater complexity of organizing production all raised the costs of disruptions and control failures. Consolidation increased the social character of production and brought with it the need for more control.

Yet just when the firm was experiencing a qualitative leap in its need for control, its traditional means—hierarchical control—became less effective as a method of managing the growing workforce, including workers in those activities especially associated with monopoly industry. In other words, hierarchical control declined because it could not cope with those characteristics—the implications of size and market power—that specifically differentiated the new giants.

The capitalists' need to exercise control over a larger and more distant workforce necessitated an intensification in the arbitrariness, discipline, and harshness of the foremen's rule. Thus extension of control led directly to conditions on the shop floor that created a more effective challenge to control. On the one hand, oppressive conditions in day-to-day work emboldened workers to engage in strikes and other concerted action for higher wages and shorter hours. On the other hand, when workers organized for high wages, their collective organization and militance also served to undermine the foreman's shop-floor control. In this way, struggle for so-called economic gains established an organization that was equally useful in fighting for relief from the oppressive conditions on the shop floor. As always, the struggle over the rate at which labor power would be transformed into labor was intimately connected with the struggle over the value (wage) of the labor power itself.

The wider labor and anticapitalist struggles of the period have been fully recounted elsewhere. But what has been largely missing from traditional accounts is the crisis of control in the sphere of production, and the relation of this conflict to the broader struggle over monopoly capitalism.

The Decay of Hierarchical Control

What is important here is that the consolidation of industry immediately produced larger workforces inside the firms. The immense capitalizations of the trusts have tended to attract the most attention, but machines are productive only when workers are harnessed to run them, and aggregating workers into ever-larger firms was an equally important aspect of the centralization of capital. McCormick Company workers, some 5,000 strong, became part of the workforce of roughly 15,000 at International Harvester. The General Electric consolidation created a firm with 10,000 employees, nearly double the size of its principal predecessor, the Edison General Electric Company. The Carnegie Company, already a large firm employing over 10,000 workers, was submerged into the vast empire of U.S. Steel; the Steel trust's average employment in 1902 (its first full year of operation) was 168,000.[4] Later, when war orders began pouring in, the labor forces of the big firms again ballooned; International Harvester in 1916 employed 15,000 workers at its McCormick Works alone.[5] As firms grew from a few hundred or perhaps even several thousand workers at one or a few plants to tens or even hundreds of thousands of workers spread out in perhaps dozens of locations, the problem of control grew more serious.

Hierarchical control, the first step in rationalizing power within the firm, had provided a means of establishing a balance of power between workers and their bosses that operated in favor of capitalists. But hierarchical control could not abolish the basic conflict between workers and capitalists; workers resisted, as well as suffered from, the capitalists' power. Close supervision amounted to an intensification of the oppressive power of the firm and, as would be expected, created in turn an intensified militance among the oppressed.

For close supervision to succeed capitalists had to establish two conditions. First, the supervisor's power had to be sufficient to dominate the activity on the shop floor—sufficient, that is, to carry out management's goals of organizing production. And second, the supervisor's power had to be employed in the firm's interest, rather than (for example) simply in the foreman's own interest. But as the firm continued to grow, the capitalists' ability to establish each of these conditions eroded.

From the capitalist's perspective, the supervisor's power was to be used to correct any perceived laggardness or "soldiering" on the part of workers.[6] The presumption was that control could be maintained only by the firm's superior force, so any slacking off in effort (much less any open resistance) was to be met with direct and open punishment. Indeed, to make workers appreciate the power arrayed against them, even open flaunting of the supervisory prerogative was useful. The foreman's command carried as much weight as the sanctions that backed it up: the foreman could dock the workers' pay, physically abuse, coerce, suspend, or fire workers; have workers evicted from company-owned housing; and in many cases blacklist workers to prevent their being employed elsewhere in the industry or even the region.

But while the weapons wielded by foremen were intimidating, they were essentially negative. They punished workers for their failure to obey, to work diligently, or to do whatever suited the foreman's whim. As a naked and clearly visible system of power, hierarchical control revealed to the workers the oppressive nature of capitalist relations. Negative sanctions provided a natural focus for resistance. Sabotage, physical threats to exceptionally tyrannical foremen, appeals to higher bosses, and collective (if informal) understandings about work paces quickly supplemented the more open strike demands for curbs on the arbitrariness of foreman and became commonplace companions to close supervision. While mostly unsuccessful in gaining redress of grievances, these efforts nonetheless pushed workers to unite in opposition to oppressive power. Hierarchical control's harsh regimen, then, tended to evoke a response from the workers that was equally harsh and militant.

What were missing, of course, were the positive attractions for workers that, in the entrepreneurial firm, had grown out of the personal ties and more intimate associations between capitalist and worker.[7] There existed few grounds for an appeal to workers based on their sense of identification with the capitalist or the company. What had been a subtle blend of incentives and sanctions in the entrepreneurial firm (varying, of course, with the particular capitalist, industry, and period) became, in the large firm, almost entirely a repressive system. The capitalist in his office was now separated from the worker on the shop floor. The internal structure of the firm thus came to mirror more accurately and more harshly the class divisions in society at large. The continued growth in the firm's workforce extended this process to crisis proportions. At both Pullman and U.S. Steel, the harsh and oppressive quality of shop-floor life and the total absence of positive incentives provoked almost perpetual conflict and, eventually, spectacular outbursts.

Intimately connected to this conflict was the increasing difficulty that capitalists encountered in ensuring that foremen would use their power in the firm's interest rather than in their own. Foremen were notoriously unpredictable in this respect, as the complaints of the workers seem to bear out. Foremen's identification with management was never assured, for they had goals of their own quite different from those of the firm, and favoritism, idiosyncracies, prejudice, and grudges all seemed to flourish under this system. The result was arbitrary and personal punishment and undoubtedly widespread abuse of power.

Although hierarchical control required personal supervision, expansion of the firm implied an increasing separation of those most motivated to supervise in the capitalist's interests (the owners and high-level managers) from the actual shop-floor supervisors. Just as earlier the growth of the entrepreneurial firm had eventually broken all personal bonds between the capitalist and the workers, so now growth in the expanded firm dissolved any personal ties between the capitalist and all but the upper fringe of the supervisory staff. In place of the personal relationship was the naked employer-employee relationship. Here again, U.S. Steel provided an illustration of the problem. In 1910 the company employed a force of over four thousand *foremen*, as well as numerous higher-level supervisors and managers.[8] Simply overseeing the foremen was too much for the top managers. So between managers and workers there emerged ever-proliferating layers of less reliable supervisors.

The top-echelon managers were further separated from the workers by the form of the expansion. Consolidation produced multiplant concerns; the scattered production facilities of the previously independent companies became linked, not through geographical proximity but through the administrative and supervisory apparatus. "Headquarters," rather than being divided among separate offices adjoining the dispersed plants, was centralized in the financial districts, away from all plants. U.S. Steel's main office, for example, was located in New York, despite the concentration of production facilities in Pittsburgh. At General Electric, the new headquarters was explicitly established near one of its production facilities in Schenectady in order to provide for the "necessary direction and control in the executive offices to keep the large enterprise functioning satisfactorily" and to "keep a close watch on the handling" of production; even so, the company relied less and less on face-to-face contact.[9] Thus, at the plant level, even the highest officials were already several tiers from the top.

Moreover, consolidation placed a new type of owner at the top of the corporation. As corporate ownership became more widely dispersed, the financial investor replaced the industrial entrepreneur.[10] But since finance capitalists tended to have less experience with and less interest in production per se, management was often left in the hands of professional managers, instituting a new managerial layer between capitalists and workers. At General Electric, the managers at each of the three manufacturing facilities (Schenectady; Lynn, Mass.; and Harrison, N.Y.) reported to the third vice president at headquarters in Schenectady. Above the vice president for production were the president and the various committees of the board of directors, upon which sat the finance capitalists who represented the actual owners of the corporation. As Harold Passer notes, the manufacturing facilities "had a surprising degree of independence."[11]

Thus, the firm's delegated power could be used to promote the supervisors' own ends quite independently of the firm's goals. Within the existing system of control, capitalists had little way of checking or channeling this power for their own interests, since the system was built on the foreman as re-created entrepreneur, with wide discretion over his workers.

"Organizational uncoupling," as it has aptly been termed, undoubtedly tended to reduce the efficiency of the firm.[12] But its biggest effect was to weaken the supervisor's power in the workers' eyes, since the boss's authority was clearly being used for personal gain rather than because production demanded it.

Even so, the crisis on the shop floor might have been contained had it not been for the larger social context in which it appeared. After all, pioneering big firms had faced these problems earlier and escaped without any strategy more sophisticated than that of intensifying close supervision (and in some cases introducing inside contracting to make the foremen even more like subentrepreneurs). What elevated shop-floor conflict to crisis proportions in capitalism's transition period was the interaction of this conflict with the wider worker revolt in society.

Shop-floor conflict inevitably became part of the struggle over the regime of monopoly capitalism because it occurred in a broader social context of sharp class tensions. And it was a crisis for monopoly capitalists, because the broader context both generalized the conflict and tended to strengthen workers. The social context thus reduced the individual employer's ability to impose solutions unilaterally on his workforce.

One part of the context was the great leap in the social character of production brought about by the centralization process. What in a small firm had been chiefly an affair to be settled among the participants became, in a huge consolidated firm, a *social* problem. In the case of a strike, all consumers of a particular commodity were affected, rather than just consumers of one small firm's output. The 1902 coal strike, for example, threatened to deprive the entire east coast of coal during the coming winter. Since the anthracite industry had been brought under the effective control of the Philadelphia and Reading and other large railroads, a strike necessarily meant an industry-wide shutdown. The big owners' insistence on forcing all mine operators to bargain together created extreme public anxiety about the strike, however, eventually forcing President Roosevelt to establish an arbitration board to settle it.[13]

Centralization increasingly meant that industrial strife could damage the entire regional economy, for other capitalists, both small and large, as well as residents of the region in which the principal works were located, city or state officials, tradesmen, shopkeepers, and so on were likely to be affected. But the interests of these groups were not always identical with those of the individual capitalist, and so successful use of the capitalist's power became less certain. The 1904 strike at International Harvester, for example, brought out the basic conflict between Cyrus McCormick II (the president) and George Perkins (the director representing the Morgan interests). McCormick was anxious to resist unionization and considered using the methods successfully employed in 1886—a lockout, strikebreakers, armed vigilantes, and the use of violence to defend the plants. Perkins feared the spillover effects on labor in the steel industry, where Morgan interests in U.S. Steel were considerably more significant than their investment in the Harvester trust, and so pressed for conciliation. Harvester officials apparently faced another constraint. They were worried about the precarious legal and political position of the trust, and because the public outcry over consolidation had made antitrust a live issue, they were forced to modify their bargaining position.[14] The increasingly social character of production thus tended to make each large firm's (and each industry's) labor battles more portentous for society, and wider forces increasingly impinged on individual conflicts.

Most importantly, of course, the context included the increasingly comprehensive organization of workers, a development that clearly resulted from struggles over wages, hours of work, and other factors as well as oppressive shop-floor conditions. Close supervision necessarily resulted in frequent threats and often mass firings and layoffs. But increasing worker organization meant that, while the firm could still safely dismiss recalcitrant *individuals* with relative impunity, it could not easily do so with rebellious *groups* of workers. Collective action, whether established in a formal union or growing more loosely out of the discipline and collective orientation of the workers, meant that firing workers to maintain discipline increasingly imposed heavy costs on the employer. The capitalists' ability to substitute labor from the pool of the unemployed was undermined not so much by shortages of labor or skills as by the power of workers in labor associations to create disruptions and prevent new workers from entering their jobs.

1894 and 1919: From Shop-Floor Resistance to Collective Struggle

The increasing costs of control mechanisms and their diminishing effectiveness were evident in many places. For those directly involved, they were most apparent in the day-to-day life on the shop floor. For workers, the arbitrariness of foremen brought daily grievances and continual resentment and resistance. For foremen, the loss of control manifested itself in the growing harshness and violence required to maintain production. At a somewhat greater distance, top-echelon managers worried about the phenomenon of organizational uncoupling—that is, the "breakdown in relationships between top and lower levels of management . . . deterioration of the top or central manager's ability to maintain effective control over subordinate managerial positions."[15]

Similarly, the immediate cause of these developments was also obvious: as capitalists extended their lines of control and attempted to intensify their grip, workers resisted. David Montgomery has provided an index of "control struggles"—that is, efforts "by workers to establish collective control over their conditions of work." He notes that since 1881 there have been three especially active periods: 1901–1904, 1916–1920, and 1934–1941. The World

War I wave in particular, he observes, "tended to be short and take on more of an outlaw quality"; that is, the struggles were increasingly "unofficial," initiated and carried out by small groups of workers without the union hierarchy's leadership or approval. Control strikes thus tended to supplement the other weapons available to workers—sabotage, self-policed limitations of work paces and output rates, insistence on craft rules, and so on—as a means of challenging the foremen's power.[16]

Yet, if workers responded to the growing oppressiveness of job conditions and arbitrary control by offering day-to-day resistance, such opposition was not the only and certainly not the most dramatic form of the struggle. Workers directly and collectively opposed capitalist hegemony at the workplace through the massive and militant strikes of the period.

The great strikes of the transition period have most often been attributed to long hours of work and low wages. Unquestionably, these were vital concerns. Yet what is rarely recognized is that the harsh and arbitrary discipline of hierarchical control was of equal importance and directly contributed to the workers' determination to strike. Nowhere was the connection between work organization and collective resistance more apparent than in the strikes at Pullman and U.S. Steel.

The Pullman Strike

In 1894, at the beginning of the transition period, the Pullman workers waged one of the fiercest and most significant struggles in American labor history. A direct cause of the strike was the oppressive and arbitrary control that foremen exercised over the workers.

In the early 1880s, the Pullman Palace Car Company had built in Pullman, a suburb of Chicago, a large car manufacturing works. From the first, the town and factories had been carefully designed

> to cause the best class of mechanics to seek that place for employment in preference to others. We also desired to establish the place on such a basis as would exclude all baneful influences.[17]

Although George Pullman boasted that he had successfully excluded saloons and brothels, the company's subsequent policy made clear that the chief "baneful influence" he wanted to banish was unionism.

The town and the works quickly spread, and despite other intentions, the rapid growth forced the company to introduce a more heavy-handed style of supervision. In part this involved the use of spies, bribery or corruption of local officials, control of credit, and the other repressive features characteristic of company towns. But it also involved more arbitrary control within the firm. Writing of his visit to Pullman in 1884, Richard Ely put it as follows:

> One just cause of complaint [among the workers] is what in government affairs would be called a bad civil service, that is, a bad administration in respect to the employment, retention, and promotion of employees. Change is constant in men and officers, and each new superior appears to have his own friends, whom he appoints to desirable positions. Favoritism and nepotism . . . are oft-repeated and apparently well-substantiated charges.[18]

Dissatisfaction apparently remained high throughout the 1880s and early 1890s. Then in 1893 the severe depression began, and in response to declining sales the company initiated a series of substantial wage cuts. American Railway Union (ARU) organizing began in March, 1894. On May 7, the workers sent a delegation to management demanding that the company rescind the wage cuts and reduce the heavy rents in company-owned housing. When three of the union committeemen were fired two days later, the workers walked off their jobs. The great Pullman strike was on.[19]

Investigation into the causes of the strike reveals that, from the first, the real income (wages and rents) issue was tied to the arbitrary and tyrannical power wielded by foremen. For each individual worker, of course, the connection between the two matters was direct: a foreman could reduce the worker's pay by reducing the worker's wage rate or simply by assigning the worker to poorly paying tasks. As one worker described her forewoman,

> She . . . had a few favorites in the room, to whom she gave all the best work, that they could make the most money on.[20]

Or, as another worker expressed it,

> The foreman's assistants have been entrusted to fix prices [wages paid for a job]. This is the result: one man gets $2.00 for scraping a door, another man receives $1.75 for the same work.[21]

By refusing to approve work already completed, providing poor materials, or making workers sit around waiting for another job rather than giving them work immediately, the foreman could effectively reduce the wages of those he wanted to punish. Nor were brutality and violence off limits to foremen, as an episode related by Thomas Heathcoate, a Pullman car-builder, illustrates.

> One of the foremen—he has a very violent temper—had a piece of work done which he had to wait for some little time on account of the workman not being able to do it in a certain length of time, and he struck him in the face, making his nose bleed. The matter was reported to the management, but they took no action whatever in regard to it. The man was going to sue the foreman, but he was told by the foreman of the department to which he belonged that if he did he would be discharged.[22]

In short, the foreman could always dismiss a worker and, if sufficiently angry, could have the worker blacklisted from the entire railroad industry. In all these ways, the control exercised by foremen directly affected the bread-and-butter issues.

But even aside from their impact on wages, conditions on the shop floor created resentment and resistance. When the workers' delegation met with the Pullman managers on May 7 to request wage restorations and rent cuts, they also demanded an end to the "constant harassment by foremen." As Reverend William Carwardine, pastor of a Pullman church during the strike and an intimate of many of the strikers, put it,

> In this whole question of wages the public must bear in mind that the wage difficulty was not the whole trouble. Other things being equal, the men could have borne with more grace the reduction of wages. But there was personal abuse and tyrannical dealing in the shops.[23]

As evidence of the workers' concern for better shop conditions, Carwardine cited several letters sent to him by Pullman workers. One Jennie Curtis wrote:

> It was very hard to have to work for such small wages [as prevailed after the cuts], which would afford a person a mere existence. But the tyrannical and abusive treatment we received from our forewoman made our daily cares so much harder to bear. She was a woman who had sewed and lived among us for years, one, you would think, who would have some compassion on us when she was put in a position to do so. When she was put over us by the superintendent as our forewoman, she seemed to delight in showing her power in hurting the girls in every possible way. At times her conduct was almost unbearable. She was so abusive to certain girls that she disliked, that they could not stand it. . . . When a girl was sick and asked to go home during the day, she would tell them to their face they were not sick, the cars had to be got out, and they could not go home. . . . We would complain of her to the foreman and general foreman, but they all upheld her and if you were not willing to take her abuse you could go.[24]

Another employee connected the shop abuses and the strike directly:

> So with a prospect of working an indefinite length of time at these prices [piece-rates] and under an *overbearing* and *profane* foreman, we struck and will stay out until the battle is fairly won.[25]

Moreover, as Stanley Buder has emphasized, the issue of despotic foremen had appeared earlier in the company's history. Discerned as a serious problem by Ely in 1884, abuse by foremen was the cause of a strike by woodcarvers in 1888. Investigating the 1894 strike, the United States Strike Commission heard five of the eight Pullman workers who testified complain of arbitrariness, favoritism, and other abuses by foremen, and several mentioned oppressive shop conditions as a major cause of the strike. Their testimony is all the more revealing since the Commission was primarily interested in wages and rents, and the workers had to bring up shop abuses on their own initiative.

Of course, the Pullman strike was significant not so much for what happened at Pullman itself, but rather for the highly effective boycott of Pullman cars by the railroad workers. Yet among railway workers too, the issue of abusive and arbitrary rule by foremen created much resentment and fueled militance. Franklin Mills, a discharged Baltimore and Ohio employee, stated the point flatly to officials investigating the strike:

COMMISSIONER KERNAN: What was the feeling among the employees on the Baltimore and Ohio with regard to striking prior to the time they struck?

MILLS: It was not very favorable.

COMMISSIONER KERNAN: Had there been any cuts in the wages about which they were dissatisfied?

MILLS: Not lately. The most of the difficulty on the Baltimore and Ohio was favoritism, pets, and maladministration of some of the petty officers.[26]

Charles Naylor, an ARU local president and a fireman on the Pittsburgh, Fort Wayne, and Chicago line until the strike, stated:

In a large number of roads there was a feeling among the employees that they were almost in a helpless condition to stand against the oppression of the petty officials, and the petty officials took advantage of that feeling and deviled the men, just as their particular temperament at the moment led them to do.[27]

Hierarchical control, implemented as a device for exercising power over workers, was reaping its fruits in kind.

The Steel Strike

When a quarter of a million steelworkers withdrew their labor power in September, 1919, they began one of the most bitter and brutal strikes in United States history. The strike's failure signaled the end of the transition period.

Fierce conflict in the iron and steel industry stretched back to the Civil War, but it grew increasingly intense at the end of the nineteenth century. The skilled ironmakers' unions maintained a firm grip on production through their craft restrictions, the limitation of apprenticeships, and the scarcity of their skills. Thus David Brody notes that the union contract at the Carnegie Company's Homestead Works included nearly sixty pages of "footnotes" specifying work rules that protected steelworkers at the job or otherwise regulated the labor process.[28] But as the industry turned from iron production, which required skilled workers, to the manufacture of steel, which could be mechanized, the strength of the craft unions was increasingly undermined.

Conflict over control of the labor process extended over several decades. The first crucial battle came at Homestead in 1892 and resulted in complete victory for the company. The Amalgamated, fatally weakened, hung on in some shops until 1903; its last gasp was the strike in 1901 against the new giant of the industry, U.S. Steel. Workers continued to resist; for example, at McKees Rocks and at the Bethlehem works in 1909 and Youngstown in 1915. But without being able to organize U.S. Steel's 60 percent of the industry, they could not expect much success.[29]

By 1919, then, the industry had been transformed from craft-dominated iron production to the mechanized manufacture of steel by masses of nonunion unskilled and semiskilled workers. The companies had made the most of their victory, and conditions in the plants reflected the workers' powerlessness. At the end of the decade that David Montgomery calls "the decisive period in the battle for the eight-hour day [for] American workers," approximately half of the steelworkers found themselves still locked in a twelve-hour day. Of the eight industries Paul Douglas studied, the iron and steel industry in 1919 averaged by far the longest hours: its 66.1 hours a week exceeded the average of the other industries (52.4 hours) by almost a full day and a half each week.[30]

On the other hand, wages—especially average weekly or monthly earnings, given the long work week—tended to be high relative to other industries. The great labor scarcity during the war had driven wage rates up quickly, so that by 1919 iron and steelworkers earned a premium of roughly 70 percent over the hourly wages prevailing in all manufacturing; average full-time weekly earnings in steel were 210 percent higher than the overall manufacturing average. Moreover, real wages in the industry, stagnant beteween 1890 and 1915, had advanced about 25 percent during the war. Manufacturing wages, even at a premium, were not very high; one study found that the annual earnings of 72 percent of all steelworkers were "below the level set by government experts as the *minimum of comfort* level for families of five." Wages were also quite unequally distributed, so that unskilled, primarily immigrant workers earned considerably less than is suggested by the averages. Nonetheless, the rapid and substantial wage increases between 1915 and 1919 were shared, albeit unequally, among all categories of workers.[31]

The relatively high pay received by the steelworkers did not mean, of course, that further wage advances were unimportant to the strikers. Still, it does raise the question of why steel, rather than other industries, should have become the locus of such protracted and savage struggle. As in the case of Pullman, much turned on the organization of work.

U.S. Steel in 1919 exemplified the tyranny and contradictions of hierarchical control within the expanded firm. The company had used its earlier victory over unionism to maintain a system of power little changed from that of the nineteenth century. As a group of progressive churchmen investigating the industry put it, "The character of the control in the Steel Corporation is plain: it is arbitrary control. The workers call it 'autocratic.' " Judge Gary, the company's top official, had emphasized to the presidents of subsidiary companies the importance of "retaining the control and management of your affairs, keeping the whole thing in your own hands." Gary's stricture was principally directed at excluding unions or other workers' groups from interfering with management prerogatives, and the company quickly discharged and blacklisted known union men.[32]

The strikers' complaints to a Senate investigating committee reveal much about the nature and extent of the control exercised by foremen and supervisors. Several workers testified to being laid off "for nothing"; one indicated that after arranging in advance for a day off, he was laid off for failing to come to work; another complained of being regularly docked an hour's pay for arriving "three-quarters of a minute late." Others declared that there was no appeal from the foreman's rule, because as soon as a worker tried to go to a higher boss, "he calls the foreman in, and he [the foreman] will make it so uncomfortable for us in there that we will have to quit." One reported that after he did quit to get away from an "abusive" foreman, the foreman blacklisted him so that he couldn't get a job anywhere else, and after three months without work, he had to return. Others reported that they had never been able to learn their rate of pay or how much tonnage they were entitled to and had to wait until payday to learn what they earned.[33] The foreman's power over his workers was nearly absolute.

And the corporation, as the churchmen emphasized several times, had little means of supervising its supervisors.[34] Indeed, one of the ironies of Judge Gary's tough attitude on control was that because foremen and supervisors exercised such vast and unrestrained power in order to keep out union men, the managers were not only relieved of but were also denied real contact with the men in the plants. As a result, the foremen's great power was largely unsupervised, leading to arbitrariness and favoritism. One discharged steelworker, an AFL official during the strike, described the situation well:

> Under the system, the present system, a man has no show at all for his rights.

Where I was working the man who discharged me had either three or four brothers come there, and they was working under him, and they got more money than I was getting, and they had not been there over more than three or four months, while I started with the plant itself. If you stand in with the boss, if you pay him something, or if you give him booze or something like that, then you can get a good job.[35]

The harsh discipline, the arbitrariness, the sense of having no say in the life of the plant made the steelworkers resentful and angry. They had neither union nor company officials to whom they could appeal their grievances. Under such conditions, hierarchical control led directly to resistance, as members of the investigating committee found out. Andy Beckel, an Austrian worker who was interviewed by the committee while he was standing on strike in the streets of Homestead, underlined the connection between control and resistance.

THE CHAIRMAN: Why did you strike? What was it that made you strike?

MR. BECKEL: Well, I strike because we did not have the right conditions, and we were only paid 42 cents an hour, and we worked like a mule, and if you ever say anything to them they will discharge you, and you didn't have no word to say. We were never treated right while we were there.[36]

George Mikulvich, an immigrant from Dalmatia employed in the coke works, was stopped and interviewed by the committee on the streets of Clairton; he declared (through an interpreter) that he and others were on strike because

they wanted to work shorter hours and get more money and better conditions in the mill; better treatment from the bosses and the foremen.[37]

P. H. Brogan said that one of the most important things he and other workers were striking for was

to get the union recognized so that we can have somebody that can talk to the bosses.

For Andrew Pido, a twenty-three-year-old Clairton laborer, arbitrary control by foremen created a personal motivation for his participation in the strike.

THE CHAIRMAN: What is the reason you struck this time?

MR. PIDO: I strike on eight hours a day and better conditions.

SENATOR MCKELLAR: What sort of conditions do you want better?

MR. PIDO: Well, when I was working I had a partner; he was on one shift and I was on the other, and I was doing all the job, and he was getting the pay. I was getting 50 cents and hour and he got 61.

SENATOR MCKELLAR: How did that happen?

MR. PIDO: Because he was a better friend of the boss than I was.

SENATOR STERLING: Did you do exactly the same work?

MR. PIDO: The same work.[38]

The strikers' comments are remarkable on two counts. The concern over arbitrary and brutal foremen was apparently pressing, because (as with the Pullman investigation) the Senate committee almost invariably wanted to question workers about wages and hours of work and considered working conditions only when workers themselves forced discussion of the issue. Moreover, most workers interviewed drew upon direct personal experience to describe the oppressiveness of hierarchical control; they felt no need to depend on other workers' experiences or on abstract strike issues. As at Pullman, the system that was supposed to control workers became one of the chief burdens motivating workers to fight back.

The Reformers' Attack on Consolidation

While workers were organizing and striking, middle-class reformers mounted a very different attack on the corporations—the antitrust campaign. Threats of antitrust enforcement hindered corporate attempts to establish collusive pricing procedures, while actual antitrust prosecutions directly threatened the existence of many of the biggest consolidations. Thus, while the corporations' second source of opposition did not challenge basic property relations (far from it—the "respectable" origins of the movement implied that it had its own property to protect), it did directly threaten the profitability of the new corporations. By challenging their right to exist, the antitrust movement made it more difficult for the corporations to deal with their more worrisome opponents, the workers.

The antitrust campaign would not have been possible if it had not reflected the needs of broad multiclass opposition to the corporations. Enforcement required mobilizing the powers of government against the biggest capitalists. Yet the state is merely an arena in which class relations take an explicitly "political" form, and it would certainly be wrong to suggest that the state during the transition period was not dominated by the capitalist class. Nonetheless, conflict *within* the capitalist class created a situation in which the state apparatus gained a relatively greater degree of autonomy, and other groups (professionals and intellectuals, for example) were able to play a greater role in determining state policies.

The transition produced a situation of intraclass conflict. Corporate capitalists faced considerable opposition from small capitalists, who allied with citizens' "reform" groups, farmers, the conservative labor unions, and others who rightly feared that their own interests would suffer from the corporate program. These groups opposed the corporations on several important questions. One issue was the corporations' access to state power to facilitate their operations—for example, state regulation to ease the corporations' entry into foreign meat markets or state subsidies to train workers in needed vocational skills.[39] The most dramatic form of the conflict, however, involved antitrust activities.

The antitrust debate primarily concerned laws and their enforcement. Common-law precedents and early interpretations of the Sherman Antitrust Act had proved to be only a temporary hindrance to consolidation. But beginning soon after the turn of the century, considerable uncertainty existed as to how freely the trusts would be allowed to operate. The dissolution of Morgan's Northern Securities holding company in 1904 first raised the basic question of "bigness," a theme that echoed in the great number of antitrust prosecutions that followed.

An early resolution to the problem was attempted by the leaders of big business, particularly the J. P. Morgan interests, soon after the Northern Securities decision. In the case of International Harvester, for example, a working agreement was established whereby I-H turned over its records to the Bureau of Corporations, and if the Bureau established any wrongdoing, I-H agreed to cease such operations. The natural imbalance between the amount of records and complexity of decisions made by International Harvester and the meager resources of the Bureau ensured that no effective action could be undertaken. Moreover, the "cooperation" amounted to what was termed an "immunity bath" protecting the corporations from criminal prosecution.[40]

The public viewed such half-measures as insufficient, however, and the prosecutions necessarily continued. In the ten or so years following the Northern Securities case, major antitrust suits were filed against Standard Oil, American Tobacco, International Harvester, U.S. Steel, Armour, Swift, and American Sugar Refining—all among the top ten industrial corporations in 1909—as well as against Aluminum Company of America, General Electric, Corn Products Refining, DuPont, and many other big firms. Standard Oil and American Tobacco were dissolved into ten and four parts, respectively. International Harvester, Corn Products, and DuPont were forced to sell portions of their operations.

This unprecedented—and unrepeated—intervention by federal agencies contributed an element of uncertainty to the operations of big corporations. For example, U.S. Steel, when incorporated, controlled 65 percent of the steel market, and for a time it appeared that the Supreme Court would define as "unreasonable" restraint of trade a situation in which (along with a number of other conditions) one firm controlled more than 50 percent of the market. Judge Gary of U.S. Steel apparently decided to forego further consolidation and even to allow some erosion of U.S. Steel's position, in order to escape antitrust action.[41] Similarly, Armour, Swift, and the other big meatpacking companies were forced to dismantle the National Packing Company, their jointly owned price-fixing vehicle. The dramatic Standard Oil and American Tobacco cases raised the possibility that all the big consolidations might, in time, be broken up.

Clearly, big business had to establish its power with regard to the state before the fruits of consolidation could be realized. Corporate capitalists needed a context in which public support and the power of the state could be swung decisively to their side. Events on the world stage were to come to their rescue.

Monopoly Capitalists Triumphant

Wars, even foreign wars, have often provided dominant classes with an opportunity to settle domestic scores. Military conflict, especially if it is successful, can generate new support for the government and groups in power. It provides a patriotic atmosphere within which the dominant class can portray its opposition as (wittingly or unwittingly) traitorous. The (perhaps inevitable) allegiance to one's own country makes such a tactic inordinately effective in mobilizing public opinion.

At no time in our history has war served more effectively as a cover for suppressing domestic conflict than it did during World War I. Recent historical scholarship has suggested that one of the principal pressures pushing Kaiser Wilhelm's government toward war was the need to deflect and stifle the growing working-class movement inside Germany.[42] As we now know, World War I broke the internationalist bonds of the Second International and ended the Social Democracy's power to demand reform at home. At terrible cost to the world and eventually to itself as well, the German bourgeoisie was saved from its own working class. Such a thesis of intentional war-mongering could hardly be sustained for the United States, yet the war had much the same effect here. Moreover, it produced an altogether more pleasing situation for American corporate capitalists. Whatever would have happened in the absence of the war we can never know, of course, and it would be a mistake of historical interpretation to assume that the resolution of conflicts worked out during the war would not have been forthcoming in a time of peace. There were strong forces pushing the corporate program that undoubtedly would have achieved the same result without war. Nonetheless, it was in the context of war that the triumph occurred.

The war period began with "preparedness" activities in 1915 and extended through "reconversion" and the dismantling of the wartime controls, many of which continued to 1920. As the war began, several things happened at once. Rising defense expenditures and huge military contracts from abroad produced a war boom, ending the prewar stagnation and holding out the prospect of high profits to big and small producers alike. Public concern with the power of the corporations, particularly among small businesses, was deflected by the war. And as tighter labor markets made workers more confident, their increased militance brought them into direct conflict with small as well as big capitalists.

The war thus intervened to destroy the line-up of political forces that had made possible the vigorous application of the antitrust law. In the first place, the war dissipated public pressure for antitrust activity. Moreover, the growing role of corporate businessmen in actually running the government made any independent federal action unlikely. Businessmen in government argued that dissolutions would interrupt the war effort, and with public attention focused elsewhere, the courts and prosecutors readily accepted the argument. All the major antitrust decisions that went against the corporations were handed down before the war. After the war, when final decisions were made in the U.S. Steel, International Harvester, and other cases, public sentiment had drastically changed, and so had the courts' opinion: no major dissolution occurred.

Equally important, the government itself directly encouraged collusion. The theory was that production losses hurting the war effort could be avoided by coordination, in effect by bringing all major producers together. Under the leadership of the War Industries Board, coordinating committees staffed by prominent businessmen were established for over sixty commodities. These committees were open, legal, and even patriotically applauded groups that were encouraged to perform for each industry what Judge Gary had earlier tried to do at his dinners. They had power to establish prices, allocate production, and determine the use of raw materials—in short, to do everything required to administer a system of corespective behavior.

Once the need for coordinated production had been accepted, it was natural that the composition of the committees should reflect the interests of the major producers in each industry. For example, the Cooperative Committee on Copper, established by the Council on National Defense (prewar predecessor of the War Industries Board), consisted of the presidents of

Anaconda Copper, Calumet and Hecla Mining, Utah Copper, and United Verde Copper, the vice presidents of Phelps Dodge and Kennecott Mines, and Murray M. Guggenheim of the powerful Guggenheim family interests. Every one of the major copper-producing firms was represented.[43] Other commodity sections were similarly constituted.

The result was the most complete coordination of production yet achieved within industry. When combined with the wartime boom, this collusion made profits soar. U.S. Steel's profits in 1916 were three times what they had been in 1912, and those for 1916–1920 were more than double the amount earned in 1911–1915.[44] International Harvester's profits, though based only indirectly on the war effort, showed an almost identical increase. In effect, the corporations were granted a crucial five- or six-year period during which they were not only permitted but actually encouraged to coordinate their policies. Even those recalcitrant producers who resisted collusion and favored old-time competition were compelled under government-sanctioned pressure to cooperate.

With the split between small and big capitalists decisively resolved in favor of the corporations, the "natural leadership" of the biggest capitalists reasserted itself. Small capitalists once again lined up with their betters, this time to face the postwar "red menace."

Corporate capitalists in and out of government took the lead in the campaign to limit working-class power. In part, this involved compromising with and coopting the conservative union leadership. Through "national interest" forums like the National Civic Federation, Samuel Gompers and other labor leaders had been brought into "responsible" relations with the corporations. When the war came, the AFL leaders proclaimed a ban on strikes for "the duration."[45]

Yet even so, the resistance did not fade. As the war effort progressed, labor actions became more frequent and more militant. Fueled by the war-generated labor scarcity, both union membership and the number of strikes reached all-time highs during 1917, 1918, and 1919. Moreover, the official AFL no-strike pledge abdicated strike leadership to the Socialists and labor radicals. The Socialist Party opposed the war, and the IWW and other radical unions refused to recognize any ban on strikes.

With businessmen actively running the government and with Wilson and the other political leaders worried about building support for the war, the burden of suppressing labor shifted from individual employers to agencies of the federal government. The government in turn relied more and more on its emergency war powers to prevent "disruption" of military production. As Selig Perlman and Phillip Taft put it,

> The decline of the I.W.W. has been attributed to the rise of communism and to

> its failure to adapt itself to postwar conditions. The decline of the I.W.W. can be more plausibly explained by the systematic removal of its leadership by imprisonment, itself part and parcel of the intensified hostility of the public engendered by war-time emotion and interested employer propaganda. The marvel is not that the I.W.W. declined, but that for seven terrible years it was able to survive without crumbling into dust.[46]

What occurred dramatically and violently in the cases of the IWW and the Socialist Party took place more quietly but no less surely throughout the entire labor movement.

The return of the Republicans to power in 1920 did not mark the "return to normalcy," but rather the end of any effective challenge to the monopoly capitalists' new regime. The unsuccessful coal miners' strike in 1923 represented the last hurrah of the opposition movement before its long decline in the 1920s.

The transition period that ended in the early twenties produced three effects of lasting importance for industrial structure. First, the big corporations established secure positions in most major industries, but they were prevented from achieving outright monopolies; oligopoly or shared monopoly became the typical industrial form. Through the wartime encouragement to coordinate the war effort, corporate collusion created the basis for corespective behavior. Big corporations learned to exploit their market power with shared rather than single-firm monopolistic control. Competition was reduced to nonprice behavior among established rivals, but it was not eliminated.

The failure of big corporations to take the final step in consolidation (as Rockefeller and Duke had succeeded in doing in oil and tobacco and as Morgan had attempted to do in several industries) can only be explained by the effectiveness of the organized public opposition to the trusts and by the antitrust activities that that opposition necessitated. While the mergers of the 1898–1902 period were horizontal, reflecting simple desires for more market control, the mergers of the late twenties were largely vertical, and those of the sixties were diagonal—that is, they increased diversification. Thus, while the opposition could not blunt the basic capitalist tendency towards centralization of capital, it did alter the form that centralization took.

The second effect of the transition was that class conflict pushed corporate capitalists to link their interests more closely to state power. This connection was partly preventative: corporations had to ensure that state power would not be turned against them, as it had been to some extent in the prewar, antitrust policies. But more generally, corporations sought to use government to establish a "stable" and "responsible" framework for negotiating with labor. The integration of Samuel Gompers, John Mitchell, and other conservative and primarily AFL labor leaders in an "industrial relations" system during the war had promised a solution acceptable to the corporations. Nonetheless, it involved a *quid pro quo*, for the labor leaders demanded in return for their compliance that the government enter the bargaining process as a "neutral" outside force. This demand did not mean much in the immediate postwar period (the 1920s), because labor was too weak to enforce its due. But the outlines of the "corporate state" would become important with the reemergence of working class power in the 1930s. Indeed, the postwar period can be considered as the first phase in that blending of corporate and "national" interests that led, in the 1930s, to the macromanagement of the economy, and, in the post-World War II period, to the worldwide defense of potential areas of corporate investment.[47] Ultimately, as the working class and its representatives gained sufficient strength to force real concessions, the politicizing process was to lead to the present crisis of democratic government.

The third result was that the brutal and violent means by which corporate capitalists defeated labor in the titanic wartime and postwar struggle was exposed as an inadequate basis for controlling workers. Capitalists came to realize that a new system of control was required and that continued reliance on military force would, in the not-very-distant future, lead to disaster for the system. Force could be used when crisis demanded it, and the half-decade ending in 1920 certainly proved that employers would call upon any means at their disposal when their class position was in jeopardy. But force could not be the *first* line of defense. As labor's organization slowly but inevitably improved, it became evident that a system of labor controls built only on force would not long survive.

By the early 1920s, then, corporate capitalists had achieved an impressive consolidation of their power. In each of the major industries, the centralization of capital had transformed the market. Competition among the many was replaced by that now-familiar combination of competition *and* collusion among the few. Moreover, the regime of monopoly capitalism was secure. The big capitalists had successfully broken up the popular antitrust alliance; they had bent the state to active support of programs servicing corporate needs; and they had smashed the dangerous elements in the labor opposition and coopted the conservative labor leadership.

The capitalists' triumph produced a kind of stability that has lasted to the present. Exceptionally stupid management might threaten individual firms, and the severe depression of the 1930s would challenge the entire system sufficiently to make major reforms necessary. But the basic operation of the system in the half-century following the transition would largely be the working out of the potentials that were promised by consolidation.

CHAPTER 5

Seeing the World: Corporations in Monopoly Capitalism

THE CONSOLIDATION of industry and the victory of the corporate capitalists established the new era of monopoly capitalism. This new context altered both what was necessary and what was possible in organizing production. Since the 1920s workers and their bosses alike have faced new prospects and new constraints.

Most importantly, the transition produced two distinct types of business enterprise in the United States.[1] A few hundred corporations with extensive market power and tens or hundreds of thousands of employees exist at the center of the economy. These firms—collectively termed the economy's "core"—control the major portion of the economy's production, profit making, and accumulation.

Around them, in industries or branches of industry that the big corporations have not yet invaded, nearly 12 million small and medium-sized firms—the economy's "periphery"—continue to survive. These firms represent a continuation of nineteenth-century capitalism. Only in one important respect have things changed: small firms now exist in a system dominated by big business. Where nineteenth-century firms were powerless in the face of the impersonal mechanisms of the competitive market, their small-fry counterparts today must also cope with the power of big firms. Thus, while small firms have many competing sellers in their own product markets, they face great monopoly power everywhere else. They may be able to sell to only one or a few firms, a situation auto parts suppliers well understand; they may use raw materials or finished products available from only one or a few manufacturers, as McDonald's franchises do; they may depend on the big capitalists for financing, for retailing their products, or for granting subcontract work. And even where small businesses are relatively independent of these pressures, they always face the chance, usually the disaster, of having a giant invade their market. Small firms today exist under either the actual dominance or the long shadow of the big firms.

The change has altered the small firms' environment and reduced their prospects. Yet it has not fundamentally altered the way they operate. Generally they must compete in markets with few barriers to the entry of other firms. Their labor forces tend to be small and quite informally organized; simple control remains characteristic of the periphery. Small firms bear a high chance of failure, and, especially during the recession phase of the business cycle, bankruptcies are frequent. The success or failure of such firms rides heavily on the owning family's ability to produce competent leadership for the firm.

Core firms, on the other hand, have developed into mechanisms for accumulation quite different from their nineteenth-century predecessors. Indeed, the history of the labor process in the twentieth century is largely the story of how new contradictions emerged within large firms and how these corporations used their resources to resolve the contradictions. That story is the subject of the next three chapters. First, however, we must explore in detail the ways in which the core firms differed from their smaller cousins.[2]

Centralization in the Core Corporation

Archimedes claimed that, given a lever and a place to stand, he could move the earth. Corporate capitalists, unwittingly manipulating the twin levers of competition and credit, hastened the process of centralization and thereby moved the world of the corporation.

It is possible for firms to grow without expanding their market power, as happens, for example, when all firms in an industry grow at a rate equal to or less than their industry's rate of growth. Similarly, it is possible for monopoly power to increase without any corresponding growth in firm size; firms can expand their market power by simply agreeing to collude, regardless of whether or not they are growing. But this is not what usually happens.

It is the linking of monopolization and growth in firm size that generates the dramatic transforming effect of centralization. As centralization occurred within the basic industries, it tended to produce monopoly. As it occurred within the context of an expanding national (and international) economy, it tended to produce firms of enormous size. The combination of monopolization and growth proved to be highly profitable. And as the core firms reaped enormous profits, they experienced inexorable pressures to spill over into new markets—through vertical integration, diversification, and multinationalism. The end results of this process of centralization have been, for the largest firms, an enduring state of high profitability and a low risk of failure. The corporation has become, in Robert Averitt's phrase, "eternal."[3]

The core firm's ability to survive and prosper grows out of its success in combining two quite different (and, in the peripheral firm, especially antagonistic) elements of investment: high return and low risk. Investment always carries with it the promise of return but also the risk of loss. Small-business owners and corporate capitalists alike seek to gain the return and avoid the risk. But small businesses usually can obtain the promise of high return only at the cost of bearing exceptional risk. A few small firms may succeed, winning at the long odds and thereby growing rapidly, but most small businesses realize low profit rates or failure, or both.

Core firms, in contrast, have been able to improve the trade-off significantly, getting, as it were, the promise of high returns with relatively low risk of loss. The success of the large firm, then, must be understood as deriving from its ability to influence both these aspects of investment.[4]

Monopolization

The core economy is in part defined by the presence of monopoly power. The growing domination of the monopoly firms in the economy as a whole is apparent in several ways. If we look at individual industries, we find that in old industries, monopoly has remained; in new industries, monopoly has emerged. If we look at all industries together, the global estimates show slowly but steadily increasing market power.

Consider first the old industries. By the 1920s, consolidation had taken place in industries producing goods such as dairy products, grain mill products, meat, bakery products, refined sugar, tobacco, soaps and toilet articles, chemicals, petroleum, tires and rubber, shoes, shoe machinery, steel, aluminum, copper, fabricated metal, electrical products, household appliances, communications equipment, motor vehicles, railroad equipment, photographic equipment, telephones, and gas and electricity, and services such as life insurance and commercial banking. Note that these early-established oligopolies continue to exist today.[5] The persistence in oligopoly is quite remarkable considering the tremendous changes, technological and social, that fifty years of rapid accumulation have wrought.

William Shepherd's sample of thirty-five "consensus" oligopolies—industries he asserted would be widely accepted as true oligopolies—provides another indication of the persistence of shared monopoly once it has been established. Comparing industrial concentration in 1947 and 1966

> yield[ed] a fairly definite answer—oligopoly concentration persists. There was no "significant" change for twenty-nine of thirty-five industries. There were four significant rises [in industrial concentration] as against two declines, and these rises were generally bigger than the declines. Of the two declines, one (electric motors and generators) at least partly reflected antitrust action. The other one (aircraft engines) reflects a statistical quirk, since in fact the industry is approaching a duopoly condition.[6]

Based on this and other evidence, Shepherd concluded that "the main body of evidence suggests that tight oligopoly and near-monopoly, once attained, tend to persist." If we extend Shepherd's analysis to the 1972 data, we find that seven of thirty-three industries showed declines in the four-firm concentration ratio of ten points or more during the twenty-five-year period. Eight oligopolies increased their market power, while most (eighteen) simply persisted.[7]

Moreover, dominant firms have appeared in new industries that have developed since the 1920s, such as computer and aircraft manufacture, air transportation, television broadcasting, photocopying, and miniaturized electronics. The trend is also unmistakable in some older industries that had not "matured" by the 1920s, including grocery retailing, lumber and newsprint manufacture, dry-goods merchandising, grain exporting, and fast-food service.

The trend towards monopolization has not been uniform, of course, and some change has occurred. Over very long periods, major technical innovations or changes in demand have undermined old markets, forcing firms either to enter entirely new markets (witness Pullman's entry into engineering and construction) or to suffer decline (as has happened to companies in railroad equipment manufacturing, leather goods production, and—until recently—coal mining). Also, some dominant firms have been unable or unwilling to increase market shares: U.S. Steel has suffered a consistent decline in its market share, and General Motors until very recently was unwilling to allow its share to go much over 50 percent. Given the antitrust constraints and other options for investment, these firms have sought oligopoly rather than monopoly.[8] In some industries, one or two new firms have pushed their way into oligopoly, as the Kaiser and Reynolds companies did in joining Alcoa in the aluminum industry. In a very few instances (for example, Cuba Cane Sugar), big firms have failed because of poor management, despite a continued strong demand for their industry's product. Nonetheless, in the vast majority of cases, relatively tight oligopoly has continued to be the rule.

The result has been increasing market concentration in the economy. The historical evidence, though fraught with severe problems of definition and conception, bears out this conclusion. By 1963, approximately 40 percent of national income arising in the private sector resulted from markets where the sellers had substantial market power (See Appendix, Table A-3). This represents a considerable increase over the "global" estimates for earlier periods. G. Warren Nutter estimated income from concentrated industries at about 17 percent of total income for the turn of the century; George Stigler and Nutter put the overall figure for the 1930s at about 20 percent.[9] More importantly, reviewing the period since World War II (for which there are reasonably good data), Shepherd concluded that "structural monopoly has apparently been increasing steadily and appreciably over the whole range of markets."[10]

Growth in Firm Size

Even in a stationary economy, the centralization of capital would imply growth in the size of the largest firms. In the expanding United States economy in the 1920s and again after 1940, centralization produced colossal aggregations.

The growth of large firms can be seen by comparing the number of such firms in 1919, at the beginning of the monopoly capitalist period, with the enterprises existing fifty years later. Any criterion for what constitutes a "large" firm is necessarily arbitrary. As noted in Chapter 2, a cutoff of $10 million eliminated all except a handful of firms in the nineteenth century; by 1919, the same criterion corrected for inflation ($25 million) would not have been nearly so restrictive. Recognizing this arbitrariness, let us choose two levels for purposes of comparison—for 1919, firms that had assets exceeding $50 million, and firms with assets of $1 billion or more. Since prices had risen approximately 50 percent by 1969, a criterion of $75 million in 1969 reflects the same real scale as $50 million in 1919; similarly, the $1 billion category for 1919 translates into $1.5 billion in 1969.

The results (Appendix, Table A-4) are quite dramatic. Whereas in 1919 there were only 166 firms in the $50-million category, by 1969 the number of firms of equivalent scale had grown to well over a thousand. Similarly, the huge firms of the billion-dollar category increased from only five or six in 1919 to nearly one hundred in 1969. Moreover, large firms are no longer confined—as most of them were in 1919—to the "social infrastructure" industries of transportation and utilities. Industrial (mining and manufacturing) firms and merchandising concerns showed the most rapid increase. These comparisons undoubtedly understate the actual explosion in the number of "large" firms because of the growth of huge enterprises in other sectors of the economy (agribusiness, services, communications, and so on).

Absolute size confers important benefits on a firm. Any remaining technical economies of scale—whether efficiencies at the plant level or marketing or transactions economies at the firm level—now become realizable. More importantly, projects once too large to be considered become serious investment candidates for the firm. One illustration is the franchising of fast-food outlets. These outlets sell much the same product as small nonfranchised restaurants, so their success owes little to new products or new technology. While initially they may attract customers through their low prices and convenience, increasingly the value of the franchises depends on regional or nationwide advertising that differentiates the product in the consumer's mind. The entry of firms with sufficient size to undertake large-scale advertising makes franchising profitable. Size, then, expands the range of profitable investments available to the firm.

Even so, the essence of centralization is the growth in the size of the firm *relative* to the size of other economic or political entities.[11] And here the process is equally visible (See Appendix, Table A-5). The top 100 manufacturing firms have increased their share of total manufacturing assets from approximately a third in 1925 to roughly half today. Sales of the 500 largest industrial corporations as a percentage of the gross national product have grown from 40 percent in 1955 to 57 percent in 1975—increasing by nearly half in a span of just twenty years.

The increasing relative and absolute size of the typical core firm equips it with many advantages. One of the most important is the ability to capture the benefits of new technology. Innovation may come either from within the core sector's own research labs or from outside (small businesses or individual inventors). But generally such technology can only be profitably *exploited* by firms of sufficient scale to produce, market, and advertise for the national market, leaving no uncontested markets to potential competitors. Even outside innovation, once it has been proven, typically winds up being sold out to core firms. In the context of a system of big firms, bigness is a prerequisite to joining the game.[12]

Another crucial advantage conferred by size is access to political power, an important resource with the increasing government role in the accumulation process. Government contracts have become an important source of corporate sales; regulatory agencies play a bigger part in setting prices, defining fair business practices, allocating markets, and setting product or work safety standards; and government policies concerning collective bargaining, interest rates, depreciation and tax schedules, pollution standards, export promotion, energy use, and a host of other issues have come to impinge directly on the prospects for corporate profit making.[13] Bigness yields political influence for corporations, permitting them to avoid damaging legislation, to shape regulatory rulings to their own needs, to enforce claims for protection of foreign investments, to undertake costly and lengthy litigation, and to demand their "rightful" share of lucrative government contracts. In an increasingly politicized economy, the ability to lobby effectively has a direct impact on the profitability of "private" investments.

Other Aspects of Centralization

If it is confined to one industry, the growing firm will sooner or later reach the limits of its growth. As it reaches a position of (shared or single) monopoly, the firm can only grow as fast as the industry's market. But usually when this happens, the firm's accumulating profits push it to expand its horizons and find a bigger world in which to operate.

Vertical integration, diversification, and multinationalization are alternate paths of growth. They can all be thought of as different ways for the firm to redefine its own industry by expanding it. The limits imposed on the firm's growth by shared monopoly in the original market are now thrown off.[14] And the tendency toward monopolization now reappears within this new and larger sphere of operation.

Vertical integration involves expansion to include more stages of production in the firm's own operations. Most large industrial firms began by manufacturing some product. Typically they purchased their raw materials from other businesses and sold their products through independent wholesalers and retailers. Seeking new areas of investment, big firms began to encroach upon the businesses of their suppliers and distributors. Thus, big firms purchased outright or gained a significant ownership position in the extractive industries, parts manufacturing, or other sources of critical raw materials. Similarly, they moved downstream to achieve more control over distribution and sales. Where products once passed through many stages of production, from farm or mine to basic processor to parts maker to assembler to wholesaler to retailer, with each stage being performed by a separate firm, now with vertical integration their manufacture was increasingly centralized within one corporation.

An illustration of forward integration was the decision by U.S. Steel and other big steel firms to move into metal fabrication. Before World War II, metal barrels and drums had largely been produced by small fabricators. But shortly after the war, the big steel companies, to ensure having markets for their lower grades of steel sheet, bought up the small companies and, in the words of *Iron Age,* "pretty much completed the capture of the entire barrel and drum business."[15]

Vertically integrated firms gain the possibility of capturing their suppliers' or distributors' profits to supplement earnings from their original industry. Whether this strategy is attractive or not depends on the investment possibilities available elsewhere. In some cases higher profits have undoubtedly been the lure, but in most cases it appears that vertical integration was primarily intended for defensive purposes, that is, to reduce the risk associated with the primary line of business.[16]

Diversification—spreading the company's activities to unrelated or only marginally related products—is another manifestation of the centralization of capital in big corporations. In contrast to earlier periods, the 1960s saw an extremely high proportion of business mergers between firms that were neither competitors nor buyers or sellers of each others' products.[17] Yet diversification has a much longer history than the recent merger wave; for example, the Federal Trade Commission (FTC) found extensive diversification as early as 1950. After studying 926 product classes to determine how frequently the one thousand largest firms were leading producers in industries *other* than their own, the FTC found that at least one of the big firms was among the leading four producers in over 28 percent of the industries studied (264 product classes). No comparable study has been undertaken since, but few observers doubt that diversification has increased substantially.[18]

Large companies have diversified their operations primarily through acquisitions and mergers rather than by simply opening new lines of business. Slightly over two-thirds of the growth in the two hundred largest corporations' share of total manufacturing assets between 1948 and 1967 resulted from acquisitions. Since the largest corporations tend to acquire firms with well-established operations—generally those with assets between $10 million and $100 million—the impact on medium-sized firms has been devastating. One study calculated that in the absence of mergers there would have been at least 40 percent more medium-sized firms.[19]

As a rule, when large firms diversify, they tend to enter industries that are competitive. There have, of course, been some notable exceptions, as when Kaiser Industries tried to break into the auto industry, when RCA and GE tried to invade IBM's computer preserve, or when Howard Hughes attempted to develop a fourth television network. Yet these attempts have been noteworthy largely for their failure and for the impressive power of the entrenched firms that they reveal.[20]

Given that it is more profitable to create a monopoly than to fight one's way into a preexisting one, firms wishing to diversify have moved into the periphery. William Shepherd calculated how frequently large firms entered major industries between 1960 and 1965 and compared his "entry index" for each industry with the existing degree of market concentration. The resulting correlation was highly negative, lending strong support to the proposition that large firms have tended to enter relatively competitive industries.[21] These findings reinforce the general point that the centralization process tends to proceed from the large corporations outward toward the competitive periphery.

Diversification not only provides the firm with new areas of potentially profitable investment, but, even more important, it also tends to reduce corporate risks by spreading investment over a greater number of industries.[22] Fluctuations in trade, changes in consumers' preferences, or technological obsolescence that adversely affects one industry will affect only a part of the diversified firm's operations.

Geographical extension represents another, and historically the most important, path for corporate expansion; in the present period such extension is necessarily multinational. United States business began producing for foreign markets as far back as the cod trade in the seventeenth century, but the distinctive feature of multinationalism—the establishment of production facilities abroad—awaited the rise of the large firms. Even then, the full flowering of multinational operations occurred only after the Second World War, when a combination of several factors—favorable monetary arrangements under the Bretton Woods agreement, devastated economies in the other advanced capitalist countries, the military and political hegemony of the United States, and, of course, the core firms' need to find new areas to reinvest their huge domestic profits—established exceptionally favorable circumstances for foreign investment.

The total foreign assets of United States investors (primarily corporations) grew from $19 billion in 1950 to nearly $200 billion in 1974. In relative terms, corporations nearly doubled their foreign investment, from 5 percent of total invested capital in 1950 to nearly 10 percent by 1972. The role of multinationalism is also evident in the rising share of profits that firms derive from foreign operations: foreign profits increased from 7 percent of total corporate profits in 1950 to nearly 25 percent in 1972.[23]

Multinationalism, like vertical integration and diversification, is directly linked to the centralization of capital in core firms. On the one hand, core firms' market power in their home markets leads them to invest abroad. They may enter foreign markets to forestall potential competition and to prevent foreign rivals from growing large enough to threaten the firms' original sphere of operations. Also, while competitive firms always have the option of expanding in their home markets, core firms find that extensive expansion at home spoils their market; hence they are more likely to seek expansion abroad. On the other hand, core firms' size seems to be an essential precondition to investment abroad. One study found that, after accounting for interindustry differences, the only factor statistically associated with whether or not firms went abroad was firm scale. Small or medium-sized firms may trade in world markets, but they rarely produce abroad.[24]

Since core firms are more attracted to foreign investment and have the resources to undertake it, it is not surprising to find that core firms account for almost all American investment abroad. In 1967 and 1968, for example, some 561 companies were responsible for 90 percent of all United States foreign investment.[25]

Multinational operations provide the core firm with several new possibilities. In some cases, the multinational enterprise may capture benefits from traditional economies of scale or comparative advantage. Also, the multinational firm can draw on capital sources in other countries; it can exploit its wider markets to even out lags or excesses in production; it can use the threat or fact of the runaway shop to discipline labor in its home operations; it can play rival governments off against each other to gain important concessions and subsidies; and it can, by rigging internal prices, avoid or largely escape taxes.[26] But at the top of this long list of advantages is the simple fact that new markets and new sources of labor provide the essential preconditions for expanded accumulation.

The primary result of these advantages of investing abroad is a higher profit rate. The higher profit rate explains why the share of a firm's profits coming from abroad typically exceeds the share of its assets invested abroad. In 1971, for example, GE's foreign profits came to 20 percent of total GE profits, while its foreign investment was only 15 percent of its total investment; similarly, IBM gained 54 percent of its profits on foreign operations while having invested only 34 percent of its capital abroad. For all corporations, the 9.8 percent foreign share of their total invested capital earned them 24.4 percent of their overall profits.

More directly, between 1950 and 1972 the average profit rate on the foreign operations of corporations ranged from 12 to 17 percent, compared to an average profit rate for all their operations of between 5 and 11 percent. Multinationalism has thus raised the core firms' profit rate.[27]

To a lesser extent, multinationalism has also reduced the risks associated with core firms' investments. By concentrating on production and sales elsewhere, the multinational firm can weather depressions or waves of labor militance in any one country. Of course, this advantage does not extend to those times, like the 1930s or middle 1970s, when the crisis is worldwide.

Once a multinational has entered a foreign market, the forces pushing toward centralization also emerge in that market. But there is a difference. The new firm is not a small competitor, requiring decades of growth to be able to dominate the market; rather, it is a huge firm with vast resources that can move quickly to capture a significant share of it.

Centralization and Profits

Centralization has altered the core firm's situation in two specific ways: it has increased the average profitability of the firm's investments, and it has decreased the risks associated with those investments. Market power and size contribute both to increasing the average profit and to reducing the risk. Multinationalization further enhances the profit rate, and vertical integration and diversification tend further to reduce risk. These results apply in general to each large corporation, and they are apparent in the statistics for individual corporations and in the aggregated data.

High Profit Rates

According to the best data available, core firms earn roughly 30 percent higher profits than noncore firms (see figure). If we take as the "core" those firms that are both large and have significant market power, core firms between 1958 and 1971 achieved an after-tax profit rate of 10.8 percent. Other categories of firms earned profits of 7.8 to 8.8 percent.

Note that neither size nor market power *alone* increases profits substantially. Indeed, size alone appears to reduce the profit rate. More cautiously, these figures are perhaps best interpreted as demonstrating that a more or less uniform profit rate (between 7.8 and 8.8 percent) existed in the economy's periphery, and that only the core firm's twin advantages of size *and* market

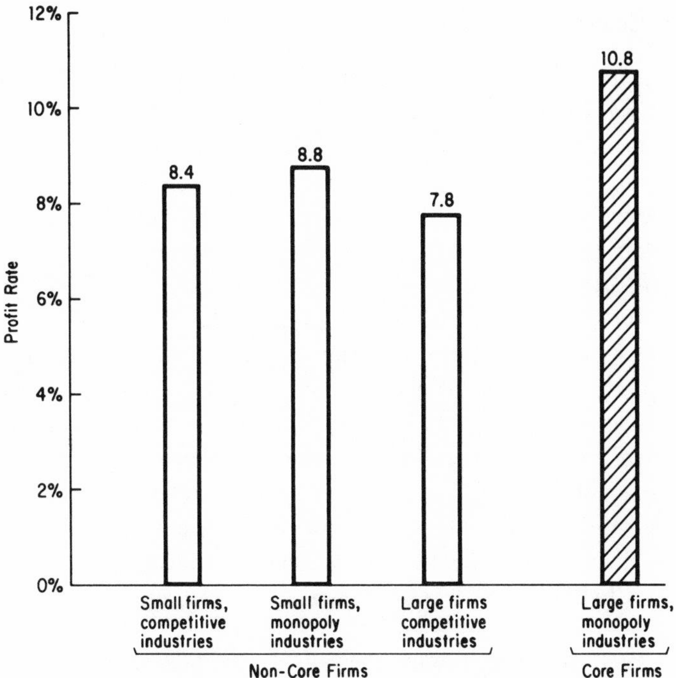

Profit Rates of Core and Non-Core Firms, 1958–1971[28]

Source: See Note 28.

power significantly raised that rate.* This finding is consistent with a careful study by Bradley Gale, who showed that only large firms could take advantage of market power.[29] The data strongly bear out the thesis that core firms, which enjoy special advantages, turn these advantages into substantially higher profit rates. Thus, not only do core firms have bigger profits, but they also have profits that are more than proportionately large.

* These profit data are consistent with the hypothesis that the categories of "large firm–competitive industry" and "small firm–monopoly industry" are in fact transitional situations. Large firms without market power either have the resources to transform their industries into shared monopoly markets (such as Texas Instruments) or they derive little advantage from size (such as Ling-Temco-Vaught). Small firms with significant market power either use that power to grow large (as did Xerox earlier) or surrender that market power to a larger firm, either due to their inability to defend the market (as many small electronics firms with a new innovation have done) or because they have been purchased themselves (for example, Hertz). Thus, the categories of "small firm–competitive industry" and "large firm–monopoly industry" would seem to represent the more enduring positions.

Low Risks of Failure

The second salient feature of core firms is that they have been able to reduce the size of the risks they face. It has long been known, for example, that large firms' profit rates vary less than do those of small firms; to the extent that such variability indicates risk, big firms are less risky.[30]

But perhaps a more significant indicator of low risk is the core firms' near-immunity to business failure. Consider, for example, the 225 corporations that in 1919 had assets equal to or greater than $50 million. During the following fifty years, only 21 firms were liquidated. (See Appendix, Table A-6). If we leave aside the small but unsuccessful category of private urban transit companies—10 out of the 15 lines went bankrupt, accounting for nearly half the big-company failures in all industries—the remaining industrial, utilities, transportation, financial, and merchandising concerns were strikingly successful. The 210 big firms from 1919 suffered only a 5 percent bankruptcy rate over the fifty-year span; every decade roughly one in a hundred of them went broke. In addition, more than 95 percent of the firms that survived to 1969 as independent businesses were able to increase their real assets.*

The core firms are not completely sure bets, of course. Urban transit stands in stark contrast to the other industries. The complete failure of urban transit companies, mainly in the 1930s and 1940s, shows that even big capitalists cannot always survive massive social and technological change, especially when that change is profitable to even larger concerns.[31] In the other industries, a few firms collapsed and others simply failed to grow. The market warfare of capitalism can be fought on favorable terrain but can never be eliminated.

Yet the result is a remarkable persistence among the big firms, especially when it is remembered that the fifty-year period included the Great Depression, several wars, and major changes in technology and life style. Big firms may not all be literally eternal, but investors can only consider such low risks of failure to be heavenly.

The combination of rapid accumulation and an extremely low failure rate could produce only one result: the increasing domination of the economy at large by big firms. This trend has been stable, persistent, and of significant magnitude. The core of the economy expands as core firms spill over into new markets and new industries, and the economy's competitive, small-business periphery declines and recedes. No wonder, then, that (in Stephen Hymer's

* Success in surviving is separate from the question of these firms' profitability, since for the latter we would need to consider dividends paid out, as well as beginning and ending asset values.

words) the capitalists in giant corporations today "rule from the top of skyscrapers [and] on a clear day, they can almost see the world."[32]

Since the 1920s, conflict in the labor process has occurred within the larger context of monopoly capitalism, which has implied two specific changes for the core firms. First, core corporations are more profitable than other firms, and hence they can devote more resources to developing structures of workplace control. It is not simply that they start with larger capitals, but these capitals also generate a perpetual and more-than-proportionately larger flow of profits, some of which can be shared with workers. Second, core corporations face smaller risks, indeed an almost negligible risk of failure, and hence they can more confidently develop long-term structures of control. The lower risk means that core firms need to worry less about their implicit long-term commitments. As we shall see, both of these features figured prominently in the corporations' efforts to revolutionize the labor process.*

Centralization and the Rise of Nonproduction Labor

Monopoly capitalism introduced an additional dimension of change in the core firms' operations that also directly affected the nature of the control problem. Big corporations found themselves employing, and becoming increasingly dependent upon, the labor of "nonproduction" workers.

It is well known that throughout this century "white-collar" workers have become an ever-larger proportion of the workforce. From a relatively small base of less than 15 percent of the total employed labor force in 1910, the number of white-collar workers grew to one-third of those employed in 1960 and to nearly 40 percent in 1975.[33]

This growth was due to a variety of forces. The rising number of federal employees, the expansion of state and municipal bureaucracies, and the increasing personnel for educational, health, and other publicly provided services constituted one part of the growth. Yet there was also a parallel (and often previous) expansion of white-collar work—or more accurately, nonproduction work—in the private sector of the economy, and what is not often recognized is that this parallel growth in large part derived from the typical core firm's new circumstances. For one thing, the firm's monopoly power and

* The core firms' higher profits and lower risks are themselves derivative in part of more successful structures of control in the labor process. The process of profit making and accumulation is dialectical, not linear.

size put it under great pressure to expand its sales and coordinate its vastly wider scale of production. And in meeting these needs, core firms increased the employment of those engaged in the sales effort (broadly conceived) and in supervision.*

The corporation's push to expand its sales effort occurred in two stages. Initially the firm simply needed to gain control over the sales process, and this required a sales force composed of its own corporate employees. Nineteenth-century firms had had clerks who took in money and wrote out shipment orders, of course, but most of the actual distribution and salesmanship was done by independent agents. Competitive firms simply produced as much as they could as cheaply as they could and threw the output on the market. There, independent sales agents made the deals, often flogging the lines of two or three competing firms at once. At GE, for example, independent agents originally accounted for most of the sales, at times earning substantial incomes in the process. But as GE began to exert its dominance in the electrical industry, it moved to take control of the sales apparatus. It established marketing and distribution networks and began assigning managers to full-time sales work. Most importantly, the independent agents were proletarianized—that is, they were made employees of the firm and sold only GE's products. The firm acquired its first wave of the new white-collar staff.[34]

The second stage in the expansion of the firm's sales staff came with the attempt to manipulate market demand. In part this involved simply expanding the numbers of sales personnel and selling more intensively. But it also involved qualitatively new activities. By the 1920s advertising and other attempts to differentiate product brands had become serious corporate activities. In addition to employees directly engaged in advertising—copywriters, commercial artists, technicians, and so on—the sales effort also called for more administrative personnel. This involved, in part, what Paul Baran and Paul Sweezy have called the "interpenetration of sales and production"; in other words, such things as product construction and design became essential elements in the *sales* effort. Automobile model changes are the best known example, but the pressure to find buyers affected all producers. And as the production process itself became increasingly subject to marketing considerations, there was a corresponding growth in the employment of product designers, style and fashion personnel, packaging experts, and others striving to make the product appealing. Another part of the sales effort expansion was due to the increasingly "scientific" approach to selling: the use of psycholo-

* Other elements also contributed to the expansion of the administrative staff: the need to reduce the costs of management; the effort to internalize training, legal, medical, and other functions; and the legal recordkeeping requirements attached to pension and benefit plans, health and safety rules, environmental regulation, and so on.

gists, market forecasting, consumer research, and so on. Thus marketing and sales became important new activities within the firm, virtually equal to the actual production.

But there was another reason why the growing scale of the firm spurred the expansion of administrative staff. As Harry Braverman has explained it, increasing size has created a rudimentary form of social planning, which appears within the firm as a need for increased administration. Each firm has become a huge aggregation of activities, separated spatially and by industrial and even national lines. Previously, these activities had been coordinated (if that is the word) through the market. Now, the firm itself needed a larger administrative apparatus.[35]

In the core firm, moreover, there was a need to impose *control* as well as to provide technical coordination. The firm could assume neither that the middle layers of foremen, supervisors, and managers would be adequately motivated by top management nor that the intervening layers would automatically proffer their best efforts for the firm. As a result, the core firm introduced increasingly sophisticated controls, primarily in the form of cost accounting, capital budgeting, inventory controls, and financial reporting. The staff responsible for the recordkeeping and data analysis of financial and cost accounts came to form a second major department within the firm.

Thus the sheer size of the corporation, both by expanding the need for technical coordination and by intensifying the demand for greater controls, pushed the firm to increase its supervisory and clerical staff. This pressure was manifest as early as the 1920s, but it has been equally strong in the postwar period, for which the data are better (see Appendix, Tables A-7, A-8, and A-9).[36] Firms of all sizes have tended to expand their non-production staffs, but this trend has gone the furthest in the largest firms. In all firms employing 2,500 or more workers, for example, the number of nonproduction workers per 100 production workers grew from 36 in 1954 to nearly 44 in 1972.

Evidence by industry confirms this trend. In all manufacturing, for instance, the ratio of nonproduction to production workers more than doubled between 1947 and 1975. These industry averages mask the even more dramatic rise in nonproduction staff within just the core firms. Although data for individual firms are in most cases lacking, the experience of two firms for which we have data (AT&T and Polaroid) may suffice. Not only have the nonproduction staffs of these firms been rapidly increasing over the past two decades, but they have actually caught up with (and in the case of Polaroid surpassed) the production staff. See Appendix Table A–9.

Thus far we have focused on those pressures pushing the individual firm to expand its nonproduction staff. But in accounting more generally for the rise of such employment, we must note that the transition to monopoly capitalism also tended to stimulate the growth of whole white-collar *industries*. Thus in 1976 advertising, insurance, banking, finance, and business services such as data processing, temporary office help, and commercial research and testing labs together employed over 5 million workers.[37] In these industries, nonproduction workers constitute the vast majority of those employed.

All of these forces have combined to produce a substantial and strategically critical nonproduction staff within the core corporations. This growth has had profound social consequences, but for the individual firm, the immediate result was to create an additional problem of control. Never as urgent as the crisis, described in Chapter 4, that erupted in the control of its production workers, the problem was nonetheless persistent and serious.

To understand the nature of this problem, consider what is involved in such jobs as supervising other workers, selling to customers, responding to a business letter, interviewing new personnel, or updating files. In none of these jobs can tasks be easily transformed into routinized operations. Thus workers respond idiosyncratically to supervisors, customers have particular demands requiring special handling, job applicants may present credentials not easily evaluated in standard categories, and so on. In all these cases, and for nonproduction work in general, the nature of the work does not lend itself to simple objective measures of productivity.

This point should not be overstated, for corporations quickly perceived the benefits of routinizing nonproduction work and have devoted considerable resources to doing so. Their efforts have succeeded in part, particularly with the lowest levels of clerical and sales work. Indeed, their very success has substantially eroded the usefulness of the blue-collar/white-collar distinction for today's labor force. Yet for a large proportion of the nonproduction employees, routinization was not possible.

The problem of control, then, was this: employers found that it was extremely difficult to carry out the second element of the control system—evaluation of worker performance—for nonproduction labor. The distinct nature of each separate task meant that it was not possible to compare it *directly* with the performance of other workers or even of the same worker at other times. Nor was it easy to tell how much effort the worker had actually put into the particular operation. Often it was not even possible to discover immediately whether the task had been performed adequately.

Instead, what nonproduction labor demanded was evaluation over a long period of time—months or perhaps years. The particularities were thus evened out: typists could be expected to have been assigned an average number of long letters and short ones, difficult ones and simple ones; sales agents should have encountered an average share of eager buyers and reluctant ones; and so on. But in the intervening time, evaluation was ambiguous. And if the worker's performance could not be easily evaluated, the third control-system element—rewarding and disciplining—could not be tied to performance.

For the nineteenth-century employer, controlling the nonproduction labor process was not a serious problem. On the one hand, such labor was a small and less critical aspect of the firm's operations than it is today. On the other hand, the small white-collar staff occupied an elite position within the firm. It generally received high pay, had considerable job security, and could look forward to regular promotion with seniority. Most importantly, there was typically a personal relation with the capitalist. As Margery Davies describes it,

> The small size of offices at this time meant that the relationship between employer and employee tended to be a very personalized one. The clerks worked under the direct supervision, and often the direct eyesight, of their employers. . . . The personal benevolence of an employer could go a long way toward making the hierarchical relations within an office more tolerable. An employer who spoke nicely to his clerks, let them leave early if they were feeling sick, or gave them a Christmas goose helped to create working conditions against which the clerks were not likely to rebel. By treating his clerks with kindness or politeness, a paternalistic employer was also likely to be able to get them to work harder for him. This personalization of the work relationship between the clerk and his employer. . . [lay] at the root of the phenomenon of employees being "devoted to the firm."[38]

Thus the personal relation with the boss that production workers had experienced in the entrepreneurial firm survived much longer for the nonproduction worker. But it could not last forever.

The expansion of the nonproduction staff destroyed these workers' elite position within the firm. For one thing, the growing numbers of such workers meant that their wage costs came to be a significant component of the firm's costs; the (relatively) high wage that in the nineteenth-century firm had purchased "devotion" now came to be much more expensive. Equally important, the growing size of the administrative staff meant that a personal relationship between employer and white-collar worker was no longer possible. Centralization of capital had rendered such vestigial small-business relationships obsolete, in the office as well as on the shop floor.

The coming of monopoly capitalism thus altered the context of workplace conflict along a second dimension. In addition to providing core firms with higher-average, less risky profits, the new system created enormous pressures upon firms to expand their nonproduction staffs. This, too, would figure prominently in how the firm approached the issue of controlling the labor process.

CHAPTER 6

Experiments, Beginnings, and Failures

AS the core corporations entered the period of monopoly capitalism, they were confronted with a conundrum. Although the resources they commanded were vast, at the same time their own workers increasingly challenged their control. The corporations' problem, then, was to figure out a way of using their accumulated resources to undermine the workers' opposition and strengthen management's control.

The labor problems arose from two different sources. First, and more urgently, there was the crisis of control on the shop floor, and here the corporations' basic response was brute repression. Yet the corporations' ability to call forth troops did not provide a stable basis for future business operation. Just as war reflects the *absence* of a stable world system, so industrial conflict reflected the failure of a viable system of control. This point was clearly understood by the early corporate capitalists, and they moved to rectify matters. Less immediate, but nonetheless persistent, was the rising burden of the nonproduction staff. Here the problem was not overt opposition from workers, but rather the need to reorganize once-elite workers into less costly but still devoted employees.

It was to solve these two problems that the major corporations launched a lengthy period of research, experimentation, and trial; extending over the first four or so decades of the century, this effort produced welfare capitalism, Taylorism and scientific management, and "employee representation" or company unions. The corporations also engaged in less direct approaches, financing industrial psychology, the National Civic Federation, training institutes for the "new" foreman, and endowed business schools at Harvard, Stanford, and elsewhere.

These programs constituted experiments, and eventually—beginning in the 1920s but attaining full force only after World War II—they would lead to the reorganization of work within the firm along lines of structural control. Yet the road ahead was by no means certain. The problems persisted.

The Failure of Welfare Capitalism

Labor problems did not emerge full-blown after the First World War; the earliest experiments in both welfare capitalism and scientific management are more properly stories of the transition era. U.S. Steel, International Harvester, and others, the biggest of the new corporate giants, early confronted and responded to the changing conditions.

Welfare capitalism arose out of the corporations' concern for finding a way of creating in their workers a sense of loyalty. Within the National Civic Federation, leading corporate capitalists had formulated a broad social strategy for "harmonizing" the interests of labor and capital; welfare programs became one specific part of this strategy. The plan was simple: corporations would provide (selected) workers with recreational services, clinics and health care, pensions, stock-sharing and other savings plans, housing, and educational and other benefits and services. These welfare benefits, it was hoped, would persuade workers of the corporations' genuine concern for their well-being and, by actually improving their existence, undermine worker militance. In a somewhat more heavy-handed vein, the participating corporations also sought to bind their workers to them by creating stronger dependence—a dependence based not only on the worker's income but also on essential services. For example, workers who joined strikes found that their leases required them to vacate company-owned housing immediately.[1] Finally, the corporations perceived the usefulness of welfare programs as a public-relations device, to convince the public that they were responsible and caring employers.

The strategy of welfare capitalism thus involved bribing workers with selected nonjob benefits to undercut the militance created by the alienating and oppressive conditions on the job. What was conspicuously absent was any attempt to reorganize existing power relations at the workplace.

At International Harvester, interest in welfare programs derived from essentially two sources.[2] At the plant level, especially at the mammoth McCormick Works, welfare programs were introduced by management to fight the resurgence of union organizing among workers. The first stock distribution plan, for example, was announced the day after a strike had broken out at the Deering Works, another Chicago plant of International Harvester. Throughout the period of the most intense strike threat, McCormick family members dangled before McCormick Works employees the prospect of substantial stock bonuses for "faithful" workers.* Similarly, the employment of the first services specialist or "betterment worker," the introduction of certain health measures such as flush toilets and pure drinking water, and other programs fit into the McCormicks' program of wooing workers.

Harvester's welfare programs also had advocates at a quite different level, however. George Perkins, the Morgan banking representative who served as a corporation trustee, was charged with mediating conflicts among the various owning families whose firms had been merged to form International Harvester. More importantly, he also acted as Morgan's watchdog, coordinating labor relations and other corporate policies with an eye toward the spillover effects on steel, shipbuilding, railroads, and the other industries in which the Morgan banks held interests. When the government attack on the trusts began, and in the case of International Harvester particularly after the Justice Department investigation of 1906 and 1907, Perkins began promoting welfare capitalism as "the labor program of 'good trust.'" A sickness and accident benefit plan soon followed.

Thus at International Harvester, different but not necessarily conflicting motives soon led to a quite elaborate range of welfare programs. In addition to the pension plan, the sickness and accident benefit program, and the stock-sharing program, I-H had by 1920 branched out into new areas: a plant safety program; a medical plan providing physical examinations for new employees, dental examinations, hospital facilities, community (visiting) nurses, and home instruction in hygiene; a supplementary profit-sharing plan; social clubs, including library facilities for workers; and a variety of other benefit programs.

The list was in many ways more impressive than the programs themselves, for numerous limitations and eligibility clauses prevented most workers from benefiting from the main provisions. The regulations of the pension system, for example, specifically reserved benefits for those workers who refused to join a union and avoided taking part in strikes:

*When the actual stock distributions were made several months later, twenty workers who had been active organizers were not given bonuses; see Robert Ozanne (1967), pp. 39–40.

> A pension may be suspended or terminated by the Pension Board for gross misconduct or other cause.[3]

In the context of the company's refusal to pay union workers their share of the 1903 stock distribution, the meaning of the language was clear. In 1919, when management was concerned that workers might have forgotten the meaning, President Harold McCormick reiterated the point in a letter to employees:

> As you know, our Pension Plan is a purely voluntary expression of the company's desire to stand by the men who have stood by it.[4]

Other programs contained similarly restrictive clauses. Thus the accident benefit program required workers receiving benefits to sign waivers releasing the company from legal liability for the accident. Nonetheless, according to one Harvester executive,

> The issuing of such policies would greatly strengthen the loyalty of employees to the company . . . the interests of his family would all bend in this direction. . . . Further than this, the physical conditions required from medical examination in the granting of such policies would greatly increase the general physical condition of the help employed, with a corresponding physical and moral effect on the household. I believe at first sight that a weapon of this kind would be much stronger than any profit-sharing proposition toward breaking up unionism.[5]

The stop-and-go history of welfarism at International Harvester revealed its experimental nature. The programs were funded and rapidly expanded during years of labor trouble and antitrust prosecution but curtailed at other times. Moreover, the company wavered in the uses to which it put welfarism. At some times, and with some programs, it sought to distribute meaningful benefits, even if the benefits were restricted to a few selected employees. But at other times and with other programs, the company failed to provide any substance to the grandly publicized schemes. The accident insurance plan, for example, was based largely on the company's calculation that it would save money by escaping adverse accident-liability judgments.

The welfare program at International Harvester was mirrored elsewhere.[6] At Pullman, in addition to such programs as a dispensary and an inspection system to reduce industrial accidents, the company established an employee health program offering "free medical advice and treatment, not only to the injured but to the sick." John Runnells, Pullman President, justified the programs as follows:

> The greater loyalty [on the part of the workers] which comes from proper sanitary precautions and medical assistance is of far greater value than the investment involved.[7]

At General Electric, welfarism started timidly in 1906 with an employee suggestion box. But GE also got caught up in the "betterment" spirit, and other programs quickly followed: a safety and health program in 1907, a pension scheme in 1912, and by 1920 a savings plan; company support of athletic and social clubs for workers; health, life, and accident insurance; workplace hot lunches; apprenticeship and training programs; and the other paraphernalia of welfarism.[8]

But it was at the huge U.S. Steel Corporation that welfare capitalism achieved its greatest refinement. Although the operating departments continued to be managed by practical men who insisted on iron-fisted labor policies, the new financial promoters took a broader outlook. The great publicity surrounding the trust's formation, as well as the long and bitter labor history of the industry, made Morgan's lieutenants particularly anxious to demonstrate that the company cared about its workers. Late in 1902—one year after the merger took effect—the company announced a stock subscription plan for its employees whereby it sold stock to workers at what was described as "the market price, or usually a little less," and the company paid a special premium on workers' shares for the first five years.[9] Chairman of the Board Gary foresaw that as a result of the plan "the interests of capital and labor will be drawn more closely and permanently together."[10]

The stock subscription program was only the first of many programs at U.S. Steel. In 1906, a safety program was begun that, the company claimed, cost $10 million during the first eight years of operation and reduced serious accidents by some 40 percent.[11] In 1910, the company began a workmen's compensation program, "Voluntary Accident Relief," that paid disabled workers several months' wages, depending on the severity of the injury, and provided the families of workers killed on the job with a minimum of eighteen months' wages. This program, like others, was introduced by the company as a "a rebuke and a rebuttal" to the notion that "workmen get nothing except by contest and struggle."[12] In the same year, the company instituted a pension plan for which the company and the Carnegie Relief Fund paid all expenses. After twenty-five years on the job, men could retire at sixty-five and women at fifty-five with a pension. The following year (1911), the firm launched a major sanitation drive, installing toilets, urinals, pure water drinking fountains, and areas for washing up. It followed this effort by providing lunchrooms and restaurants, safety equipment and protective clothing, first-aid stations, and medical facilities and personnel.

Not content with betterment programs in the plants, the corporation also engaged in widespread welfare work in the steel-making communities. It built churches, schools, social clubs, playgrounds, swimming pools, athletic fields, dwellings, boarding houses, and medical facilities for workers' use. It provided visiting nurses, land for vegetable gardens, training schools for children of workers, "practical housekeeping centers" with instruction in homemaking skills, and "Americanization" classes for immigrants.

Whenever possible, the company engaged in strenuous publicity efforts to show off to the public its concern for its workers. The company proudly listed its welfare expenditures in the decade after 1912 as a whopping $112 million, a figure representing over 8 percent of the profits during the period. Judge Gary never failed to mention the betterment expenditures when testifying before Congress or talking with the press. The *Bulletin* published by the firm's Bureau of Safety, Sanitation, and Welfare recounted for employees the many programs in which they could participate. And the company's annual reports were absolutely aglow with these efforts.

Programs at International Harvester, Pullman, General Electric, and U.S. Steel were the most elaborate and costly examples of a whole wave of betterment programs at major corporations. A 1919 Bureau of Labor Statistics special report on industrial welfare indicated the breadth of the employers' efforts. Of 431 establishments surveyed, 375 had begun some type of medical program and 265 reported having hospital facilities, 80 had established disability benefit plans, 75 had pension plans, and 152 had constructed recreation facilities for their workers. Literally hundreds had engaged in some form or other of welfarism.[13] Publicity for these broader efforts was also intense, seeking to show that capital and labor had more in common than in conflict.

The movement continued to grow into the mid-1920s, when it reached the peak of its popularity. A 1926 survey of fifteen hundred of the largest United States companies reported that 80 percent had some form of welfare program and about half had "comprehensive" schemes. Another study showed that the average annual welfare expenditure was about $27 per worker, or about 2 percent of the average worker's annual income.[14]

Welfare capitalism, then, represented a sophisticated, well-financed, and widely implemented plan for controlling labor. It reflected the large capitalists' awareness of the need for positive incentives in hierarchical control in order to attract workers' sympathies. It promised considerable tangible benefits to those who submitted to the company's paternalism, and it especially rewarded those who over long periods refrained from union activity and remained "loyal" to the firm. Yet it failed.

The first indications of failure were dramatic. Robert Ozanne, historian of industrial relations at the McCormick Works, makes the point this way:

> By 1916 [International Harvester] officers could look back on twelve years of

labor peace marred only by the strike at the Auburn Twine Mill in 1913. Had the combination of repression and welfarism achieved permanent immunity from unionism? A labor explosion in 1916 proved welfarism no more than a veil spread over the basic, unmet needs of the Harvester workers.[15]

In April of 1916, a spontaneous walkout shut down the Chicago plants of the company; bitter struggles broke out between the "harmonious" partners—management and the workers—as workers ignored the "progress" made through the company's betterment programs. Similarly, in August 1918, workers at GE's mammoth Lynn plant struck, again without much organization but undeterred by the advantages of welfarism. In the words of one unsympathetic contemporary observer, their solidarity was

> so complete that it resulted in an entire walkout and in practically 100 percent of the workers joining the various craft unions.[16]

The strike lasted three weeks before the federal government intervened, leaving very bitter feelings among the workers.

But it was at U.S. Steel, right at the citadel of welfarism, that the most intense struggle of all began. In September 1919, thousands of workers risked their jobs and in many cases their lives to build the union and improve working conditions. For them, the benefits of having first-aid supplies near their work stations or getting pensions when they retired were undeniable gains, but of little consequence when compared with pressing issues like shorter hours of work and relief from oppressive and arbitrary foremen. For these concerns, welfarism provided no answers. One contemporary observer summed up U.S. Steel's difficulty by noting:

> The trouble is that the Corporation's labor policy is still in the stage of detectives and toilets.[17]

Strikes at International Harvester, GE, and U.S. Steel were only symptomatic; what is significant is that they came at precisely those companies in which welfarism had been pushed the furthest. The corporations responded to strike demands with long dissertations on the vast sums of money they had expended in gaining better conditions for the workers. For example, the Senate Committee investigating the steel strike was presented with pages and pages of such figures. Much of this evidence, like much of welfarism itself, was intended for public consumption. Yet, in reading the transcripts of the company executives' statements, one also senses something more than calculated play-acting, more even than honest anger at the ingratitude of the workers. What one perceives is the capitalists' realization of the bankruptcy of welfarism as a method of coopting and controlling workers.

Indeed, in the late 1920s the corporations began to rid themselves of the financial burden of their unsuccessful effort, and as Stuart Brandes has noted, welfarism failed to survive the Depression.[18] Some programs were scaled down, others dismantled; where possible, as in the case of workmen's compensation and later with pension plans, employers shifted the costs to the government through publicly financed benefits. Only those programs that directly contributed to productivity, such as physical exams and industrial safety measures, tended to be retained.

Welfare capitalism failed because it did not deal with the fundamental issue of power within the firm. Although it was a sophisticated and highly publicized attempt to bribe workers into accepting the existing authoritarian and paternalistic relations, the renewed militance of the workers indicated that welfarism did not do the job. To reorient the workers' allegiance from their peers to the corporation, capitalists needed something that reformed relations in the workplace itself. For this, welfarism was too peripheral to be effective.

Even in defeat, however, employers recognized certain possibilities. Welfare capitalism's twin principles—using positive incentives to attract worker loyalty rather than relying only on sanctions to compel obedience, and making the rewards stand in some systematic relation to each employee's demonstration of the desired behavior—would be remembered in later attempts at control.

The Ambiguous Results of Scientific Management

A second set of control experiments focused directly on the workplace and aimed at strengthening the employer's hand in the struggle to speed up production. Frederick Winslow Taylor, founder and chief propagandist of the movement, diagnosed the problem as essentially one of "soldiering"—that is, of workers habitually choosing to produce at less than their maximum possible rate. Taylor and the "efficiency experts" who followed him believed that, through a careful study of individual jobs and judicious selection of incentives or bonus pay, employers could structure the workplace so that soldiering (or soldiering workers) would be eliminated. Their efforts, variously known as "Taylorism" or "scientific management," promised to resolve the crisis of control through scientific study.[19]

It has become fashionable to interpret scientific management as an enormous breakthrough in the history of work relations. Thus it is said that

"Taylorism dominates the world of production" and that "work itself is organized according to Taylorian principles."[20] But this view overestimates scientific management's impact. For one thing, not all those elements of which Taylor wrote were new with the Taylor system. The thrust toward standardization of tools and tasks, the fragmentation of jobs, and the increased use of semiskilled or unskilled workers—all of which the Taylorites stressed—were tendencies that had long been evident in American development. A second error has been the tendency to confuse Taylorism as a management theory (and it did cause considerable stir among the professionals who advised businesses) with Taylorism in practice, where its impact was considerably more limited. Finally, the Taylor movement has been confused with the broader reorientation of management that occurred during the transition period; many parts of this reorientation, however, had little or nothing to do with scientific management per se.[21]

Closer analysis suggests that scientific management played a more circumscribed, though still important, role. Its significance was that it showed the possibilities of applying corporate resources to the control problem in a systematic way. Although widely debated among professional management theorists, it was not introduced into industry on any broad scale, and by the First World War its potential as a workplace panacea had been destroyed by the intense labor opposition that it generated. Like welfare capitalism, it failed to solve the crisis of control in the firm. Yet, also like that other movement but perhaps more directly, scientific management contributed experience and ideas to corporate capitalists that eventually led them to modern forms of control.

Scientific management presented both an analysis of work relations and a new philosophy of the workplace—that is, it made both a material and an ideological assertion. In its analysis of work, Taylorism asserted that the managers' inability to control soldiering resulted from their inadequate knowledge of the actual techniques of production. Most of the specific expertise—for example, knowledge of how quickly production tasks could be done—resided in the workers and to some extent in the foremen, many of whom had come up through the ranks. But higher management had no access to it. Taylor wrote that he

> realized that the greatest obstacle to harmonious cooperation between the workmen and the management [Taylor's euphemism for greater management control] lay in the ignorance of the management as to what really constitutes a proper day's work for a workman.[22]

How could management bargain for a "fair day's work" if it didn't even know how much could be done during the workday? Thus, for management to control production, employers had to dispossess workers of their special knowledge and gain for themselves mastery of specific production expertise.

Taylor's analysis of work grew directly out of employers' experiences with piece-rates. Piece-rates always carried the allure of payment for actual labor done (rather than for labor power), thus promising an automatic solution to the problem of translating labor power into labor. Two difficulties invariably intervened to spoil this solution. First, when workers used their employer's machinery, capitalists had as much stake in seeing that the machinery worked hard as in inducing workers to speed up. Paying workers only according to their self-established pace (as piece-work attempted to do) became unattractive if it meant that the machinery ran at less than full speed; in this case the piece-rate would cut down on the labor cost, but it would not necessarily bring profits. Thus, capitalists could never be indifferent to the worker's pace, even if the piece-rate meant that the employer was only paying for work done.

The second, more serious difficulty was that piece-rates always contained an incentive for workers to deceive employers and restrict output. Since the pay structure was necessarily anchored on some expectation of how quickly a job could be done, the system clearly led workers to make jobs appear to take as long as possible. On the other hand, if all or most workers responded to the piece-rates with enough production to raise their wages substantially, then the expected job completion time would fall, and the piece-rate would be adjusted accordingly. To prevent this, workers tended to restrict output.

As long as management depended on its workers for information about how fast the job could be done—that is, as long as workers had a monopoly on that "special knowledge"—there was no way to make the piece-rate method deliver its promise. Scientific management directed its material assertion at exactly this issue and offered "scientific study of work" as a new independent source of special knowledge.

The Taylorites' ideological assertion was that both workers and employers would benefit from increased production. Thus both had a stake in seeing that "science" and "scientific methods" were used to determine the one best way that each task should be done. As Taylor himself put it, "What constitutes a fair day's work will be a question for scientific investigation, instead of a subject to be bargained and haggled over."[23] Since the real objective was to wrest from workers control over special knowledge, and since "scientific investigation" was likely to be employed (literally) by management, the results of such a procedure could hardly be in doubt. Yet the effect of this maneuver should not be minimized: the objectivity of science was being appropriated to bolster management prerogative.

Thus science was to produce a new body of special knowledge, and this new learning would be lodged in management's hands. The methods by which this change was to be effected involved all three elements of control systems, but by far the most revolutionary concerned the first, the direction of work tasks.

Taylor and his followers understood that unless management knew in detail how production occurred, precise direction of work tasks was impossible. To achieve an understanding of production, the Taylorites proposed time and (later) motion studies and, more generally, systematic study of the production flow. "Scientific analysis" produced a vast body of task standards, best or quickest techniques, and the like, and the stopwatch became the most important tool in the efficiency engineer's kit. The data were so vast, in fact, that individual managers could not be expected to master them, so Taylor recommended establishing a company planning department that could systematize and thereby effectively use such information. Finally, the newly defined tasks needed to be communicated to the workers who were to carry them out, and this involved specifying to workers exactly what they were expected to accomplish each day. Taylor recommended that each worker receive an instruction card at the beginning of each workday, giving explicit written form to this communication process. In other words, direction of work tasks was to emerge from orderly processes of information discovery, organization, and communication.

Scientific management also proposed revision of the second control system element, the evaluation of work done. In prior systems, of course, the foreman himself had monitored performance in a more or less capricious way. Under the new system, piece-rates constituted the chief form of pay, so at one level judging each worker's performance was to be merely a matter of measuring output. Yet Taylor realized that this was much too crude a measure of performance and proposed "functional foremanship" instead. The traditional foreman's job was to be fragmented into eight parts or functions and a separate individual assigned to undertake each part. Three of the new foremen were kept busy directing the work and one meted out punishment, but the remaining four were all put to the task of performance evaluation: checking to see that machines were driven at proper speeds, inspecting the quality of work, ensuring that workers took proper machine maintenance measures, and recording the times and costs of work. The point was to systematize the evaluation process.

Finally, the matter of reward and punishment—the third control element—was entrusted to what was termed the "differential rate piece-work" system. As with all the piece-rate methods that had been so fervently promoted during these years, Taylor's system attempted to avoid the pitfalls of deliberate deception and output restriction. Taylor's idea was to split the rate structure, with a considerably higher piece-rate—30 to 100 percent higher, as Taylor so frequently repeated—applying to workers who met the established time standards for the task. (Since the higher piece-rate typically required a 200 or 300 percent increase in output, employers were pleased to make this offer.) Work study was intended to eliminate the possibilities for deception by providing a new source of special knowledge, so the piece-rate could be unambiguously aimed at inducing higher production.

Scientific management thus presented an ambitious agenda. It proposed a thorough-going change in all three elements of control, designed to eliminate soldiering. More broadly, it claimed to eliminate the conflict between workers and employers, rendering labor unions—with their "bargaining and haggling"—unnecessary. Taylor often boasted that "during the thirty years that we have been engaged in introducing scientific management there has not been a single strike."[24] Here, clearly, was a promising solution to the control crisis in the firm.

Yet if we look at Taylorism as a management practice rather than as an idea, the promise was never fulfilled. For one thing, the system was complicated, and employers often grew impatient long before the final elements were ready to be installed. At the American Locomotive Company, for instance, one of Taylor's early converts, David Van Alstyne, began introducing elements of the efficiency system. But higher management, which saw the program as experimental, was not ready to undertake the scale of changes required for full implementation. Under pressure to obtain results, Van Alstyne began taking shortcuts, and the full system was never installed. This experience repeated the past—at Bethlehem, Taylor himself had been fired before he was able to complete the job—and foretold future difficulties.[25]

More significantly, Taylorism failed to solve the crisis of control because most big corporations failed even to give it a try. The extent and incidence of scientific management has always been something of a mystery, but the available evidence suggests that Taylorism was largely confined to smaller, usually nonunionized enterprises.[26] In any event, the new industrial giants—U.S. Steel, International Harvester, and the others—showed little interest in it. Of the twenty-five "representative" firms using scientific management that Robert Hoxie investigated in 1915, only two (Westinghouse and Jones & Laughlin) ranked among the largest industrial firms.[27] Other big firms experimented with bonus systems and time and motion studies, but none appeared willing to undertake large-scale reorganization along Taylorian lines.

One reason for the big firms' coolness may have been that Taylorism seemed to express a philosophy that ran counter to the image so carefully contrived in the other labor programs of the big firms. Despite Taylor's rhetoric of labor-management cooperation, workers and bosses alike understood that stopwatch methods constituted a real challenge to the workers. The Taylor system, when stripped of its "scientific" veil, attempted to remove the decisions over work pace and sequence from the bargaining between foremen and workers—bargaining in which workers participated and exercised some power. In order to impose the new Taylorized standards, management had to break the workers' power to resist. On the other hand, welfare capitalism (and later the "plans of representation") attempted to convince workers that harmony, not conflict, would bring rewards to workers.

One place where the tension between Taylorism and welfarism was clearly visible was the textile firm of Joseph Bancroft and Sons of Wilmington.[28] An entrepreneurial firm, Bancroft had grown slowly through the second half of the nineteenth century, but in the 1890s the firm's labor force nearly tripled, as merger and internal growth rapidly extended its scale. The old paternalistic relations of entrepreneurial control no longer held the expanded workforce in sufficiently tight harness; a "crisis of control" loomed, and a new system was required.

The Bancroft management chose not one but two new approaches: Elizabeth Briscoe was hired in 1902 to introduce welfare work, and Taylor's disciple H. L. Gantt was retained in 1908 to begin reorganizing production along scientific lines. The first effort sought to rebuild a sense of personal bonds between employer and workers. The second effort attempted simply to introduce more efficient methods of production. Since welfare work did not directly affect the production flow—it focused on workers' housing, plant safety and sanitation, medical services, and so on—whereas Taylorism was aimed only at the work process itself, Bancroft managers saw no conflict between these two approaches.

Yet the company's experience demonstrated that Taylorism and welfarism coexisted uneasily, if at all. As Gantt began reorganizing production, speeding up work, and dismissing recalcitrant (or "non-first-class") employees, the workers became resentful. Directly undercutting the intent of the welfare programs, the efficiency methods provoked conflict between management and workers. The road jointly taken seemed to diverge: the company was forced to choose between the strong-arm tactics needed to install Taylorism and the positive incentives embodied in welfarism. (In this case, welfarism won and Gantt was dismissed, although soon after, Briscoe was demoted as well.)

The main failure of Taylorism, however, was that it failed to solve the crisis of control in the firm because workers simply fought it to a standstill. Taylor's claim that scientifically managed shops had never suffered a strike was contradicted by the record. At American Locomotive, for example, Van Alstyne's attempt to introduce Taylorism had been met with serious union opposition. The unionized boilermakers secured an agreement that exempted them from the new system, and unorganized machinists were so provoked that they established an International Association of Machinists local and promptly went out on strike. Later, when the company went back on its agreement with the boilermakers, they struck and stayed out for three weeks. The strike was settled only by the removal of Van Alstyne and his system. Similarly, as we have seen, the new arrangements at Bancroft and Sons were abandoned in the face of rising worker frustration and resistance, manifested in the higher turnover and growing in-plant conflict.[29]

The decisive battle came at the government's Watertown (Mass.) Arsenal. The War Department used the arsenal both to produce military materiel and to provide an independent check on the costs of similar equipment procured from private producers. But it was old, its machinery was obsolete, and its manufacturing costs were too high to be useful for either competition or comparison. So in 1909 the Army called in efficiency experts to improve the situation. The installation of scientific management proceeded smoothly for two years, during which time a planning department was established, engineering studies completed, inventory control improved, and so on.[30]

When the Taylorites moved into the shops to introduce the bonus-pay plan and to begin stopwatch timing of particular jobs, however, conflict immediately flared. The skilled molders, whose jobs were chosen as the first to be timed, walked out. Their strike immediately galvanized the International Association of Machinists into renewed opposition to Taylorism—the machine shops were, after all, the principal locus of applications of Taylorism—and the government ownership of the arsenal provided an opening. The Watertown strike was settled by an agreement for a public investigation, and in fact several actions followed: a Congressional inquiry, mobilization of AFL opposition to Taylorism, a serious academic evaluation of Taylorism in practice, and a legislative ban on the introduction of stopwatch and premium-pay methods into military enterprises.[31] Most importantly, the strike alerted all organized labor to oppose Taylorism.

The growing labor opposition to scientific management, especially after the highly publicized troubles at Watertown, ended the possibilities for a scientific management solution to the firm's crisis of control. It would be implemented in some cases—one optimistic contemporary estimate suggested that about 1 percent of all industrial workers labored under the system—and in certain firms it would be dominant. But labor, especially the highly organized machinists, had learned to be on the lookout for the appearance of the "time-and-motion man" on the factory floor. Their opposition disproved the claim that "science" could eliminate the worker's ability to soldier or, more accurately, that Taylor's system could build worker-boss harmony and could decisively turn the shop-floor battle in management's favor.[32]

Yet the scientific management movement was one of those failed (or only partially successful) experiments from which much was learned. First, the chaff needed to be discarded: daily instruction cards, the silliness of extreme time and motion studies, functional foremanship, the differential-rate piece-work plan all had to be abandoned or heavily modified. One important element that did endure was the aggressive attempt to gain management control over the special knowledge of production—what Harry Braverman has brilliantly described as the "separation of conception from execution."[33] Another element that survived was the notion that each worker's job should be carefully defined, including standards of "adequate" performance. The basic impulse to define jobs in terms of output rather than simply obedience to the foreman's orders would be picked up later by the structural control systems. Yet another lesson was the need to subject management itself to management control, specifically by breaking the power of foremen to act as absolute rulers of the shops. Functional foremanship would never catch on, but the transfer of hiring, disciplining, wage-setting, work directing, and other functions to personnel departments and planning or industrial design offices would take hold.

Undoubtedly the greatest lesson that capitalists learned from the efficiency engineers was that rational methods and large resources could be devoted to the management process and be made to pay handsome dividends. With their investments in welfare capitalism, employers sensed that they had obtained little return on their money. Scientific management had not really paid off either, but the prospects seemed much more promising. The difference was no doubt due to the fact that scientific management directly addressed the issue of power relations in the workplace, whereas welfarism seemed peripheral. If the Taylorites had not found quite the right mechanism, they were at least looking in the right place.

The Limits of Company Unions

Toward the end of the First World War and during the 1920s, big companies turned eagerly to a third type of experiment, termed "plans of representation" or "works councils" by the companies but known more generally as "company unions."[34]

The chief stimulus to company unions derived from the labor settlements handed down during the war. The dramatic rise in labor militancy had threatened to cripple military production, and after the United States entered the war President Wilson established the War Labor Board (WLB) to arbitrate disputes. Soon after, the outlines of the new policy emerged: labor would be guaranteed the rights to organize and bargain collectively but be denied the right to strike. The *type* of labor organization was not specified, however, and company unions were interpreted as being qualified labor organizations; indeed, the WLB frequently mandated a works council in its arbitration decisions. Companies rushed to set up councils before real unions could become established; between 1919 and 1924 some 490 firms established representation plans.[35]

The idea of the company union was simple: establish a formal grievance procedure within a context of rigorously defined limits. Given a channel for expression of legitimate grievances, "loyal" workmen would not be driven into the ranks of the unions. The corporations did not overlook the fact that the plans also offered extensive possibilities for propaganda, and the "American plan" of industrial democracy was much bandied about. Yet the importance of works councils did not lie primarily in the publicity battle; company unions represented a real roadblock to independent unions.

The plan at GE was instructive. The huge Lynn works had been hit by a strike in August, 1918, halting work on war contracts. The War Labor Board quickly entered the scene, inducing workers to go back to their jobs in return for what amounted to binding arbitration. When the award was handed down several months later, it included a provision for "shop committees," and GE moved aggressively to implement the plan before outside unions could take up the workers' cause. Thus was born the "Lynn Plan of Representation."[36]

Under the Lynn system workers in each shop elected employee representatives who, together with an equal number of management appointees, served as a shop committee. Voting was by secret ballot, and only workers (no foremen or "leading hands") were allowed to serve as representatives. The representatives in turn elected various adjustment or appeals committees, as well as safety committees and the like.

The principal function of the Plan was to provide a grievance or appeals procedure. Grievances in the shops were to be taken up initially with the appropriate foreman, but if the grieved worker failed to find the foreman's decision satisfactory, the Plan opened the way for appeal to the shop committee. If the worker was dissatisfied with the shop committee decision, he or she could appeal up the ladder to the department head, the general works joint committee, and the works manager. Although the Plan also envisaged certain other activities (joint investigations into work safety, fuel use, and so on), grievances remained the first concern.

GE reaped a considerable publicity bonanza from its Lynn Plan, and the crowing was not entirely unjustified. In the first two years of operation, representatives were elected, rules of procedure established, and some 274 cases appeared before the shop committees. Roughly half were settled in the employee's favor. But more importantly in the company's eyes, the Plan seemed to deter independent unionism. From 1918 until 1933 (at Lynn) and 1936 (at Schenectady), the GE plants had only company unions. Indeed, GE management felt so confident of its company union that its chairman, Gerard Swope, met secretly with AFL President William Green to suggest that the AFL organize and control the Plan. Having concluded that unionism could not be indefinitely delayed, Swope hoped in this way to forestall a more militant force that could be "a source of endless difficulties." (The Federation refused the offer.)[37]

GE's faith in its Plan was well-founded. Representation at Lynn provided for equitable treatment of workers only within a larger framework devised by management. True, the joint committees, with their equal numbers of workers and management representatives, maintained the final right to dispose of grievance cases. Their power, however, was sharply limited in two respects. First, the Plan carefully spelled out the rights reserved to management, most specifically the right to set the work pace and pay rates, establish all policy relating to work routines, and determine the general and specific rules of the enterprise. Thus the shop committee's authority was limited to determining whether these policies had been properly interpreted and applied by the foremen and whether individual workers had been unjustly treated *relative* to established corporate policy. Clearly the company's power to make the policy loomed as much more important than the committee's power to redress misapplications of policy.

Second, while the Plan treated the grievances of individual workers, it provided no mechanism for workers to press their collective interests. It included no bargaining mechanism for establishing overall wage structures and rates, for setting work standards and paces, or for the other vital concerns of worklife. In the very process of establishing a "union," the plan of representation tended to dissociate workers from their peers, putting them instead in individual relation to GE.

If the GE Plan offered carefully limited but nonetheless positive benefits to entice workers away from unionism, International Harvester's Works Council provided a grimmer experience. Harvester's plan, like GE's, was a war baby, born after the labor pains of the strikes and turmoil of 1918. Harvester officials considered the council as an important defense against the immediate threat of outside unions, but their memos also indicate a broader concern with "anarchical and 'bolshevik' activities" and with "the world-wide unrest of . . . the 'working classes.'" Against these combined evils, Harvester management saw a need for "the adoption of clearer statements of fair and democratic principles by leading industries."[38]

The Harvester Works Council followed the general lines of the other plans of representation, with certain minor modifications. As with other plans, the council handled primarily *individual* grievances. Robert Ozanne notes that "the plan seems to have been carefully designed to keep rank-and-file employees from ever getting together." There was no provision for employee meetings, for representatives to meet with their constituents or by themselves without the management appointees being present, or for representatives from different plants to meet together; in short, each council or committee worked with the corresponding management structure, not with parallel workers or groups of workers. Another common feature was that the scope of the council and the finality of its decisions depended on management approval; it had no independent power. Finally, and perhaps more strongly than in other plans such as GE's, the Harvester plan restricted participation. Only American citizens were allowed to be representatives, although at the crucial plants such as McCormick and Wisconsin Steel, foreign-born workers constituted 50 percent or more of the workforce, and few of these had been naturalized. The Council thus consisted of the privileged workers, and its actions indicated that they often represented their own interests rather than those of the wider labor force. In all these ways, the Harvester plan emphasized how limited was the workers' maneuvering room inside company unions.[39]

But what marked the Harvester plan as especially ominous and oppressive was the use to which Harvester management put the Council. Top Harvester officials saw the plan as a way of getting workers to govern other workers in the interests of the company, and to a considerable extent they succeeded in making the idea a reality. The first test came in the wake of the unsuccessful strikes of 1919, when management saddled the Council with the task of choosing which strikers to rehire. Although there is no record of the employees' representatives ever having requested this power, it immediately made the Council into a formidable body: elected workers and their company counterparts were now deciding who kept and who lost their jobs. In subsequent years, the Council was called upon to resist cost of living increases during the inflation of 1919–1920, to recommend wage cuts during the recession of 1921–1922, and to support several other proposals that were, in effect, antiworker decisions of management. This management bias was made possible by the superior resources of the management representatives, the inherently unequal positions of the two sides (one side drawing upon the power of the employer, the other reflecting the disorganized state of the workers), and the dependence of the entire scheme on management support of the plan.

Even in these forbidding circumstances, workers fought back and forced International Harvester to gut the program. In the mid-1920s, the workers elected representatives who insisted on wage increases and refused to bow to management pressure to be "realistic," so that the Council was consistently deadlocked. Since all disputed measures went to the company president to be resolved, Harvester was placed in the position of repeatedly turning down the workers' demands. The unreliability of Council support eroded management's enthusiasm for the plan, and the workers also lost interest when they saw how truly weak their representatives were. In the late 1920s the system lapsed into somnolence.

The plan revived somewhat in the 1930s, when the growing workers' movement once again led both workers and management to jockey for control of the Council mechanism. Management used the councils to circumvent the Wagner Act, and as late as 1937 Harvester had effectively resisted the entrance of genuine unions. Even after a 1936 National Labor Relations Board decision had declared that the plan was a company-dominated organization rather than a union, the company held on: "independent" unions—that is, unions independent of any national labor organizations—were established in each Harvester plant by the former Council representatives. Truly independent unions gained recognition in the Harvester plants only in the 1940s.[40]

Thus company unions survived from the end of World War I until the labor gains of the late 1930s. Although they were highly effective in delaying unionism (Irving Bernstein termed them "the most important device employers used to prevent or undermine labor organization"), they were too transparent for the intense workplace conflicts of the 1930s.[41]

Still, valuable lessons had been learned. For one thing, the experience with company unions persuaded corporate capitalists that formal grievance and appeals procedures were quite useful. Rather than being a threat to management prerogative, they reinforced it. On the one hand, the company could redress petty individual grievances at little cost to itself; indeed, if such efforts made workers happier, and particularly if they prevented grievances from festering into union militance, employers gained by resolving them. Disputes over "grievable" issues focused attention on individual cases rather than on collective concerns and on exceptions within established policy rather than on the policy itself. On the other hand, a formal grievance procedure provided an independent check on the arbitrariness of foremen; workers were being enlisted, as it were, in an alliance with management to ensure that foremen carried out company policy. The elaborate elections and council constitutions created unrealistic expectations among the workers, but company unions demonstrated the worth of the joint employee-employer committees for investigation of grievances.

More broadly, the plans of representation pushed corporate leaders to see their firms as institutions best governed by "laws" or rules rather than by management whim and command. Once again, the company unions, though weak in substance, communicated the lesson through their exaggerated form. The widely emulated Leitch Plan, for example, established a House of Representatives elected by workers, a Senate elected by foremen, and a Cabinet composed of management. "Laws" were established when passed by both houses and approved by the cabinet.[42] More concretely, at GE, International Harvester, and elsewhere, company policy had to be formulated and codified before councils could pass on whether grievances were valid or not.

The analogy to democratically established laws was false, of course, since management in every case retained the right to determine what the laws would be. Nonetheless, the corporations found attractive the concept that a pseudo-legal structure might have useful control consequences, not only directly by compelling behavior but indirectly by legitimizing employer-imposed work procedures. Company unions had indeed been a useful experiment.

Welfare capitalism, scientific management, and company unions all failed as efforts to bring new systems of control into the firm. For, as we shall see, the modern core corporation has achieved stability through quite different means, through what may be termed "structural control" of the work activities themselves.

Yet each of the experiments contributed to the making of structural control. If corporate leaders had drawn up a list of the lessons they had learned from this long period of experimentation, they would have noted that control must emanate from a legitimate overall structure, that it must be concerned with the work itself, that jobs must be defined precisely on the basis of management's control over special knowledge, that there must be positive rewards for proper work, and that management itself, especially foremen, must also be subjected to systematic control. In a general way, these lessons constituted the agenda for structural control. Undoubtedly the list is easier to construct in hindsight than it was to perceive in advance, and no corporate leader was convinced or even conscious of all the entries.

The follow two chapters show how, on the basis of their incomplete understanding but facing real problems, corporations imposed structural control. The organization, coordination, and assignment of work tasks became embedded in a larger structure of work. The pace of work, along with the specific direction of work tasks, emanated from this structure. Two possibilities existed: the control mechanism could be embedded in the technological structure of the firm, or it could be embedded in the firm's social-organizational structure. Corresponding to these two possibilities are the systems of technical control and bureaucratic control.

The firm's overall structure, being both more comprehensive than the immediate workplace and having been imposed from a higher level, removed control over the flow of work from the foreman's hands. The foreman's role in the production process became one of merely enforcing a prestructured flow of work activities. Rather than being exercised openly by the foreman or supervisor, *power was made invisible in the structure of work*. Thus, structural control became the modern-day manifestation of a more ancient but enduring capitalist phenomenon, the yoking of alienated labor to the pursuit of profits.

CHAPTER 7

Technical Control: An All-Around Adjustor and Equalizer

HOW SOMETHING is produced is in large part dictated, of course, by the nature of the product and by the known and available technologies for producing it. Thus, lumbering takes place in the forests, while food processing tends to be concentrated indoors, and building jet liners involves a stationary work object while radio assembly uses a moving line. Considerations of technical efficiency (for example, the number of times steel has to be reheated as it is processed) distinguish superior from inferior methods. Yet by themselves these types of technical considerations are insufficient to determine what technologies will actually be used.

It is well known that most industries confront a variety of possible techniques, and that the relative costs of required inputs will influence which is chosen. For example, steel making can be performed in huge automated factories with much machinery and little labor, as it is in the advanced countries where labor is expensive; or it can be produced in primitive hearths, with greater labor inputs and less machinery, as it is in many underdeveloped countries today and as it was in the United States seventy-five years ago, when machinery was expensive. Thus, *within* the known and available technologies, choice based on cost considerations is necessary.

What is less well known is that there is also an important *social* element in the development and choice of technique. Firms confront a range of techniques that differ not only with respect to required inputs, but also in the possibilities for control over their workforces. A superior technology may be one that facilitates the transformation of the firm's labor power into useful labor, even if that technology entails a larger bill for other inputs or even a larger wage bill per hour of operation.

While it remains true that capitalists undoubtedly seek those technologies that are most *profitable*, we now must admit that there are several considerations that enter into the calculation of profitability. One is technical efficiency, the ratio of the physical outputs to the physical inputs; another is the cost of the various inputs and the value of outputs; yet a third is the extent to which any technology provides managers with leverage in transforming purchased labor power into labor actually done. The way in which this third consideration—control—came to be considered is revealing of the whole process that has revolutionized work in the capitalist era.

Any system of control embodies the three elements introduced earlier: direction of work tasks, evaluation of work done, and rewarding and disciplining of workers. *Technical control* involves designing machinery and planning the flow of work to minimize the problem of transforming labor power into labor as well as to maximize the purely physically based possibilities for achieving efficiencies. Thus a social dimension, the inherent class nature of capitalist production, is added to the evolution of technology.

Technical control is structural in the sense that it is embedded in the technological structure or organization of production. It can be distinguished from simple mechanization, which merely increases the productivity of labor without altering the elements of control. For example, the use of an electric rather than a manual typewriter increases the speed with which a secretary works, but it does not alter how the secretary is directed to the next task, how his or her work is evaluated, or what the rewards or disciplines will be. Mechanization often brings with it technical control, as the worker loses control of the pace or sequence of tasks, but this consequence must nearly always be understood as the result of the *particular* (capitalist) design of the technology and not an inherent characteristic of machinery *in general.*

Technical control can also be distinguished from simple machine pacing, although the two are obviously related. Machine pacing occurs whenever a worker must respond to, rather than set, the pace at which the machinery is being operated. Employers have often built a production pace into machinery to try to gain control of the labor process. Yet as long as the machinery affects just one worker or one work team, the conflict over pace and rhythm continues to revolve around just these workers and their boss. For example, machinery can typically be operated at various speeds; it requires bonus schemes, piece-rates, incentive pay, and the like to set the pace. Even where machinery has only one speed, boss and workers can nonetheless agree to turn it off for rest periods, if the machinery in question utilizes only workers in this particular workplace. The social organization surrounding such machine pacing continues to be that of simple control. Technical control emerges only when the entire production process of the plant or large segments of it are based on a technology that paces and directs the labor process. When that happens, the pacing and direction of work transcend the individual workplace and are thus beyond the power of even the immediate boss; control becomes truly structural.

The Origins of Technical Control

Although popular mythology has the assembly line springing from Henry Ford's inventive genius, the basic idea of continuous flow production goes back much further. At the beginning of the nineteenth century, Rhode Island textile merchants viewed the factory as simply a place to collect (and hence better supervise) previously dispersed workers. But these employers were soon taught a costly lesson by their Boston-based competitors, who introduced superior (even if still rudimentary) continuous-flow production. And here, from the moment the spindles and looms were attached to the water-driven central power shaft, machinery harnessed the workers.[1]

What the Boston manufacturers discovered, of course, was that continuous-flow production permitted them, rather than their workers, to establish the pace of work. The spindles and looms (and later machines to card raw cotton and to dye finished cloth) could be set to operate at a given rate, and the attending workers could be forced to keep up. The first element in controlling labor (directing workers in which tasks to perform and when) was handled mechanically.

This first use of technical control brought severe consequences for the affected workers. Most important, of course, was the high speed of the work. Manufacturers anxious to achieve cost advantages over their competitors continually sought to increase the output of their machines and their workers. Accounts of textile mill history tell of the gradually increasing pressure. Norman Ware, for example, explained that

> the tendency of the factory system was to increase the strain and discipline under which the work was carried on. Both the management and the workers had, in earlier

years, been unaccustomed to thinking in terms of machine discipline. . . . [As the system advanced] increasing tension was the result of both . . . the development of a policy of speeding up and of improvements in the machinery that permitted greater efficiency.[2]

As the machinery was refined, and even more as the employers realized the potential of machine discipline, work became more frantic. In contrast to the so-called laxity of the early days, textile workers from the 1840s onward faced increasing pressure.[3]

Nor was greater speed the only change. With machinery driven at a uniform rate, workers could no longer create their own work rhythms. Independent spinners and weavers, just like farmers, coopers, shoemakers, and other workers, tended to produce in spurts, working furiously for a while and then slacking off or even stopping entirely to rest.[4] Now, the machine-established pace was uniform.

Before the midcentury speed-up, it was still possible for the workers to impose some of their own rhythms on work. They did so simply by the expedient of "doubling-up"—that is, one worker would do his or her own job and also, by frantic effort, another's; the released worker could then relax for a while until it was time to turn about. As intensifying competition imposed a speed-up, each worker's job required his or her full attention and even this source of variation was lost.

Equally important for the worker was the effect on mobility while at work. In the early shops the spinners and weavers needed to move around, to obtain materials or to dispose of finished goods. Contact and conversation with other workers was natural in the process. But in the new power-driven mills all machines operated together, and the operative had neither any cause nor any right to move about the mill. Instead, the worker became nearly as much locked in place as the machinery.

With each worker fixed to a physical location in the production process, contact among workers virutually ceased. Whereas before workers had made the workday pass more quickly by talking or reading to each other, now each worker simply tended his or her machine. Of particular importance to their employers, workers had little opportunity to discuss common grievances, compare foremen, or exchange views on pay rates or job conditions.

Thus, the textile factories early developed machine pacing and technical direction as a method of structuring the first of the three control elements. The other elements were less well worked out. The second aspect—evaluating the workers' performance—was relatively trivial, since the machinery actually performed the carding, spinning, and weaving, and hence the quality of every operative's output was more or less identical. Some variation did exist, mainly in the quantity produced but also in other ways, such as the knots used to join broken threads. Yet these differences were quite visible and easy for the foreman to discern. The third control element—disciplining and rewarding workers—rested on traditional hierarchical control principles. Piece-rates effectively punished operatives who lagged behind the output standard, but alongside the piece-rates stood the foremen's power. Chronic laggards, as well as troublemakers and strike organizers, were quickly fired and blacklisted.

As the earliest large-scale capitalist enterprises, the textile mills developed the production basis for technical control. In these mills, workers found themselves yoked to machinery that determined their work pace; there was little room for resistance in the workplace, and, lacking a strong union, they accepted the work or left.

Yet despite this early success in textiles, few other industries in the nineteenth century followed the mills' lead. Although rapidly improving machinery quickly raised production levels in many industries, only in rare cases did it provide a means of controlling workers. In shoemaking, for example, several inventions (most notably the McKay and Goodyear stitchers) provided capitalists with sufficient cost savings to crush competition from independent shoemakers; yet shoe factories remained more like the early Rhode Island mills—collections of closely supervised but separately engaged producers—than the continuous-flow mills.

Thus in railroading, in iron and steel production, in metal products fabrication, in brewing and distilling, in the garment trades, in shipbuilding, in glassworks, in sawmills and barrelmaking and other industries, the "shop" form of organization—simple control—prevailed. The introduction of machinery revolutionized the techniques of production, making prior craft skills obsolete and mightily raising productivity. But machinery did little to change the social organization of the workplace. The foreman's empire remained intact, because his role in directing production remained central.

Technology and the Direction of Work Tasks

Toward the end of the nineteenth century, the crisis created by the contradictions of simple control set off the search for more powerful and sophisticated mechanisms. Most of the discussion of control in scholarly journals has been devoted to the more self-conscious experiments: welfarism, scientific management, and company unions. But in the plants and offices of the large corporations the notion of technical control was by no means ignored. The advantages of continuous-flow production beckoned.

While all the corporations at the turn of the century groped toward new structures to control their workers, each firm and each industry faced somewhat different circumstances. In some the product, whether a blast furnace heat (as at U.S. Steel), a harvester (as at I-H), or a sleeping car (as at Pullman), involved single-unit or small-batch production; here employers saw little chance to exploit technical possibilities for control. These employers did engage in a titanic struggle to break the power of the skilled crafts workers. And as hierarchical control was solidified in these industries, the corporations turned to the bribes of bonus schemes, incentive pay, and welfare capitalism for their more sophisticated control structure.

But in other industries, notably meatpacking, electrical products production, and auto manufacturing, the flow of production was more direct. Here technology was first recognized as a basis for wider, structural control.[5] Meatpacking was one of the first industries to adopt continuous flow, this time as a disassembly line. When Swift, Armour, and others began using refrigeration to revolutionize slaughtering and meatpacking, the old shop-based, small-batch techniques of the abattoir gave way to continuous flow. Investigating the packing houses for a British medical review, one journalist put it as follows:

> outside the big factory buildings there are long, inclined, boarded passages up which the animals are driven. Thus the pigs are brought up to the height of the second floor. As they enter the main building each pig is caught by one of the hind legs. With rope and loop-knot and hook it is slung up, the head downwards and the neck exposed, at a convenient height for the slaughterer to strike. With great rapidity the suspended pigs are pushed on to a sort of passage about four feet broad where their throats are slashed open as they pass along. . . . Within less than a minute the dying pig reaches a long tank full of scalding water and in this the palpitating body is thrown. . . . Standing in the damp and steam men armed with long prongs push the swine along. By the time when the hogs have floated down to the other end of the boiling-water tank they are sufficiently scalded for the bristles to be easily extracted. They are now put on a movable counter or platform and as the hogs pass along other workers scrape the bristles off their backs. . . . At a subsequent stage the body is opened and the intestines are removed.[6]

From the perspective of control, the benefits of such production were immediate and obvious. By establishing the pace at which hogs were driven up the passages and onto the slaughter platform, managers could set the pace of work for the entire workforce. There were limits, of course, both physical and worker-imposed ones, but supervisors no longer had primary responsibility for directing the workers. Instead, the line now determined the pace, and the foremen had merely to get workers to follow that pace. Our observer makes this point quite explicit:

> When [the animal is] strung up, the machinery carries [it] forwards and men have to run after it to cut its throat, while others follow with great pails to catch the blood; and all this without interrupting the dying animal's journey to . . . the next process of manufacture. . . . On they go from stage to stage of manufacture and *the men have to keep pace with them.*[7]

Thus by 1905 the essentials of continuous-flow production, including the possibilities for controlling workers, were established in meatpacking.

While continuous-flow production appeared first in textiles, meatpacking, lamp production, and elsewhere, it was the Ford assembly line that brought the technical direction of work to its fullest potential. The automobile industry had its origins in the bicycle plants, where each team (a skilled mechanic and his helpers) performed all the operations necessary to assemble bicycles from separate parts. Carried over into auto plants, this organization slowly gave way as the assembly process began to be broken into parts, each team now adding only a limited range of parts to the product before the product was passed on to another team. But when the Highland Park plant opened in 1913, the endless conveyor finally abolished the craft pretensions of the Ford workers.[8]

The Ford Company's phenomenal success grew out of more than its efforts to impose a new way of controlling its workforce. The company produced a product for which public demand expanded rapidly; each year roughly 90 percent of all Ford cars had been purchased before they were built. Moreover, Ford (emulating successful manufacturers in other industries) was adept in applying mechanization to production. The introduction of machinery eliminated high-wage skilled labor and achieved big increases in labor productivity and large declines in labor costs. As one factory observer reported:

> The foundry superintendent asserts that if an immigrant, who has never seen the inside of a foundry before, cannot be made a first-class molder of one piece only in three days, he can never be any use on the floor; and two days is held to be ample time to make a first-class core maker of a man who has never before seen a core-molding bench in his life.[9]

Thus, in large part Ford's success arose from the same developments that fueled the growth of other firms.

Still, there was also something quite revolutionary about the Ford plants, and it was recognized as such at the time. Like the famous Lowell mills of the early nineteenth century, the Ford plants (and especially Highland Park) attracted widespread attention as the models of progressive capitalist industry. This attention derived most fundamentally from the Ford assembly line.

The Ford line resolved technologically the essential first control system task: it provided unambiguous direction as to what operation each worker was to perform next, and it established the pace at which the worker was forced to work. Henry Ford himself emphasized this aspect of the line by stating as one of his three principles of progressive manufacture, "the delivery of work instead of leaving it to the workmen's initiative to find it."[10] Ford might well have added that the line's "delivery of work" also relieved his foreman of having to push work onto the workers, as was necessary in simple control. H. L. Arnold studied the plant in great detail in 1914, when Ford introduced the first chain-driven "endless conveyor" to assemble magnetos:

> The chain drive [continuous assembly] proved to be a very great improvement, hurrying the slower men, holding the fast men back from pushing work on to those in advance, and acting as an all-around adjustor and equalizer.[11]

Whatever the sequence of tasks chosen, the new setup transformed that order into a technological necessity. Even if many assembly sequences were physically possible, the line left the workers no choice about how to do their jobs. The chassis or magneto or engine under construction came past a worker's station, lacking the part inventoried at that station; it would soon move on to other stations where it would gain every other part. The obvious necessity of adding the part stocked at this station was thus established. Arnold (and co-author L. F. Faurote) expressed the consequences of this point as follows:

> Minute division of operations is effective in labor-cost reducing in two ways: first, by making the workman extremely skillful, so that he does his part with no needless motions, and secondly, by training him to perform his unvaried operation with the least possible expenditure of will-power, and hence with the least brain fatigue.[12]

Thus the line hemmed the worker in by establishing a situation in which only one task sequence was possible and "needless" motions were avoided.

Similarly, the line established a technological presumption in favor of the line's work pace. Struggle between workers and bosses over the transformation of labor power into labor was no longer a simple and direct *personal* confrontation; now the conflict was mediated by the production technology itself. Workers had to oppose the pace of the *line*, not the (direct) tyranny of their bosses. The line thus established a technically based and technologically repressive mechanism that kept workers at their tasks.

The substitution of technical for human direction and pacing of work simultaneously revolutionized the relation between foreman and workers. Arnold and Faurote explained that:

> [The Highland Park plant] has applied team work [that is, division of labor] to the fullest extent, and by this feature in conjunction with the arrangement of successive operations in the closest proximity, so as to minimize transportation and *to maximize the pressure of flow of work, it succeeds in maintaining speed without obtrusive foremanship.*[13]

In effect, the line eliminated "obtrusive foremanship," that is, close supervision in which the foreman simultaneously directed production, inspected and approved work, and disciplined workers. The line relieved the foreman of responsibility for the first element of the control system.

The significance of this change is indicated by the small number of straw bosses and foremen needed to supervise the Ford workforce. In 1914 about 15,000 workers were employed at all the Ford plants. Leaving aside the top management, this large force was overseen by just 255 men ranking higher than workman, including 11 department foremen, 62 job foremen, 84 assistant foremen, and 98 straw bosses or subforemen. Thus there was one foreman (all ranks) for each 58 workers, an impossible ratio except in the situation where the foremen no longer directed the sequence or pacing of work.[14]

American Telephone and Telegraph (AT&T) provides a more recent illustration of this same phenomenon. Bell System workers fall into three broad groupings: telephone operators; craft workers (linemen, installers, and others); and clerical and sales staff. Since the operators' duties mainly require them to respond to routine incoming calls, AT&T has been able to subject their work to technical control. Between 1958 and 1976, the number of operators per supervisor varied between 14.9 and 18.9, a span of control twice that of AT&T's other (nontechnically controlled) workers.[15]

This change in foremen's status is confirmed by studies of how foremen spend their time at work. For example, John Yanouzas used on-the-job observations to compare foremen in two types of work situations: shops doing "job-lot" work (hierarchical control) and workplaces using assembly lines (technical control.)[16] Reanalyzing his data in terms of our three elements of control, we find two interesting results. First, while foremen on the assembly line still spend most of their working time on activities relating to control, they spend less (72 percent of their day) on such activities than do foremen in hierarchical control (83 percent); apparently the line itself assumes some control functions. Second, of the time spent on control activities, foremen in

Allocation of Foremen's Time Spent on Control

Control System	Control Element, Percent of Time Spent On: #1 Directing Work	#2 Evaluating Performance	#3 Disciplining
In Hierarchical Control	77.5	15.5	7.0
In Technical Control	56.3	30.6	13.1

technical control spend less time on the first element and about twice as much time on the second and third elements as do foremen in hierarchical control. As Peter Blau and W. R. Scott put it:

> Assembly line production tends to reverse the flow of demand in the organization. . . . Since the presence of the conveyor assures coordination and a certain level of productivity, it obviates the need for supervisory direction to achieve these ends.[17]

The foreman is thus transformed into an enforcer of the requirements and the dictates of the technical structure. On the assembly line he monitors workers to keep them at their tasks; he no longer initiates tasks. The foreman penalizes exceptions to the normal flow of work, rather than personally directing that flow. Moreover, the larger structure tends to legitimize the foreman's role. Exceptional circumstances aside, the foreman cannot be held personally responsible for the oppressiveness of the production process. If the legitimacy of the line is accepted, then the necessity for the foreman's job follows. The actual power to control work is thus vested in the line itself, rather than in the person of the foreman. Instead of control appearing to flow from boss to workers, control emerges from the much more impersonal "technology."

But while the Ford assembly plant established a technical basis for the first control element, the rest of the control system remained quite primitive. Inspection and evaluation of each worker's performance was relatively simple; generally, either the part had been added to the product or it had not, but even so, foremen and a small army of inspectors had to keep a sharp watch on production. Unfortunately, few records survive concerning the amount of sabotage or substandard work, but Arnold and Faurote noted that,

> constant supervision of workmen, constant work inspection and constant watching [of work] . . . give skilled overlooking to the work of every man. . . . Every workman is perfectly aware that he is under constant observation, and that he will be admonished if he falls below the fast pace of the department.[18]

When inadequate work (or insubordination or union activity or any other unwanted behavior) was detected, the old mechanisms of hierarchical control came into play. All supervisors had the power to discharge workmen immediately and at will. With relatively high pay, especially after the $5-a-day wage was announced, these conditions (according to Arnold and Faurote),

> make the workmen absolutely docile. New regulations, important or trivial, are made almost daily; workmen are studied individually and changed from place to place with no cause assigned, as the bosses see fit, and not one word of protest is ever spoken, because every man knows the door to the street stands open for any man who objects in any way, shape, or manner to instant and unquestioning obedience to any directions whatever.[19]

Thus, although the direction and pacing of work were technologically established, the Ford plants reflected hierarchical control in managing the other aspects of the control system.

Even here, however, the revolutionary effects of technical control began to be felt. With foremen holding less responsibility for the direction of work, they needed less power. Their power of arbitrary dismissals had been essential as long as the battle between workers and bosses was a directly personal one. But this power was costly; by 1914 so many workers were fired or quit that five hundred new workers had to be hired each day to replenish the fifteen thousand-person workforce; the payroll office maintained records on nearly one hundred thousand persons previously employed at Ford.[20] With the line, however, the worker-boss struggle was mediated by technology, and the bosses were no longer responsible for actively directing workers in the sequence or the pace of their tasks. In late 1914 subforemen lost their right to fire without worker appeal, and although each subforeman could dismiss workers from his own department, often they were simply transferred elsewhere. Thus control operated as a system of related parts, and change in the first element brought in its wake an important erosion of arbitrary foremen's rule elsewhere.

The consequences of technical control were no less severe in the auto plants than they had been elsewhere. In textiles and meatpacking the new system had restricted workers' ability to move about and communicate with other workers, and it had the same effect among auto workers. The findings of the famous *Man on the Assembly Line* study illustrate this point. Although the auto plant in the study employed over a thousand production-line workers, Charles Walker and Robert Guest found that in the most typical case, a worker had "verbal interaction" with only eight or ten other workers. Each worker tended to have almost no communication (interaction less than three times a day) with workers as close as three work stations away, a distance of no more than forty or so feet. The reason for the limitations on social contact was simple: the line moved fast, and

> Each worker is restricted because of fixed equipment to a limited range of movement along the line. He has a [tool] which is suspended above him by wires. It cannot be moved at will to any location in the section, but runs along the overhead track only up to the point where the workers in adjacent groups begin their operations.[21]

By having the product rather than the workers move around the factory floor, technology required that each worker remain at his or her post. The privilege of free movement across the production area had been eliminated, not (as in hierarchical control) by a foreman's arbitrary rule, but rather by the dictates of technology. Workers were thus isolated; since they did not need to move about, their work was more regular and easy to monitor, and hence they were more firmly controlled.

Moreover, the limitations on social contact appear to become more severe as plants have become more fully automated. In the 1950s, William Faunce studied auto workers who, about fifteen months prior to his interview, had transferred from older plants to a "highly automated" plant in the same company while continuing in the same job classifications. Faunce investigated five variables he thought would affect social interaction: the amount of attention required by the job, the distance between work stations, the extent of worker control of the work pace, machine noise, and the number of jobs that involved teamwork. In each case he found conditions in the automated workplaces more isolating. Workers reported that the automated jobs required much closer and more constant attention, that work stations were further apart, that workers had less chance to vary the work pace and thereby establish opportunities for conversation, that the new factory was noisier, and that there were fewer jobs involving teamwork. In short, workers had become "virtually isolated socially on automated production lines."[22]

Extensions of Technical Control

Today, of course, technical control is based upon a much more sophisticated technology than was available when the Ford line was first introduced. Yet, rather than producing qualitative differences, the new technology simply expanded the potential contained in the concept of technical control.

The most dramatic changes in technology are the result of new devices to control or program machinery. Numerical control, whereby machines are fitted with control devices that read preprogrammed tape, has thus far achieved the most widespread application, although by itself it is clearly one of the more primitive of the known techniques. If the same tape is reused, the task sequence or machine speed or operation is repeated; if the tape is reprogrammed, a new task can be performed. Thus, either through the creation of a bank of tapes or through new programming in the design department, numerical control tends to remove from the shop floor some of the initiating and directing of work tasks. Now the operative must follow the pace and pattern set into the machine by the tape.[23]

Still, numerical control, at least up to the present, represents simply an advance in machine pacing of individual workers. The technique tends to be applied to single machines or groups of machines, and the social organization surrounding a numerically controlled workplace is not significantly different from that in other workplaces.

Much more portentous are the emerging feedback systems—controls that are computer-linked, minicomputer controlled, or based on microprocessor technology. In the computer-linked systems, the operations in large segments of a factory (or even an entire factory) are tied to a large central computer such as the IBM 370. In direct numerical control, for example, many machines, each individually fitted with numerical control devices, are linked directly to a central computer.[24] The computer can send instructions (according to its preprogrammed routine) as to what operations or activities workers are to perform, and upon successful completion of the task the central computer will receive feedback information that will permit it to send out instructions for the next operation. Through central programming the computer (that is, management) can follow production through its various stages, controlling the flow of work.

Many firms have begun using minicomputers to oversee particular segments of the production process. Minicomputers are simply small computers with much less capacity than the large mainframe machines, and costing only a tenth or a hundredth as much. They were developed to handle small or simple operations when the immense capacity of the large computers was not needed. For example, minicomputers control the cranes that stack and simultaneously inventory crates of cigarettes in a new Philip Morris warehouse.[25] A principal advantage of the minicomputer is that its size and cost make it flexible enough to be introduced into an existing factory without redesigning the entire facility. Minicomputer technology appears to be ideal for the lower-level controls.

Yet even the minicomputer has not been the final step: microprocessor technology threatens to raise controls to an even higher level of sophistication. A microprocessor is described as a "computer on a chip," and it is perhaps better understood as the basis for microcomputers: tiny, cheap machines that can process information and perform simple logical operations. For example, a microcomputer-equipped scale, when programmed with postal rates, zip codes, and the location of the scale itself, can weigh a package and compute the postage if the operator merely types in the destination zip code. Microprocessor technology makes it technically possible and financially feasible to link every machine or operation in the factory, no matter how mundane, to computer controls.[26]

While initially these various technologies appeared as alternatives, the next step in harnessing the burgeoning technology was obvious in hindsight. Microcomputers, minicomputers, and mainframe computers were combined in one sophisticated, interconnected system. Feedback systems have thus evolved to the point where a computer hierarchy to control work takes its place alongside the human hierarchy. Just as foremen watch over particular shops, so microcomputers control the operations conducted on particular machines. As with real foremen, these mechanical foremen (perhaps aspiring to become IBM 370s?) are themselves directed, evaluated, and corrected by higher-level (larger brain capacity!) minicomputers that control and direct many processes at once. Yet the minicomputers are but the technical middle management, reporting to the really big brains that can "understand" the entire production process. If the central computer fails to operate properly, the minicomputers can continue to run their preprogrammed default routines, keeping their workers and machines usefully busy until the mainframe machine comes back on duty.[27]

All this new technology has extended the potential for management control almost faster than employers have been able to utilize it. Dramatic price declines have made computing power almost free, relative to other costs of production.[28] The result is that control devices—from simple numerical control up through computer hierarchies—are now pouring into the factories.

Thus computer technology gives a giant boost to the earlier methods of technical control. An essential advantage of this technology over older systems is its flexibility. Whereas the actual machines on traditional assembly lines had to be redesigned and retooled in order to change the production process, under computer-directed production the programs only have to be rewritten. Aside from making product alterations easier, this programming capacity makes it possible to adapt technical control to small-batch (machine shop) operations. In this respect, computers have extended technical control to previously untouched processes.

Computer-based controls extend and make more powerful the direction of work activities by technical means, but the feedback systems also contribute one genuinely new element to technical control, and in this respect they constitute qualitative advance over Henry Ford's moving line. As their name implies, feedback systems not only send out instructions but also receive back information from the chain of the computer hierarchy. On the basis of this information, evaluations of work progress can be made. Computers have begun subjecting to technical control the second element of a control system, the monitoring and evaluation of work performed. On the early Ford lines, such inspection and the detection of inadequate work were primarily the responsibility of the foremen and inspectors, and disputes over work quality quickly created direct confrontations between workers and their supervisors. Now, however, with machines testing the quality of work as well as directing workers, technical control spreads to the first two control functions.

To achieve successful technical control over the monitoring and evaluation of work performance, corporations have stimulated a technology termed "automatic testing." At the simplest level, automatic testing merely mechanizes the quality control process. For example, as an automobile engine is assembled, it is subjected to continuous tests to determine leaks, parts malfunctions, or missing parts.[29] In more sophisticated applications, automatic testing provides continuous management information about productivity, labor costs, spoiled work, wastage, and so on.[30] All this provides top management with much quicker feedback for the monitoring (and control) of the production process.

In this dazzle of new technology the workers are almost lost from sight. With their activities and productivity constantly being directed and monitored by the computer hierarchy, workers find even less opportunity to exercise any control over their work lives. Their immediate oppressor becomes the programmed control device, the programming department, the printout—in short, the technology of production. In this environment, the human hierarchy and the capitalist organization of production that has produced the technology appear to recede. Control becomes truly structural, embedded in that hoary old mystification, technology.

Technical Control and the Firm's Workforce

The imposition of technical control marked the firm's first serious step toward structural control. The impact of technical control could not be expected to be limited to individual workplaces, and it was not. The entire firm's workforce was affected and, in turn, the working class at large.

First we should note one way in which the new system did not change matters. As observed earlier, technical control did not alter the third control element (the disciplining and rewarding of workers). It is not surprising, then, that technical control did not directly alter those social consequences primarily associated with the mode of discipline. In particular, technical control continued and perhaps strengthened the tendency for the workforce to become more homogeneous.

In its early days, technical control, like hierarchical control before it, motivated its workers mainly through the fear of punishment. The carrot was largely absent, the stick ever-present. The chief weapon, often even a first-resort disciplining device, was the reserve army of the unemployed. Less drastic penalties (such as suspension or docking of pay) also existed, but their usefulness varied directly with the potency of the supervisor's major sanction, dismissal. Rebellious workers or those who simply refused to work as hard as the most eager replacement faced the sack.

But if dismissal was to be fearful, either as a threat or as a fact, it was necessary that there be many substitute workers available and able to fill the jobs. It was precisely the lack of suitable replacements that had given the old skilled workers their power and had led, by way of reaction, to their demise. Similarly, in times of tight labor markets (such as wartime), workers were relatively confident both that replacements could not easily be found and that, if they were fired, they could find other jobs.

In technical control no less than in hierarchical control, employers had a powerful incentive to make their workers as interchangeable as possible. Continuing mechanization eroded the need for skills anyway, making the workforce more uniformly composed of unskilled and semiskilled machine operatives. But the strictly *control* aspects of work reorganization contributed a further impetus to the homogenizing process.[31]

The tendency to create a common (and degraded) status for all workers was evident in the labor policies of the early Ford plants. The famous Five-Dollar Day that Ford announced in 1914 was not necessary to fill the company's vacancies; it did, however, create an enormous labor surplus. The day after the announcement was made, there were ten thousand people outside the gates clamoring for jobs; for months afterward, as Francesca Maltese reports, the job-seekers "continued to clog the entrances to Ford's employment offices."[32] The lesson was not lost on the people employed inside the gates: the company would have no trouble finding replacements for recalcitrant workers.

Similarly, other Ford labor policies attempted to generate a ready reserve of surplus labor. Thus it is no coincidence that the first large-scale entry of blacks into northern industrial employment occurred in the Ford plants.[33] By 1926 Ford employed ten thousand black workers, over 90 percent of Detroit's black industrial labor force. The company cast its net even further, drawing into potential employment the physically handicapped (generously labeled "substandard men"), young boys, and others. It was energetic in establishing a recruiting bureau to attract workers from other cities. Technical control both continued the need for surplus labor as a ready disciplinarian and strengthened its derivative, the increasing interchangeability and homogenizing of the labor force.[34]

The attempt to generate highly visible pools of surplus labor was a response to the crisis of control on the shop floor, and it affected primarily blue-collar workers. But technical control's influence extended also to the lower-level clerical staff, and here technical control introduced a new stimulus towards homogenization.

The corporation in part addressed the problem of controlling the white-collar staff by reorganizing their work along the lines of technical control. The routinization of clerical work has been extensively investigated elsewhere, and it need not be repeated here.[35] The essential point is that many clerical workers—those performing keypunching, typing of standard forms, and other routinized operations—were transformed into operators of simple machines. High school education had become nearly universal by 1930, and the large pool of educated workers meant that as these workers could be more easily replaced, they became subject to the discipline of the reserve army. They had been reduced to the level of homogeneous labor.

But even as the new system solved some of the corporation's labor problems, it created other, more serious ones. Technical control yoked the entire firm's labor force (or each of the major segments thereof) to a common pace and pattern of work set by the productive technology. In so doing, technical control resolved for the individual workplace and the individual foreman the problem of translating labor power into labor. But it did so at the cost of raising this conflict to the plantwide level. Thus the basic conflict was displaced, not eliminated.

At first, this displacement was not realized. Throughout the 1910s, and even more in the relatively conflict-free 1920s, technical control appeared to have decisively turned the power balance in favor of the capitalists. Individual sabotage, disputes between workers and their foremen, and grumbling over wages continued, of course, but it was thought that these could be managed while the power of technology drove the work pace.

The flaw in this naive thinking was exposed dramatically and at heavy cost to the capitalists. Irving Bernstein describes what happened in the auto plants:

> On December 28 [1936] a sudden sit-down over piece-rate reductions in one department in Cleveland swept through the plant and 7,000 people stopped work; Chevrolet body production came to a complete halt.
>
> On December 30 the workers in Flint sat down in the huge Fisher One and the smaller Fisher Two plants. Combined with the stoppage in Cleveland, this forced the closing of Chevrolet and Buick assembly operations in Flint. On December 31 the UAW sat down at Guide Lamp in Anderson, Indiana. . . . By the end of the first week of the new year, the great General Motors automotive system had been brought to its knees.[36]

The costs of lifting the shop-floor conflict out of the individual workplace and raising it to the plantwide level were now apparent. Technical control linked together the plant's workforce, and when the line stopped, every worker necessarily joined the strike. Moreover, in a large, integrated manufacturing operation, such as auto production, a relatively small group of disciplined unionists could cripple an entire system by shutting down a part of the line.

Technical control thus took relatively homogeneous labor (unskilled and semiskilled workers) and technologically linked them in production. The combination proved to be exceptionally favorable for building unions. The Flint strike was not the first sit-down, nor were such strikes confined to plants with moving lines. But the sit-downs were most effective in the mass production industries like autos, electrical products, rubber, and textiles. More broadly, "quickie" sit-downs (strikes of a few minutes or an hour or two), sabotage, wildcat strikes, and other labor actions were much more effective in plants organized according to technical control.

The Congress of Industrial Organizations' success of the 1930s clearly resulted in part from wider factors not considered here—the Depression, the increasing concentration of industry, and the conscious activity of militant union organizers. Yet technical control significantly enhanced the chances of industrial unionism, and such organization marked the beginning of an effective limitation on the new form of control.

Limits on technical control were nowhere more clearly revealed than at

General Motors' Lordstown (Ohio) Vega plant several decades later. GM had come to Lordstown with the intention of achieving a dramatic speedup in output. Its strategy was two-pronged. First, the company redesigned the plant and machinery to accommodate the production of roughly one hundred cars per hour (one every thirty-six seconds); this rate represented a 40 percent increase over the one-a-minute average that prevailed in most of its plants. Second, GM recruited a new labor force, one without long traditions of fighting to restrict industrial output. The plan didn't work.[37]

The 1972 revolt at Lordstown gained much publicity and even notoriety, and justifiably so; but mostly the event attracted attention for the wrong reasons. On one side, Lordstown was declared atypical (and hence not really worrisome) because of the youthfulness of the workers (the average age was twenty-four), because of the plant's counterculture ambience, and because of the workforce's lack of industrial experience and discipline. On the other side, Lordstown was heralded as the new wave of working-class revolt for precisely the same reasons. Yet what really should have been noted was that Lordstown may have represented technical control's final gasp as an ascendant control system. The most advanced industrial engineering went into the design of the plant, but only resistance and the breakdown of control came out.

Machine pacing and deskilling through the use of "smart" machines will continue, and it is even expanding in the lower-level clerical occupations. Moreover, in new areas of investment—the South and the Third World, for example—technical control remains a first principle of factory organization. In the economy's small-firm periphery, such organization remains equally important. But technical control can never again *by itself* constitute an adequate control system for the core firms' main industrial labor force. The presence of unions with effective (even if circumscribed) countervailing power is forcing a change, as we saw in the case of Fred Doyal's job at GE's Ashland plant. In both its white-collar and blue-collar applications, technical control is already being combined with elements of another structural system—bureaucratic control.

CHAPTER 8

Bureaucratic Control: Policy No. 1.1

THE monopoly corporations' first efforts at establishing control were, on the whole, unsuccessful. By the 1920s, welfare capitalism had been tested and found wanting. It would not be completely abandoned, of course; pension funds, worker health programs, and the like continued to exist, even if many were dropped and others were switched to public agencies at the taxpayers' expense. Yet the 1919 steel strike and the labor troubles at International Harvester and other large firms that had relied on welfare schemes to appease workers demonstrated that fundamental antagonisms remained.

The same thing was true of Taylorism and employee representation plans. Enthusiasm for these methods waned in the 1920s as corporate leaders perceived their limited success. Again, some parts would be kept, and in certain cases these methods would remain essential. Yet mostly they would come to be seen as ancillary rather than central to control.

Technical control marked a much more substantial step, as shown by its persistence into the post-1945 period. But even here success was partial; the 1930s ended the illusion that technical control would resolve the labor problem. Assembly lines and other technologically based ways of supervising workers transformed workplace conflict into broader and ultimately more dangerous plantwide struggles. In tire making, auto parts production, radio and auto assembly, electrical machinery manufacture, and other technically controlled operations, the plants were first paralyzed by sit-downs and then quickly unionized. The very presence of unions guaranteed that some accommodation would be necessary. True, technical control would continue to be used in particular industries and would be employed for some tasks in nearly all industries. Yet a fundamentally new system was required.

That system, developed essentially during the post-1945 period, was bureaucratic control. Bureaucratic control, like technical control, differs from the simple forms of control in that it grows out of the formal structure of the firm, rather than simply emanating from the personal relationships between workers and bosses. But while technical control is embedded in the physical and technological aspects of production and is built into the design of machines and the industrial architecture of the plant, bureaucratic control is embedded in the social and organizational structure of the firm and is built into job categories, work rules, promotion procedures, discipline, wage scales, definitions of responsibilities, and the like. Bureaucratic control establishes the impersonal force of "company rules" or "company policy" as the basis for control.

In its most fundamental aspect, bureaucratic control institutionalized the exercise of hierarchical power within the firm. The definition and direction of work tasks, the evaluation of worker performances, and the distribution of rewards and imposition of punishments all came to depend upon established rules and procedures, elaborately and systematically laid out.

Bureaucratic control attempted to routinize all of the functions of management in the way that technical control had routinized the first function. Capitalists were to retain overall control of the enterprise's operations through their power to establish the rules and procedures. But once the goals and structure were set, the management process was to proceed without need of, and (except in exceptional circumstances) without benefit of, the conscious intervention or the personal power of foremen, supervisors, or capitalists.

Bureaucratic control first emerged in firms such as IBM and Polaroid, where management enjoyed a virtually free hand to introduce the new relations from the top down. Management saw bureaucratic control as a way of avoiding unions and as a basis for labor-management relations that was an alternative to the dual power, collective-bargaining model that had emerged from the 1930s. For management, bureaucratic control eliminated the weakness of technical control.

In most firms the new form of control did not necessitate a sharp break with past practice. Rather, the new procedures were introduced piecemeal, more in response to actual problems than as part of a master plan.[1] Moreover, the new form of control could never completely eliminate prior forms. The shift to bureaucratic control was therefore a shift towards relatively greater dependence on this organizational method, and bureaucratic control came to exist alongside and be reinforced by elements of hierarchical and technical control. Bureaucratic control became the predominant system of control, giving shape and logic to the firm's organization, but it did not completely eliminate elements of other systems of control.

As we shall see later, a different (though in some ways parallel) development occurred in firms where unions already existed. Here, the inadequacy of technical control and the subsequent bargaining between unions and management led to a modification of technical control that pushed it towards bureaucratization. Management sought to use bureaucratic control to limit the impact of the unions, to draw them into joint disciplining of workers, and to regain some of its lost initiative. Unions turned to bureaucratization of the workplace to codify and thereby defend their negotiated gains. This dynamic led to quite different results, however. Most notably, management retained many more prerogatives where unionism was excluded than where joint administration was accepted.

Even though it was by no means a new invention, bureaucratic control constituted the most important change wrought by the modern corporation in the labor process. Just as technical control had emerged from the factory floor to be applied not only to blue-collar but also to lower-level white-collar work, so now bureaucratic control appeared first in the office and was later applied to production work. The new system transcended its white-collar origins and, in the corporations discussed below—IBM, AT&T, U.S. Steel, Polaroid, GE, and others—came to organize manual as well as mental work. This was the "managerial revolution" of the modern corporation. Technical control is now seen to be but half—and the lesser half at that—of the full story of the transformation of the workplace in the twentieth century.

Bureaucratic Control in Operation

The Polaroid Corporation, best known for its instant photography, provides a detailed case history of sophisticated bureaucratic control. The corporation was large enough to rank 230 on *Fortune's* 1977 list of top industrial corporations. In 1975, despite the worst layoffs in Polaroid's history, it employed over nine thousand persons.*

Polaroid's major activity is manufacturing, and in this respect it is typical

*All data, quotations, and other material on Polaroid, unless otherwise noted, are taken from conversations and internal documents the corporation readily provided. Indeed, it is a mark of the sophistication of Polaroid's management and of the success of its version of bureaucratic control that the company showed little hesitation in making this information available. Some of the details (e.g., the number of job families) may have changed since the interviews, but these changes in no way affect the essentials.

of big business in general. While the hobbyist and family-snapshot uses of Polaroid's products provide most of the company's sales, its cameras have also proved useful for many industrial needs, most notably in issuing identification cards. To meet these demands, Polaroid itself manufactures the equipment and supplies sold under its brand.

Polaroid activities also extend beyond manufacturing. Until the still-unfolding and quite shaky effort by Kodak to challenge Polaroid, the corporation had the instant-photography market entirely to itself. As a result, Polaroid carries out all those activities that monopolistic, multinational firms find necessary to maximize their profits. For example, the company makes a large sales effort; rather than relying on the market to generate demand, it has pursued an aggressive and costly advertising strategy. Similarly, it maintains a huge research and development program to devise new products, partly to attract new consumer dollars and partly to defend itself from competition. In addition to its basic manufacturing force, Polaroid employs a substantial number of workers in sales, research, legal, and other tasks. In 1977, 45 percent of the firm's workforce (4,879 employees) were classified as production workers; another 23 percent (2,523 workers) were engaged in office work; and 32 percent (3,509 employees) were assigned to supervisory, research, and other professional jobs.

Polaroid is thus a middle-sized manufacturing giant, with considerable market power, international operations, an active sales effort, and a large production staff. In all these respects, it is typical of "smokestack America." Its employees are not unionized.

Polaroid's system of control is built on a finely graded division and stratification of workers. The divisions run both hierarchically (creating higher and lower positions) and laterally. They tend to break up the homogeneity of the firm's workforce, creating many seemingly separate strata, lines of work, and focuses for job identity.

The workforce at Polaroid (as elsewhere) is divided into two different groups: those supervisory and professional employees who are exempt from the provisions of the Fair Labor Standards Act and the production workers who, in Polaroid's terminology, are "nonexempt." The exempt employees (numbering 3,016 in September, 1975) are paid on a salaried basis and are subject to a separate set of compensation procedures. The nonexempt workers (some 6,397 strong in September, 1975) are paid on an hourly basis.

Two points of importance emerge from a comparison of these groups. First, despite superficial distinctions in procedures, pay scales, methods of evaluation, and the like, there are no essential differences in the way Polaroid controls the two groups. Both are enmeshed within a highly articulated bureaucratic control system. Second, the existence of two groups with superficial and formalistic distinctions, and with real differences in pay and power, creates an important division among Polaroid workers. Thus a first step is taken in the divide-and-conquer strategy.

But the stratification of workers into separate groups and subgroups goes much further than division into salaried and nonsalaried status. The nonsalaried employees are first divided into "job families"—eighteen groups of jobs such as "general clerical," "metal trades," or "chemical mixing and processing" that are "similar in nature and involve similar skills." Within every job family, the proliferation of job titles permits a far more fertile basis for distinguishing each worker from his or her coworkers. The Materials Control and Movement job family, for example, includes a Section Leader, a Materials Aide, and some fifteen other job titles. General Clerical-Administrative has roughly thirty-five titles. Overall, the company has about three hundred job titles for its hourly staff alone. Polaroid thereby takes a second and somewhat larger step toward making each job slot appear individual or distinct.

Then there is the pay scheme. Each individual job is assigned a "Polaroid Classification Value" (PCV)—a designation in yet another, and subordinate, classification scheme. In Polaroid's theory, as many as twenty or twenty-five PCV levels are possible, although only fourteen were actually in use in 1975.

With eighteen different job families, three hundred job titles, and fourteen different pay grades, not to mention the dichotomy between salaried and hourly workers, it might appear that Polaroid had gone far enough in dividing and redividing its workers. Not so: each job is now further positioned along the pay scale so that for any given job (or PCV value), seven distinct pay steps are possible, from entry-level through 5 percent increments to top pay for the job. Thus are established many more distinct slots. Of course, workers are not so conveniently arranged as to ensure that no slots are overpopulated, but taking just the job titles and pay steps and ignoring the job families classification, Polaroid has created roughly 2,100 (300 times 7) individual slots for its 6,397 hourly workers. And that leaves out a number of ancillary means of further subdividing workers—the seniority bonus, "special pay" status, the incentive bonus, and so on.

The salaried or exempt employee compensation scheme at Polaroid is similar in all essentials to that for hourly workers. Employees are grouped into ten grades, each of which is subdivided further into nine steps. Organizationally, salaried employees are divided among the various branches (engineering, marketing, and so on) of the company.

The consequences of this highly stratified job structure extend far beyond the amount of money each worker receives, though wage differentials are by no means trivial. Most importantly, the narrow categorization of workers lays the basis for differences in job autonomy, power over other workers, working conditions, and chances for job placement or being laid off.

The point is simply that bureaucratic control makes possible a vastly greater stratification of the firm's workforce. Stratification is no longer limited by the firm's ability either to divide delegated power or to find technologically rooted differences. Now *social* or *organizational* distinctions (always supplemented, of course, by differences both in power and in technical function) become the basis for ranking and advancement.

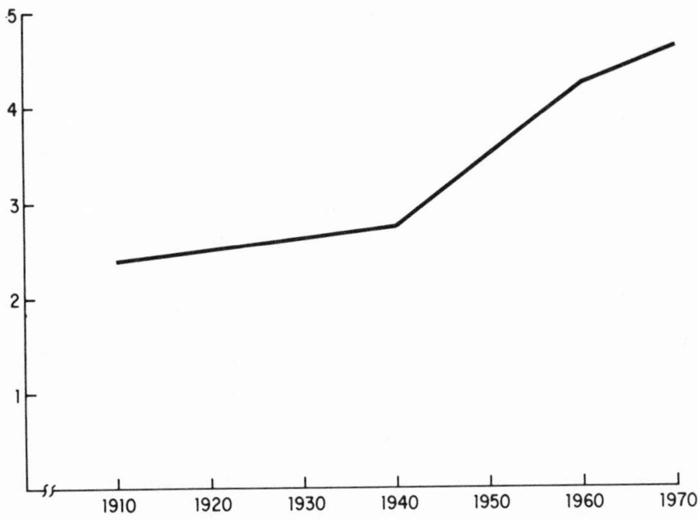

Number of Foremen per One Hundred Workers in All Manufacturing Companies[2]

One important consequence of this new stratification has been the rapidly growing number of employees who supervise other workers, not only at Polaroid but elsewhere as well. Several observers have noted that among all manufacturing companies the number of foremen per one hundred workers has been rising throughout the century, but few have pointed out that most of this growth has occurred in the post–World War II period. Indeed, between 1910 and 1940 the number per one hundred workers in all manufacturing grew by only 15 percent, but between 1940 and 1970 it jumped by 67 percent (see graph). Polaroid's experience therefore seems to be typical, as the increasing numbers of supervisory and professional employees create greater stratification in the manufacturing workforce generally.

Given Polaroid's stratified structure, then, we can see how each of the three elements of the control system operate.

Defining Work Tasks and Directing Workers

Each job within the Polaroid plants has been analyzed and summarized in an "approved description" (or in the case of salaried employees, an "exempt compensation survey"). Such descriptions, in addition to stating pay, location, and entry requirements for each job, set forth in considerable detail the tasks that the worker must perform.

The approved description for a machine operator who assembles SX-70 film provides a useful example. All the regular duties of such operatives are set forth in considerable detail, including the operation of the automatic assembly machine and responsibility for clearing jams and making adjustments, monitoring the machine's output, and maintaining the machine. For example, duty number seven (out of eighteen) states that the operator must

> make adjustments for web tracking (using automatic Servo control units for adjustment to tapered mask), and component feed failures. Check for proper operation of missing components detectors.

In addition, precise directions are given for responsibilities in the event of the crew chief's absence (the operative is responsible). Finally, even the irregular duties are spelled out: training new operators, conducting special tests for management to improve productivity or quality, and so on.

It might be thought that the company would find it profitable to make such a careful listing of duties and responsibilities only for management or skilled positions. But the job description indicates that an SX-70 Film Assembly Operator is rated only at the level of PCV-13, and roughly half of Polaroid's hourly workers (not to mention the salaried employees) have higher-level jobs.

The company thus formalizes and makes explicit the content of each job—what the worker is supposed to do while at work—in these approved descriptions. In large part these are written rules and directives, although they sometimes also include unwritten procedures that the company inculcates during training programs. Of course, bureaucratic control never fully replaces direct and personal command, and the Polaroid manual is careful to point out that any approved description "does not attempt to define all elements of a position. It defines Main Function, Regular Duties, and Irregular Duties." Implicitly, irregular Irregular Duties or even the occasional Exceptional Circumstance may require efforts outside the job description, and as we shall see, the evaluation procedure permits plenty of scope for supervisors to reinforce cooperation in such matters.

Yet the fact that bureaucratic specification of tasks is less than complete should not obscure the tremendous importance of what it does accomplish. The fine division and stratification of Polaroid's workers, in combination with the carefully articulated job descriptions, establish each job as a distinct slot with clearly defined tasks and responsibilities. A presumption of work and its specific content, that is, a presumption of what constitutes a "fair day's work," has been established.

We can see parallel processes at other firms, since for most workers in large corporations, job requirements are summed up in detailed job descriptions by means of which the firm directs job performance. Elinor Langer gives us an elegant and insightful account of how AT&T inculcates each job's criteria. Describing her job as a Customer Sales Representative at the New York Telephone Company, she notes that her supervisor

> is the supervisor of five women. She reports to a Manager who manages four supervisors (about twenty women) and he reports to the District Supervisor along with two other managers . . . . A job identical in rank to that of the district supervisor is held by four other men in Southern Manhattan alone. They report to the Chief of the Southern Division, himself a soldier in an army of division chiefs.[3]

In training for the Representative's job, the new employee is put through a programmed instruction course,

> so routine that every employee can teach it . . . [and] every part turned out by the system will be interchangeable with every other part. The system is to bureaucracy what Taylor was to the factory.

Langer describes how the training experience teaches a set of rules and procedures that narrowly prescribe how the work is to be done. For instance, lessons explain specific ways of responding to requests for changed service (attempt to sell additional service using the concept of the "well-telephoned home"), what to say when a customer asks for a particular Representative (never allow the customer "to identify his interests with any particular employee"), and so on. As Langer makes clear, the training program was primarily intended to acquaint the new employees with the *organizationally imposed* requirements of the job. AT&T uses the training period to announce the formal rules, to articulate and rehearse the unwritten procedures, and to teach the implicit expectations of the job.

Once on the job, the worker finds additional mechanisms to reassert the duties of the job description. Langer notes, for example, that

> every Representative is assigned a selling quota—so many extensions, so many

Princesses—deducted and derived in some way from the quota of the next largest unit. In other words, quotas are assigned to the individual because they are first assigned to the five-girl unit; they are assigned to the unit because they are assigned to the twenty-girl section; and they are assigned to the section because they are assigned to the district: to the Manager and the District Supervisor. The fact that everyone is in the same situation—expected to contribute to the same total—is one of the factors that increase management-worker solidarity.

Other corporations have followed Polaroid's and AT&T's lead. In some cases, union negotiations have provided an impetus toward detailed job descriptions, but even here the corporations have pushed far beyond the requirements of any contract. GE is a case in point. The company operates a tough system of job classification and analysis. As one worker explained,

> Believe me, there is a description of every job that anyone does at GE, a *detailed* description. There's a number for [every job], a written description, and so forth. It specifies *exactly* what you're supposed to do in your job.[4]

In part, these job descriptions are used to specify pay rates, work loads, and other matters in the union contract; to this extent, the union participates in establishing and writing the job descriptions. But the company also maintains an even more detailed set of work criteria than the union, laying out the specific tasks to be performed, the specific model numbers of company products to be worked on, and the specific machines and materials to be used. Together with the more general company rules, these job duties direct the actual work to be done.

Bureaucratic rules set out in the most explicit fashion possible the requirements for adequate job performance. In his study of production workers at a gypsum mining and processing plant between 1948 and 1951, Alvin Gouldner notes that "Like direct orders, rules specify the obligations of the worker, enjoining him to do particular things in definite ways." Rules specify the worker's duties less ambiguously "than a hastily worded personal command." Thus, they

> serve to narrow the subordinates' area of discretion. The subordinates now have fewer options concerning what they may or may not do, and the area of "privilege" is crowded out by the growing area of 'obligation.'

Gouldner observes that bureaucratic rules provide a substitute for the personal repetition of orders by a supervisor; once a standing rule exists, there is no need for the supervisor to repeat the instruction. Moreover, bureaucratic rules allow the supervisor to appear to detach his own feelings from his capacity as supervisor. "He can say, 'I can't help [enforcing the rules]. *It's not my idea*, I've got to go along with the rules *like everyone else*.'" So rules serve as an impersonal control technique.[5]

Formalizing the job descriptions, the assignment of workers to jobs, the task sequence appropriate to each job, and the pace and quality of work does not remove these matters from the realm of workplace conflict. Nonetheless, the bargaining now comes to focus on the application of particular rules and procedures, that is, on the interpretation of the "laws" that are to govern the workplace. Such conflict does not threaten the overall structure by which the labor process is controlled. Thus does bureaucratic control perform its first management function.

Supervising and Evaluating Workers' Performance

When it comes to the monitoring and evaluating function, bureaucratic control again marked a departure from previous practice. The vehicle for supervision remained, of course, the foremen, supervisors, and managers who together constituted the supervisory staff. But the new system drastically transformed their role and power.

The new method of evaluation was built on two elements. First, it introduced the principle that the workers should be evaluated on the basis of what was contained in the job descriptions. And second, those who were formally charged with the responsibility of evaluating—foremen, supervisors, and managers—were themselves subjected to bureaucratic control; that is, they were directed and supervised in how to evaluate their subordinates by the job descriptions for their own jobs.

Polaroid appraises every worker's performance on a regular schedule. Undoubtedly, supervisors on the job constantly monitor, assess, and reprimand or praise workers as production occurs. But more formally, at least once a year supervisors must evaluate each employee's performance. The bureaucratic direction of work provides the structure for evaluation, since workers are evaluated on the tasks and duties laid out in the job description. Although the significance of any particular task or the severity of the assessment undoubtedly varies with the supervisor, the job description provides a limited, explicit, and controlled basis for rating each worker's performance. Just as the job descriptions are known to both worker and boss, so too is the evaluation. Evaluation is an open process, with the final supervisor's rating available for the worker's inspection.

The content as well as the form of Polaroid's evaluation provides insight into its control system. Each worker is rated in each of four equally important categories on a seven-point scale; the seven levels are defined as performance appropriate to each of the seven pay steps built into every job classification. Of the four categories, the fourth ("skill and job knowledge") measures whether the employee is capable of doing the assigned job. One category treats the quantity of work done. The remaining two categories—"quality" (meaning the worker's dependability and thoroughness) and "work habits and personal characteristics"—are concerned with work behavior rather than with the actual production achieved. A separate category in the evaluation checks up on attendance and punctuality. Here mere judgements are not enough, and the form demands more precise information: a space is left for percentages and frequencies. The main concern seems to be not measuring output but instead checking compliance with the rules.

Polaroid's system, though notable, is hardly atypical. At General Electric, where in many ways bureaucratic control was more self-consciously worked out than elsewhere, the company's Directive Policy No. 1.1 set forth the principle that "Compensation Should Be Based on Performance in Meeting the Expected Contribution from the Work Designed into Positions." This principle was then explained as follows:

> The principle observed in General Electric Company is that *compensation* is based on the value of the measurable, intended *contribution expected* from the work as designed into individual positions, adjusted for the actual resultful *performance* of such work. Application of this principle reduces the effect of subjective criteria such as personal opinion about the value of the experience, education, age or length of service in the Company of a particular person.
>
> As part of the process of implementing this principle, work is designed into positions to be filled by *normally available* individuals who have the requisite knowledge and skills to do that work, rather than primarily around the capabilities or interests of any particular individual who happens to be presently available. . . .
>
> The level of worth to the Company of the contribution expected from the position is then objectively determined.[6]

Similarly, union contracts covering the organized employees at U.S. Steel and International Harvester also attach wage scales to fixed job descriptions and job classifications. In this way, unions attempt to fix both the wage (the value of labor power) and the labor actually performed. Any worker becomes entitled to the assigned pay by performing his or her job as stated in the appropriate description. To pay a lower amount makes the matter a subject for grievance procedure. To specify greater work requires the filing of a formal notice of change of job description. The conditions for both the sale of labor power and its consumption are thereby regulated by job descriptions. Whether company-imposed or a product of collective bargaining, then, job descriptions become the basis for evaluation of workers' performance.

The second change inherent in this new way of supervising and evaluating workers involved restructuring the jobs held by foremen, supervisors, and managers. These, too, were now subject to formal definition and description, as the content of the job descriptions for supervisory staff formally laid out the bases and methods for supervision and evaluation of workers. Thus the function of supervision itself was subject to the rules and procedures of bureaucratic control.

This change altered the position and role of the supervisor in the production process. The superior was now charged with judging the subordinate's performance according to specified criteria rather than the supervisor's own standards. The supervisor's judgments attained a degree of "objectivity" that served as a basis for their legitimacy. If the worker being judged did not agree with the supervisor's evaluation, he or she could appeal to outside review, either through union channels or, if no union existed, through the company's own appeals process. Undoubtedly the appeals process partially relieved the worker from the foreman's capriciousness, especially where a strong union could enforce the worker's rights. But generally, the worker was in the position of an accused traffic violator trying to convince a judge that the court should not accept the arresting officer's account of the violation: only rarely will the higher-up agree.

Real change in the system occurred because bureaucratic control brought the supervisory staff under much more meaningful control of the top echelons of management. Under the new system, evaluation of performance could be done at several levels higher in the organization, thereby allowing higher supervisors actually to regulate behavior in a way that personal direction would not permit. Thus promotion procedures, use of sanctions such as reprimand, suspension, or dismissal, and assignment of workers to particular tasks all came under top management scrutiny.

For example, at Polaroid a production manager normally supervises ten to twenty-five production workers. In addition to directing and monitoring production, he or she must

> interpret and administer personnel policies. Select, train, and evaluate individual and team performance. Initiate actions on merit increases, promotions, transfers, disciplinary measures.

Yet in all these activities, the production manager reports to a general supervisor—production, whose job it is to

> select and train first-line supervisors. Evaluate performance of supervisors and determine actions on salary and promotion. Review and approve supervisor determinations on merit increases, promotions, disciplinary measures.

Hence the first-line supervisors' room to maneuver is restricted by the impositions of inspection by higher command.

The result was a much more systematic and predictable evaluation of workers. As foremen lost much of their arbitrary power, they could no longer supervise workers according to their own idiosyncratic needs or desires or ideas of how to get things done; instead, company policy in the form of the established rules, procedures, and expectations stood as the guide. The supervisor had to follow the book, for the higher echelons held the lower supervisory staff accountable to their own job descriptions. The formal system of evaluation does not perfectly mirror the actual system, of course, and personality clashes, favoritism, and jealousies remain. Yet formalizing evaluation provided a structure for the corporation's power.

Eliciting Cooperation and Enforcing Compliance

As a system of power, bureaucratic control must also provide for rewards and sanctions, a channel or structure in which management can "maintain [the] discipline of employees," to borrow the language of the International Harvester workers' contract. Here again, bureaucratic control represented something new.

In line with the general logic of bureaucratic control, reprimand, suspension, dismissal, and other punishments became fixed penalties for specified categories of offenses. Punishment flowed from the established organizational rules and procedures. Sanctions were still applied by the foremen and supervisors, of course, but their application was subject to review by both higher levels of supervision and the grievance machinery. Punishment, like other elements of control, became embedded in the organizational structure of the bureaucratic firm.

But perhaps even more important was the institutionalizing of *positive* incentives under bureaucratic control. Not only was "bad" behavior punished, but "proper" behavior was rewarded.

In the entrepreneurial firm, positive incentives derived from the workers' personal ties to the entrepreneur. But both hierarchical and technical control relied almost exclusively on negative sanctions, for the firm was too large for personal ties to be decisive, and other potential incentives (promotion policies, higher pay) were haphazard, erratic, and subject to favoritism. No established career ladders existed, for example, to promise regular promotion to good workers. Wage differentials in fact were often set by foremen, who used their power to classify workers or measure output arbitrarily.

Bureaucratic control brought an organizational logic to the systematic dispensation of higher pay, promotion, more responsibility, access to better or cleaner or less dangerous working conditions, better health benefits, longer vacations, assignment to work stations with more status or comfort, and the other privileges that corporations now bestow on favored employees. Positive incentives greatly heightened the workers' sense of the mobility *within the firm* that lay in front of them.

These aspects of the new system can be easily seen at Polaroid. The company's power to hire and fire underlies its ability to get purchased labor power transformed into labor done. This power comes into play in a couple of ways. Insubordination and other explicit "violations of company rules and of accepted codes of proper behavior" (to use the company's language) can trigger immediate dismissal. Dismissal also threatens workers who get poor evaluations. The company states that the evaluations are designed to weed out mediocrity and, of course, mediocre job performance is determined by how faithfully the worker fulfills the job descriptions. In addition to periodic reviews—new employees after three months, other workers at least once a year—both old and new workers are on almost continuous probation. So the penalty for failing to comply with stated performance standards is evident.

Yet, even though bureaucratic control at Polaroid continues the historic capitalist right to deprive workers of their livelihood, this right has been reshaped by the bureaucratic form. Exceptional violations aside, workers can be dismissed only if they continue to "misbehave" after receiving written warnings specifying the improper behavior. Moreover, higher supervisory approval is required and any grievance can be appealed. Even the process of dismissal has become subject to the rule of (company) law.

Bureaucratic control has brought even greater change by introducing elaborate positive rewards to elicit cooperation from the workers. At Polaroid, the structure of rewards begins with the seven pay steps within each job. Each of these steps represents a 5 percent increment over the previous level. Once hired into a particular job, the worker is expected to pass through the first two ("learning") steps over a period of months. What is actually to be learned is not so much job skills as "work habits, attendance, attitude, and other personal characteristics" that Polaroid deems necessary for dependable performance. Moreover, the learning may occur more on the side of the company (learning whether the new worker has acquired the proper work habits through prior schooling or jobs) than on the part of the employee.

As the worker demonstrates mastery of the normal work routine, he or she moves up into the middle three ("experienced") pay steps. At these levels, the company expects that work "quality can be relied on," that the worker is "reliable," and that "good attendance [has been] established"; or more simply, that "personal characteristics are appropriate to the job." Progress is by no means automatic, but the worker who tries reasonably hard, makes little trouble, and is an average performer moves, in time, through these steps.

Finally, there remain the last two ("exceptional") pay steps for workers who set "examples . . . to others in methods and use of time" and who suggest ways of "improving job methods" and "increasing effectiveness of the group." These workers need to show "cooperation, enthusiasm, [and exceptional] attitude." Supervisors are reminded that there must be "special justification for 'outstanding' ratings such as these."

The pay steps within each job classification thus establish a clear reward—up to 30 percent higher pay—for workers who obey the rules, follow the job descriptions, cooperate, and in general do their jobs without creating difficulty. Yet the pay scales within job classifications are merely a prelude to the rewards available to those who move up to new job categories in the corporate hierarchy.

The company states that it "is [Polaroid's] general policy to fill job openings by promotion from within the Company," and the mechanism for doing so is a posting system. The company lists each job, along with skill requirements and other job characteristics, on bulletin boards. Employees wishing to move to the new job can bid for it, setting in motion a process of application, interview, and selection. Unlike many union plants, Polaroid does not base its selection solely on seniority, although "seniority should always be considered"; instead, jobs are filled by "the persons considered to be among the most qualified"—with qualifications including, among other things, work habits and attendance. Stanley Miller's career, described in the first chapter, illustrates this system.

Thus, through the posting system, Polaroid's fifteen hourly and ten salaried grades of jobs come to represent a second scale of rewards for the enterprising employee. Although no employee can realistically expect to start at the bottom and rise to the top (such stories better support myth than represent reality) the salary differential nonetheless suggests the range of rewards available to the employee who accepts the system: the top pay, at $160,664 annually (in 1975), is over twenty-eight times the lowest pay of $5,678 a year. More to the point, the top hourly pay ($9.26) more than triples the bottom ($3.01), and the lower salaried grades rise from the top hourly pay.

Yet even the salary differentials are not the only positive incentives that Polaroid dangles before its workers. Every employee who stays at the job for five years earns an additional 5 percent bonus. Seniority, as we have seen, is also a factor in being able to obtain job transfers and promotions. Finally, the company's layoff policy is based on an elaborate "bumping" system in which seniority is the key criterion. For example, during the 1975 recession nearly sixteen hundred employees were laid off; employees in departments where there was no work bumped less senior workers in other departments or even other plants.

Polaroid's structure thus provides tremendous rewards—higher pay, more rights, greater job security—to workers who accept the system and seek, by individual effort, to improve their lot within it. Moreover, the considerable rewards offered to workers who stay for long periods at Polaroid provide a real basis for the workers' long-term identification with the company.

The positive incentives, the relief from capricious supervision, the right to appeal grievances and bid for better jobs, the additional job security of seniority—all these make the day-to-day worklife of Polaroid's employees more pleasant. They function as an elaborate system of bribes, and like all successful bribes, they are attractive. But they are also corrupting. They push workers to pursue their self-interests in a narrow way as individuals, and they stifle the impulse to struggle collectively for those same self-interests. All this elaboration of job titles, rules, procedures, rights, and responsibilities is, of course, neither accidental nor benevolent on Polaroid's part; it is simply a better way to do business. There is no union at Polaroid, despite several attempts to form one.

The Institutionalization of Power

Above all else, bureaucratic control institutionalized the exercise of capitalist power, making power appear to emanate from the formal organization itself. Hierarchical relations were transformed from relations between (unequally powerful) people to relations between jobholders or relations between jobs themselves, abstracted from the specific people or the concrete work tasks involved. "Rule of law"—the firm's law—replaced rule by supervisor command. And indeed, the replacement was not illusory. To the extent that firms were successful in imposing bureaucratic control, the method, extent, and intensity of sanctions imposed on recalcitrant workers were specified by organizational rules. Foremen, supervisors, and managers were to apply such regulations, not formulate them, and in so doing, they objectively participated in the exercise of organizational, not personal, power.

By establishing the overall structure, management retained control of the enterprise's operations. Once the goals and structure had been established, the system could operate under its own steam. Of course, work activities could never be completely specified in advance by job descriptions; new situations continually arose for which prior regulations are not appropriate. Moreover, the workers' continual resistance to regulations meant that a rule, once promulgated, was not necessarily followed. Yet the ability to establish rules provided the capitalists with the power to determine the terrain, to set the basic conditions around which the struggle was to be fought. That power was decisive. As workers were isolated from each other, and as the system was made distinct from the bosses who supervise it, the basic capitalist-worker relation tended to shrink from sight. The capitalist's power was effectively embedded in the firm's organization.

Such a structural view of control goes a long way towards clearing up the issue of whether bureaucratic organization is an effective control device or not. Popular opinion strongly suggests that "bureaucracy" is wasteful, slow, and ineffective. Expert opinion often agrees. Alvin Gouldner, for example, noted that while bureaucratic rules specify the minimum level of acceptable performance, the rules also detail how little the worker can do and still remain secure.[7] Still other observers, most notably Max Weber, saw bureaucracy as the most highly developed and purest form of rational authority.[8]

Yet both popular opinion and expert insight miss what is essential here. The core corporations survive and prosper on their ability to organize the routine, normal efforts of workers, not on their ability to elicit peak performances. The entrepreneurial firm often depends on exceptional efforts, and the workers on occasion may put forth such efforts because of their personal ties to the capitalist or as an expression of their interest in keeping the firm in business. But the large firm generally has no claim on such efforts and (aside from virtuoso performances in the executive offices) has little interest in them. Instead, it seeks to raise as high as possible the standard for minimal acceptable performance. Michel Crozier has observed that,

> people have power over other people insofar as the latter's behavior is narrowly limited by rules [or other constraints] whereas their own behavior is not. . . the predictability of one's behavior is the sure test of one's own inferiority.[9]

Bureaucratic control made workers' behavior more predictable, and predictability brought with it greater control for the corporation.

Thus while bureaucratic control may in certain cases give up the prospect of exceptional performance, it instead achieves for the firm a high level of standard performance. Management's control is less than perfect, but compared to realistic alternatives, it is considerable. It is so considerable, in fact, that virtually all large corporations use it.

Understanding control in this sense also permits us to distinguish between workers' self-direction and autonomy. Several investigators have confused the lack of immediate external controls (self-direction) with the freedom to make decisions in one's own interest (autonomy).[10] From the firm's perspective, all that is required is that workers perform according to the enterprise's criteria. Whether they do so because they have internalized the descriptions of their jobs (and hence want to perform well), or because it is in the worker's own self-interest, is immaterial to the enterprise. It is not immaterial, however, in deciding whether workers have autonomy in their jobs. Alienated labor—workers forced to work according to the capitalist's criteria—is alienated no less because it has internalized these criteria, and its consequences are no less damaging to the workers.

The "Good" Worker

Bureaucratic control has not only transformed relations among the various strata of workers and between workers and their employers, but it has also altered the attributes that the firm expects of, and rewards in, its workers. It brought with it a new image of the "good" worker.

In previous control systems, there was little direct connection between personal attributes and control. Employers in all systems undoubtedly rewarded hard workers more than those who soldiered on the job, but the point is that the behavior demands arose directly from production and not from the control system itself. In entrepreneurial control, the personality of the capitalist set the tone, and, aside from a general deference to the employer's power, no generalization can be made about what was required. In hierarchical control, capitalists placed primary reliance on negative sanctions to discipline workers; workers needed to obey the boss and be sufficiently deferential, but the required behavior varied greatly according to the particular foreman, the circumstances of employment, and so forth. In technical control, the system forced workers to respond to machine pacing, but it left them relatively free from other demands on their behavior. In all these cases, bosses demanded that employees work regularly and that they defer to their superiors. But beyond that, no particular attributes were systematically reinforced, and foremen rewarded and punished worker behavior arbitrarily and idiosyncratically.

Thus, while severe in regulating output-related behavior, these earlier systems of control left considerable leeway or tolerance for the workers to express other behavior to create their own ambience or culture in the workplace. There existed a certain breathing space inside prebureaucratic control. In some cases the workers' culture resulted in weekly observance of the unofficial holiday Blue Monday, in other instances it resulted in bullying and routine displays of aggression, ethnic identifications, formation of informal groups that restricted output or punished overzealous foremen, exaggerated male chauvinism, and patterns of humor, anger, and other ways of expressing the workers' identity. Most importantly, the workplace culture tended to build on an image of "them" and "us," in which workers were clearly distinguished from bosses. Workers brought many of these cultural patterns with them from their communities, of course, but the point is that the workplace organization made room for such elements.[11]

With the imposition of bureaucratic control, much of that changed. The new organization of work produced change in required behavior comparable to the changes wrought by the coming of the factory. Particular work traits and patterns of interaction associated with bureaucratic control were rewarded, and in general the system intruded more insistently on the development of the worker's behavior and personality. The breathing space was reduced. Symptomatically, under bureaucratic control the workplace culture tends to express less of the workers and more of the firm. Working-class orientations and patterns of interacting yield to more bureaucratic, so-called middle-class ways. The notion of a family ("the IBM family") that includes both management and workers resurrects a concept not relevant since the entrepreneurial firm. The workers begin to use the first person plural differently; "we" now means "we the firm," not "we the workers." The workers' ability to create a workday culture begins to fade, just as, on a grander level, the working class loses its ability to make its own class culture.

Bureaucratic control tends to be a much more totalitarian system—totalitarian in the sense of involving the total behavior of the worker. In bureaucratic control, workers owe not only a hard day's work to the corporation but also their demeanor and affections.

Closer imposition of the firm's demands can be seen in the extensive range of incentives designed to mold the worker's behavior. The employer's goal remains the translation of labor power into useful labor, and some incentives in bureaucratic control—Polaroid's evaluation category of quantity, for example—directly reward more effort. But what distinguishes bureaucratic control from other control systems is that it contains incentives aimed at evoking the behavior necessary to make bureaucratic control succeed. It is this *indirect* path to the intensification of work, through the mechanism of rewarding behavior relevant to the control system, rather than simply to the work itself, that imposes the new behavior requirements on workers.

Workers who consistently behave properly (that is, in accord with the established criteria) are valuable to the corporation. Such workers have attributes much akin to technical skills. Just as technical skills make possible the operation of the firm's physical technology, so these behavior traits facilitate the firm's control. Employers seek out and reward workers with the right behavior traits.

What kinds of behavior get rewarded? Relevant here is the increased importance of the work habits and types of behavior deriving from the form of control, rather than from the content of the job descriptions.* Thus, the new requirements flow directly from the way firms seek to elicit compliance from their workers. For example, in Polaroid's evaluation system, the quantity check counts for only one-fourth of the total evaluation, and of equal importance is the category covering work habits and personal characteristics. The instructions for the remaining two parts (skill and job knowledge and quality) indicate that these items measure both actual job performance and personal attributes. Finally, in a completely separate evaluation, attendance and punctuality are recorded. Actual work output, then, counts for half or less of this evaluation.[12]

We can distinguish three principal types of behavior that bureaucratic firms reward. These are the work habits or behavior traits that the system of control seeks to elicit:

• Since the simplest way that institutionalized power is used to direct work tasks is through the establishment of work rules, the corresponding behavior trait that the firm rewards can be called "rules orientation"—an awareness of the rules and a sustained propensity to follow them.

Explicit rules are typically the first part of the normal work routine that any worker must learn. Employers' most common and general rules have to do with regular attendance and being on time. For example, at Polaroid the first two pay steps for every job (those steps at which the worker is learning the job) stress mastering the normal work routine and attendance. Here, the supervisor's evaluation of attendance and punctuality plays an especially important role. The company's personnel policy includes special guidelines on "excessive absenteeism," and the rules are very strict. At a Ford assembly plant, rules regulate absences, tardiness, gambling, horseplay, refusing assigned jobs, wilfully ringing the clock card of another worker, smoking, thefts, and careless or malicious destruction.[13]

More specific rules and procedures exist in every workplace. These rules

* As the firm evolved, the actual tasks performed at work changed in response to the firm's productive needs, not as a consequence of bureaucratic control. Thus as IBM's business changed from making card-tabulating machines to providing computer services, the company hired fewer card-sort technicians and more electrical engineers. Mapping changes in the content of job descriptions would only demonstrate the changes in job skills required of the labor force. What bureaucratic control changed was the worker traits required for the manner in which work tasks were done.

may govern the sequence of tasks, who has access to materials, how workers are assigned to various duties, safety regulations, and so on. As Elinor Langer observed, at AT&T the established procedures rehearsed in the training program regulate virtually all of a sales representative's contacts with customers.

• A more sophisticated level of control encourages workers to be dependable in their work. This goes beyond rules orientation, because it means more than just obeying the letter of the law. Dependability involves performing at a consistent level and at a regular pace, being reliable and practical about the work, and getting the job done even where the rules need to be bent or applied in new ways. Correct work behavior in this sense implies performing tasks in a reliable, predictable, and dependable manner. Thus we might term the second behavior trait "habits of predictability and dependability."

At Polaroid, pay steps III, IV, and V for every job are lumped together and reserved for the experienced worker. At this stage, "good attendance [has been] established," and the issue is whether the worker is "now sufficiently experienced to handle changes, new situations, and emergencies with competence." The accompanying descriptions indicate that experience really means dependability and reliability. In this sense, the dependable worker is one who works diligently within the rules in normal situations ("requires special help and direction from the supervisor infrequently") and who carries on in the spirit of the job description in situations where the rules do not quite apply. Most of the rating categories on the supervisor's evaluation stress such items as "effective use of time," "thoroughness and accuracy," "attitude and cooperation," "orderliness," and "dependability."

• The most sophisticated level of control grows out of incentives for workers to identify themselves with the enterprise, to be loyal, committed, and thus self-directed or self-controlled. Such behavior involves what may be called the "internalization of the enterprise's goals and values."

The worker who identifies his or her own fortunes with those of the company moves a stage beyond merely being dependable. Other workers often consider such workers to be rate-busters, but in the employer's eyes they become valuable models for other workers. At Polaroid, "exceptional" workers (those in the top two pay steps in their job classifications) not only show work whose "quality stands out," they also actively promote the company's needs: "examples are set to others in methods and use of time," and "good ideas for improving job methods and for increasing effectiveness of the group are frequent." The company sees this worker as "a recognized leader-type, although there may be no occasion for [leadership] in an official capacity."

Several studies demonstrate that bureaucratic employers do in fact reward these three types of behavior and that they are not only important to personnel managers but also have practical significance on the shop and office floor.[14] When workers are tested and assigned scores on the three behavior traits, for example, the scores predict rather well how the workers' supervisor will rate them; moreover, they also contribute significantly to explaining differences in wages. The results seem to hold for both women and men.

The mixture of incentives changes, however, at different levels within the enterprise. In the lowest-level jobs, employers tend to stress rules orientation most heavily. In the middle-level jobs, workers are more rewarded for habits of predictability and dependability. At the upper levels, employers appear to reserve rewards for those who have internalized the enterprise's goals. The hierarchy of rewarded behaviors within each job (the stress on rules orientation for learners, on dependability for experienced workers, and on internalizaton for exceptional workers) is thus supplemented by a corresponding hierarchy between jobs. Such a result is not surprising. At Polaroid, strong emphasis is placed on rules (especially absence and tardiness rules) for hourly workers, but up in the ranks of the salaried, rules have less import. Evaluations turn on "organizational loyalty" and on being a "real self-starter" and an "enthusiastic worker."

Bureaucratic control establishes not only a real hierarchy of persons but also an ideal hierarchy of traits characterizing the good worker. While it might be possible to infer such a hierarchy in earlier control systems, in bureaucratic control the ideal is made explicit and formal, and rewards are in large part geared to them. These incentives are designed to push workers up the levels of control, eliciting cooperation and even loyalty as evidence of the worker's ever-increasing reconciliation to the firm's power.

Bureaucratic control thus provides a long-run framework for the exercise of power. In contrast to other systems of control, where the methods of gaining compliance succeed as well with new employees as with old ones, bureaucratic control requires time—time for workers to learn rules, procedures, and expectations; time for workers to respond to the attractions of positive incentives; and time for employers to weed out troublesome, rebellious, or, to use Polaroid's term, "mediocre" workers. This long horizon is consistent with the core firms' ability to achieve relative immunity from the fear of short-run collapse. Corporations have moved to guarantee their long-run futures in all aspects of their operations, from ensuring raw materials supplies to making their markets safe. Controlling their workforces is merely part of that strategy.

To make the scheme work, however, corporations must reward seniority, and this puts their operations into sharp contrast with earlier systems of control. In the other systems, high turnover served to remind workers of the reserve army. Bureaucratic control's attention to the longer term produces one striking consequence: for the worker, seniority and tenure pay off. In the studies referred to above, supervisors tended to rate older workers less highly than younger workers (all other things being equal), yet the older workers received higher pay. Taken together, the studies suggest that by providing higher pay to older workers, employers reward them despite the fact that they are less valuable than younger workers. These results run directly counter to the currently fashionable wage theory of neoclassical economics. That view sees the higher pay for older workers as evidence for the unmeasured and largely unobservable quantity, "on-the-job investment in human capital."[15] Instead, positive benefits for seniority seem to be the result of employers' attempts to control their workforces. Older workers may be paid more than what their productivity would justify because seniority systems create stability in the firm and provide incentives for loyalty and dedication, workforce traits not relevant to efficiency but extremely profitable nonetheless.

Bureaucratic control impinges on the behavior of individual workers in part by providing strong and systematic incentives to obey company rules, to develop work habits of predictability and dependability, and to internalize the enterprise's goals and values. These are the new behavior requirements imposed on bureaucratic control's workers. Hard work and deference are no longer enough; now the "soulful" corporation demands the worker's soul, or at least the worker's identity. Remembering Michel Crozier's observation about power—"the predictability of one's behavior is the sure test of one's own inferiority"—we can begin to perceive the repressive essence of modern structural control.

The Contradictions of Bureaucratic Control

The success of bureaucratic control makes it seem the first capitalist organization of power that successfully eliminates its opposition. But this is an illusion, for beneath the surface the contradiction between social production and private appropriation, between the interests of labor and the interests of capital, remains. The contradiction has not generated new mass-based resistance, yet already minor cracks in the edifice appear here and there, and in these openings we perceive hints of deeper structural weaknesses. From external clues we can suggest (but not stipulate) which flaws may tear the entire structure apart.

The Contradiction in the Workplace

The transition from earlier forms of control to bureaucratic control brought with it a substantial increase in the employment security of core-firm workers. To implement bureaucratic control, capitalists acceded to or independently introduced a series of job protections and personnel policies that tended to shield workers from immediate displacement. Individual workers are by no means guaranteed employment, of course; they are subject to dismissal for failing to do their tasks or for insubordination to superiors, and fluctuations in demand may bring furloughs. But these enduring and last-resort fundamentals of corporate employment should not obscure the real changes in the way core employers operate. Grievance procedures, seniority provisions that concentrate layoffs among workers in entry-level jobs, and the general policy of fostering low turnover create expectations and real experiences of long-term, perhaps lifetime, employment. For these employees of large corporations, jobs tend to be long-lasting and stable.

Capitalists introduced the new scheme for their own purposes, yet they could not control all of its consequences. Job security and job ladders were intended to break up the sense of solidarity that united a firm's workers in collective opposition to their employer; moreover, the workers' long-term identification with the enterprise was necessary to establish the context in which the firm could elicit compliance and cooperation. These objectives were frequently realized, but job security and a long-lasting identification with the company also provide precisely those conditions that are most likely to foster demands among workers for more say in establishing the rules by which the enterprise is run. Secure workers expecting to stay with their corporate employers over long periods turn to issues of the quality and control of work. Thus, in establishing those conditions most favorable for bureaucratic control, capitalists inadvertently have also established the conditions under which demands for workplace democracy flourish. Such demands constitute a potentially fundamental challenge to employers' power.

It cannot be claimed that the new conditions have yet raised the issue of worker control to the level of a mass demand among American workers. But they have spawned two different responses, so far largely independent of each other: a growing interest among some union leaders and socialists in workplace democracy; and, among workers, a growing discontent with their jobs.

Increasingly, socialist organizers and other working-class activists have looked upon workers' control as a possible building-block for a decentralized socialist economy. Local decision-making processes promise to be a way around the stifling of initiative that accompanies top-down central planning. Yet, self-conscious efforts to introduce workplace democracy have remained external to the principal working-class demands and organizations.

The workers' response to bureaucratic control, in the United States at least, has resulted primarily in individual and small-group discontent rather than in collective action. Individualistic opposition emerges in part from the failure of the labor movement to challenge new forms of control; in the absence of a well-articulated critique of capitalism, the systemic roots of the experiences producing individual resentment remain obscure. The lack of a collective response can also be traced, however, to the inherent properties of bureaucratic control; its stratification and redivision of workers make collective action more difficult. The workers' failure to respond collectively is, then, a measure of bureaucratic control's success in dividing them. Together with the lack of a self-conscious movement challenging it, bureaucratic control has resulted in individual, not collective, opposition.

Bureaucratic control has created among American workers vast discontent, dissatisfaction, resentment, frustration, and boredom with their work. We do not need to recount here the many studies measuring alienation; the famous Health, Education and Welfare commissioned report, *Work in America*, among other summaries, has already done that. That report argued, for example, that the best index of job satisfaction or dissatisfaction is a worker's response to the question, "What type of work would you try to get into if you could start all over again?" A majority of both white-collar workers and blue-collar workers indicated that they would choose some different type of work. The overall result is consistent with a very large body of literature on the topic.[16]

Rising dissatisfaction and alienation among workers, made exigent by their greater job security and expectation of continuing employment with one enterprise, create problems for employers, one of which is reduced productivity. Workers, denied participation in setting the goals of their work, develop their own goals; the new goals may be quite at variance with the enterprise's goals. More openly, dissatisfaction combined with bureaucratic rules provides a new weapon for workers' resistance, the "work to rules" strikes. At Lordstown, for instance, both assembly line workers and maintenance workers conducted extensive inside-the-plant strikes before the 1971 wildcat strike that received so much attention. The technically controlled assembly line workers employed various forms of sabotage; but sabotage was a dangerous tactic, because where it could be traced, the responsible worker was quickly dismissed. The bureaucratically organized maintenance workers, on the other hand, pursued an alternate strategy: "We got real busy, following the rules." It was practically impossible to stop this protest.[17] Declining productivity, and especially the work-to-rules job action, indicate the continuing contradiction of social production and private appropriation even inside bureaucratic control.

By itself, however, individual or small-group opposition cannot seriously challenge employer control. Such opposition has existed throughout the history of capitalism without posing a real problem; only the *collective* power of workers can effectively threaten the organized power of capitalists. Moreover, lowered productivity by itself is not so serious either, since capitalists depend on average, not peak, productivity. What makes the rising individual frustration with capitalist control a source of potential revolutionary change is the fact that an alternative, higher productivity method of organizing work beckons. That truth emerges from the many experiments with worker self-management. An astonishingly high proportion of such experiments resulted in relaxing of management's prerogative to make the rules and higher productivity.[18] The first is the peril that capitalists face in introducing workers' management; the second is the lure, and it has proved to be a powerful attraction.

Capitalists themselves are led, even forced, to introduce the very schemes that threaten their grip. They have been the most important force behind actual experiments in workplaces. They have sponsored innumerable efforts in job enrichment, job enlargement, worker self-management, worker-employer comanagement, and so on.[19]

Thus, the logic of accumulation increasingly drives capitalists to try to unlock the potential productivity that lies inside economically secure producers who both identify with their enterprise and govern their work activities themselves. Capitalists try to obtain this higher output cheaply, by granting limited amounts of each of the needed components: some security within the overall capitalist context of insecurity, partial identification with work within the framework of private ownership, and limited self-government within an authoritarian enterprise.

The trouble is that a little is never enough. Just as some job security leads to demands for guaranteed lifetime wages, so some control over workplace decisions raises the demand for industrial democracy. Thomas Fitzgerald,

GM's Director of Employee Research and Training at its Chevrolet Division and a former GM first-line supervisor, stated this point directly. Fitzgerald explained to readers of the *Harvard Business Review* that, once workers begin participating,

> the subjects of participation . . . are not necessarily restricted to those few matters that management considers to be of direct, personal interest to employees. . . . [A plan cannot] be maintained for long without (a) being recognized by employees as manipulative or (b) leading to expectations for wider and more significant involvement—"Why do they only ask us about plans for painting the office and not about replacing this old equipment and rearranging the layout?" Once competence is shown (or believed to have been shown) in, say, rearranging the work area, and after participation has become a conscious, officially sponsored activity, *participators may very well want to go on to topics of job assignment, the allocation of rewards, or even the selection of leadership*. In other words, *management's present monopoly [of control] can in itself easily become a source of contention.*[20]

Polaroid, in an experiment in the 1960s, had discovered other problems for management. The company set up a special worker-participation project involving some 120 machine operators. The production requirements did not seem especially promising for the experiment; making the new film packs called for the skillful operation of complex machinery in the face of a pressing deadline. Workers on the project spent one hour each day in special training, two hours doing coordinating work, and five hours operating the machinery. According to Polaroid's organizational development consultant, the film was brought into production on time, and "most people think we would never have gotten it out otherwise." Nonetheless, the experiment was liquidated, not for efficiency reasons but because democracy got out of hand. Ray Ferris, the company's training director, explained:

> [The experiment] was *too* successful. What were we going to do with the supervisors—the managers? We didn't need them anymore. Management decided it just didn't want operators that qualified.[21]

Whether two now-separate elements—growing resentment with the present system and a vision of an alternative—will ever link up to create a genuine threat to management prerogatives remains uncertain. To create a real challenge, workers would have to raise participation as a mass demand, supported by a conscious political movement; to the extent that it remains experimental and confined to individual workplaces, it will retain its stench as a management device. Moreover, the continuing high unemployment of the 1970s certainly retards the advance of such a movement, since the recession weakens all workers' movements. Yet in Britain, France, Italy, and elsewhere, workplace democracy appears well on the way to becoming a mass demand, and the revolutionary potential seems great. In Chile under Salvador Allende, the workers' seizure of factories and their direct operation of them proved to be one of the most direct blows against the old relations of production.[22] Thus, in other contexts at least, the demand for participation has served to mobilize opposition to capitalism itself.

The Contradiction in the Firm

For the firm, bureaucratic control threatens to become a pact with the devil that, while offering temporary respite from trouble, spells long-term disaster. The reason is simple: bureaucratic control speeds up the process of converting the wage bill from a variable to a fixed cost.

The tendency for wages to become quasi-fixed costs results from a number of forces operating in the firm. The most important cause is undoubtedly the implicit commitment that core firms make to provide long-term employment for their workers. The commitment is not a legal one, of course, and it does not extend to all workers, lower-level production workers being the most prominent exception. Yet it has some force nonetheless, because it is only on the perceived reality of such a commitment that the firm can evince the workers' loyalty in response. Layoffs or permanent force reductions regenerate hostile relations between employers and workers. A second reason for the increased rigidity of wage costs results more directly from the system of control. Bureaucratic control requires training workers according to the job descriptions, and it demands considerable time for the firm to assess the workers' performance. Unlike technical control, in which a new worker can be trained and evaluated in a matter of a few days or weeks, bureaucratic control functions on a longer time span. Dismissing workers during the business downswing becomes more costly.[23]

In the conditions of the long postwar boom (from 1945 to about 1972), corporations encountered few cyclical dangers from the increasing rigidity of their wage commitments. The period was a remarkably prosperous one for American business, and business downturns were relatively slight. Moreover, while bureaucratic control was gradually extended to more and more layers within the firm, initially it applied only to the aristocracy of the most educated and skilled workers. Only as an increasing proportion of workers achieved some kind of employment guarantees did the new system create serious inflexibilities.

Both of these conditions had been reversed by the 1970s. The extension of bureaucratic control had come to incorporate most of the core firm's workers, while the sharp decline of the mid-1970s created serious problems even for entrenched corporations. The results were predictable. There appeared for the first time a serious tension between the job guarantees of bureaucratic control and the firm's need to be able to adjust the size of its workforce.

The conflict between the need for flexibility and the need to provide job security has been put off in several ways. One of the chief attractions for firms to invest abroad is precisely the ability to provide U.S. workers with employment security and still maintain a cushion of workers abroad who can be easily dismissed. Subcontracting to small producers provides another expendable labor force; the core firm can simply cancel contracts during a recession, thereby only indirectly firing workers.

Nonetheless, these remedies have generally not proven sufficient, and the renewed intensity of the business cycle may require periodic workforce reductions. The crunch appears greatest in the weaker core firms; Chrysler, for example, fired nearly one-third of its salaried staff in 1975, and at some plants it dismissed everyone hired after 1965. The crunch may affect even the stronger firms in depressed industries; in steel, Bethlehem's 1977 layoffs cut into masses of formerly protected workers. At General Dynamics' Electric Boat Division, the company did not even spare managers, and it dismissed many long-term employees. But even strong companies experience the contradiction; in 1975, Polaroid put some sixteen hundred workers (15 percent or so of its workforce) "on furlough," and many had little hope of ever being rehired. IBM avoided layoffs only by means of massive employee transfers, combined with moving back into the firm work that had previously been subcontracted out; unemployment was thus shifted to firms in the economy's periphery. In all these cases, workers were laid off only after huge losses had compelled drastic—and, it was feared, loyalty-destroying—action. In the crunch, workers of course were jettisoned, yet not without a recognition that the firings eroded the basis for control.[24]

Even in cases where companies can restrict firings to low-seniority, part-time, or other nonguaranteed workers, the problem persists. As protected workers bump lower workers and move into the vacated slots, they typically take their benefits with them, and often their higher wages as well. Thus, as if it were a corporate dream turned nightmare, high-priced labor replaces low-priced labor.

The danger for the firm, of course, is that bureaucratic control creates both more secure workplace control and a new cause for profits to disappear in downswings of the business cycle. An investment in plant and machinery that looks profitable during a boom period may turn out to be unprofitable when the downswing idles production. Formerly, workers were dismissed and the losses resulted from idle capital, but now, in addition to the outlays for plants and machines, corporations must continue their outlays for (some) unneeded workers as well. Thus have core firms discovered a new vulnerability to the effects of the cycle.

The transformation of labor costs from variable to quasi-fixed costs may well also contribute to the economy's tendency toward simultaneous high unemployment and high inflation. It is well known, for example, that core firms' prices have fallen less or risen more during recent recessions than have periphery firms' prices.[25] Although little is known about the movement of labor costs and productivity over the cycle, it is certainly reasonable to infer that the (secularly) rising importance of quasi-fixed labor costs in the core firms contributes to "stagflation."

The contrast between the promise of job security and the reality of furloughs and layoffs resulting from demand fluctuations itself produces resistance and opposition. The 1976 auto contracts were concluded, for example, by an agreement to share work through increased days off. Similarly, the United Steelworkers hierarchy declared that a guaranteed annual wage would be its next major target. Both of these big unions were, in fact, following the lead of others—typographers, garment workers, East Coast longshoremen, and railroaders, among others—who demanded and obtained job guarantees, often, unfortunately, at a high price in terms of long-run employment levels.

Thus, employment guarantees in the context of a rejuvenated business cycle create real dangers to any firm's profits and may even jeopardize its survival. Rather than diminishing the conflict, however, the cycle is likely to intensify workers' demands for extension of such employment guarantees. Bureaucratic control is thus without contradiction only if capitalism itself is without crisis.

Employers have tried to build within the firm a context in which they could profit from employment guarantees—profit, as it were, from the benefits of a planned society. Such a feat would have been possible only if the dominant position of the core firms protected them from the anarchy of capitalist production. The 1970s revealed the flaw in that assumption.

The Contradiction in the Private Sector

Bureaucratic control has also speeded up the erosion of the "natural" boundaries between the private and public sectors, thereby fueling new conflict over public intervention in the private realm of business. Bureaucratic control replaced direct and highly visible capitalist-worker relations with a structure or institutionalization of power, transforming the firm in the workers' experience and consciousness from a creature of its capitalist owners to a social institution.

Corporate capitalists have successfully extinguished the differences between IBM or Ford and the state government or the church or the school system or HEW. All are hierarchical, all have rules and procedures, all accord their members certain rights and responsibilities, all represent legitimate organizations in our society. The much-ballyhooed corporate citizenship of the big firms and the perennial tripartite definition of society (business, labor, and public) merely emphasized the corporation's rightful claim to a place in society.

The point, of course, was to bring home to the firm's workforce the "corporatist" ideal of society. In this respect bureaucratic control was only one, perhaps the most important, among several factors transforming the corporation from personal moneymaker to pillar of society. Society survived and prospered, the corporatist ideal proclaimed, because hallowed institutions persisted. The "American way" was built on these institutions, and they were what separated U.S. society from the totalitarian, class-ridden, and poorer societies of Europe. Included among the essential institutions, of course, were not only governmental structures deriving from the Founding Fathers but also the giant corporations that traced their origins to equally distant times. The corporations not only *were* eternal, they *ought* to be.

The blurring of the distinction between the private character of the corporations and the public sector was not simply an ideological illusion; in large part it was based on capitalist reality. After all, Americans depend on GM, Ford, and Chrysler to produce their basic means of transportation; how, when, and to what extent they carry out this task is certainly of greater public significance than anything the Department of Transportation does. Such could not have been said of each of the hundreds of auto producers in the early decades of the century, but centralization of capital has changed all that. Capitalist development has, in fact, made the private corporations into truly social institutions, with society-wide consequences.

Thus, the attempt to make the corporation over into a revered social institution was by no means far-fetched. And the pay-off for capitalists came in having the structure and operation of the corporation legitimized in society. The corporation achieved legal rights comparable to citizenship, and questions of what was "fair" to the corporations (as, for example, in recent debates over energy and tax programs) assumed a solemn place in public discourse.

But if, on the one hand, the corporation became a social institution and attacking it was equivalent to attacking society, on the other hand the corporation became subject to public regulation and control. The beauty of the laissez-faire ideology, which persisted in Supreme Court rulings at least into the 1930s, was that, no matter how much an agreement was compelled by unequal economic circumstances, whatever people were willing to agree to in a "voluntary contract" was legal. When the firm ceased to be merely a vehicle for voluntary contracts between capitalist and workers and instead became a social institution, it lost its private-sector protection and became subject to the dictates of the public sector.

The increasingly social character of corporations is a broad feature of twentieth-century capitalist development, but for the particular questions of the organization of work, job conditions, and the rights of workers, bureaucratic control tended to hasten political intervention. Bureaucratic control's reliance on formal rules and procedures, on explicit and established evaluation, on open criteria for promotion, and so on—on rule of corporate law in place of rule by command—invited political struggle to alter those rules. Given the successful effort by capitalists to identify corporations with society at large, it became appropriate on the capitalists' own terms to struggle in the political arena over corporate work conditions.

One result is that, whereas unions were seen as appropriate mechanisms for struggle when what was to be settled was a voluntary contract, the political arena became appropriate when the governing of the corporation as social institution was concerned. Increasingly, the working class has turned away from unions and looked instead to government to regulate, protect, and provide. Unions continue to be important in this process, but their role has changed: more and more what is important is their political strength and not their industrial puissance.

More generally, workers turn to the state to amend, shape, and dictate the rules of bureaucratic control. The Equal Employment Opportunities Commission, the Civil Rights Commission, the Federal Contracts Compliance Office, the Justice Department, and the various state attorneys-general and antidiscrimination commissions in the past decade have begun restricting employers' rights to discriminate, and they have penetrated deeply into corporate hiring, promotion, training, and layoff policies. The big antidiscrimination settlements ($45 million in damages from AT&T and a smaller amount from GE) indicate the possibility for significant penalties. The Occupational Safety and Health Administration has begun setting standards—bureaucratic rules—for what constitutes a safe workplace. The Pension Reform Act provides standards for company pension plans. Tax laws encourage the integration of workers into company ownership through Employee Stock Ownership Plans. The Fair Employment Practices Act defines, among other things, what constitutes overtime for nonsupervisory employees. The National Labor Relations Board (NLRB) is charged with ensuring fair play in establishing a union; it may provide relief for anyone fired for organizing activities, supervision for elections to choose bargaining agents, and so on. One could expand almost indefinitely the list of governmental regulation and restriction of workplace and production decisions. In all these ways, governmental regulations encroach upon or replace the bureaucratic rules that were initially imposed unilaterally by corporations. Many observers have noted the corporations' "appropriation of public power for private use," by which is meant the continuing and successful demands of the corporations for public policy to serve their interests; what is not so frequently recognized is that there is a parallel working-class appropriation of public power for private use, especially as a way of altering the rules under which bureaucratic control operates.

The point here is not that government regulators or even well-intentioned legislators will wage class war on the capitalists. Clearly they will only do what they are pushed to do, and the spotty record of regulation demonstrates that point. The NLRB's ineffectiveness in the drive against J. P. Stevens, described in an article in *The Nation* called "How 7,041 Got Fired," is an exemplar.[26] But neither can such legislation be seen merely as capitalist attempts to rationalize industries or reproduce capitalist society, however much capitalists might scramble to subvert reforms to these purposes. In each case, regulation provides some restrictions on what capitalists can do and offers the potential for much more. The extent of enactment and enforcement depends on the organization and militancy of those groups outside government pushing for reform.

Bureaucratic control thus establishes an explicit structure around which broader struggles in the political arena coalesce. These struggles provide an immediate avenue for improving the conditions of wage labor, and they may have more revolutionary consequences by linking workplace struggle with class conflict in society at large. For bureaucratic control is merely the latest form in which capitalist development socializes the process of production; by constructing formal rights and responsibilities, capitalists have abolished the individual capitalist's responsibility for working conditions and replaced it with a social accountability. Thus does modern control resolve the problem of local conflict only at the cost of raising it to a more general level.

CHAPTER 9

Labor Re-Divided, Part I: Segmented Labor Markets

STRUCTURAL CONTROL has cast a longer shadow than is visible from within the firm itself. The new system of control has contributed to the redivision and segmentation of the American working class. Both exogenous divisions (especially racial and sexual ones) and new distinctions of capitalism's own making have become embedded in the economic structure of society. And the divisions within the working class have distorted and blunted the class opposition to capitalism, making for a weak socialist movement and a long period of relative stability within the regime of monopoly capitalism.

This marks a clear reversal of the tendency dominant in the nineteenth century. During American capitalism's first century it inherited and recruited a highly heterogeneous labor force, but it reshaped its wage laborers into an increasingly homogeneous class. In the twentieth century, the economic system has attracted groups as divergent as before, but capitalist development has tended to institutionalize, instead of abolish, the distinctions among them. In particular, the dichotemizing of the economy into core and periphery has introduced a new structural division in the conditions of employment. The rise of the large administrative staff, with its middle position between employers and manual workers, has further fractured the common class basis. Moreover, institutionalized racial and sexual discrimination has served to deepen the splits within the working class. In all these cases, capitalist development has not only splintered the working class, it has also institutionalized the divisions. It has created distinct and enduring "fractions."*

* In each period there have been pressures toward both homogenization and segmentation, as, for example, capitalists played upon ethnic divisions in the last century to break up working class solidarity, and they have integrated black auto workers into the mainstream white male labor force in this century. But the dominant trend in the last century was homogenization, and, in this century, redivision.

The various lines of division can be seen in the operation of labor markets. Just as with other commodities, so with labor power, conditions in the market determine the circumstances of its *sale* (including the price received and the allocation of the commodity among various potential buyers). On the other hand, the way in which any purchased commodity is *consumed* depends upon the use to which it is put by its buyer after purchase; in the case of labor power, its consumption occurs in the labor process, the control of which has been the subject of the analysis of the previous several chapters. The distinction between sale (through labor markets) and consumption (in the labor process) permits us to assess the role labor markets play in segmenting the working class.

Labor markets constitute the principal means of segmenting the working class, because it is through labor market processes that workers are hired into their various jobs. We can see the differential treatment of labor force groups as the operation of distinct markets—the job market for factory operatives being quite distinct, for example, from the job market for middle-level administrative staff. Thus, the way the working class is segmented is clear: it is segmented through the operation of segmented labor markets.

Why segmented markets exist is a deeper question, however. In theory, labor markets could be segmented because buyers with great market power (*monopsonists*) can achieve a more profitable overall settlement by bargaining separately with distinct groups in the market than if they treat everyone similarly.* In this case, segmentation can be explained as an attempt to lower the overall price (wage) that the buyer has to pay.

While employers would undoubtedly wish to act as monopsonists and reduce the wages they are forced to pay, this explanation for segmentation is distinctly unlikely for one important reason: there exist many employers, and few have monopsony power. With relatively minor exceptions, employers cannot act as monopsonists.

Similarly, labor markets could be segmented because some workers are able to act as monopolists in the sale of particular types of labor power, establishing barriers to entry into some occupations and closing off these occupations to other workers. Here again, the issue is not so much whether workers might *want* to achieve such protection from wider competition (undoubtedly they do) but rather whether they are *able* to do so. With a few noteworthy exceptions, competition also prevails on the supply side of the labor market, and so the notion of worker-enforced segmentations does not

* Similarly, utility companies as monopolists segment their service markets, selling at different rates to residential and commercial buyers, thereby achieving higher profits than they could attain by selling to all at the same rate.

seem plausible. Perhaps a few of the stronger craft unions can act to limit the number of new entrants into their occupations (although their power to do so seems quite suspect), but such power is clearly absent in most occupations.

All this suggests that segmentation arises not from market forces themselves but rather from the underlying uses of labor power. If this is true, it means that to understand why segmentation occurs, we must look to how labor power is consumed in the labor process.

This chapter will describe one feature of the redivision of the American working class: segmented labor markets.* The next chapter focuses directly on the fractions of the working class.

The Three Labor Markets

The idea that labor markets treat groups differently needs little new justification.[1] Most people know, even if too few care, that the unemployment rate of blacks regularly runs at least double that of whites. At the other end of the spectrum, new Harvard Business School graduates can on average look forward to an annual income of $50,000 (or is it now $65,000?) within five years. Women's earnings, despite antidiscrimination legislation, have remained steady (within a few points) at 60 percent of male earnings throughout the postwar period. Between a third and a half of teenage black job-seekers normally cannot find work.

More novel is the notion that the various groups and the cross-cutting and overlapping divisions in the labor market can reasonably be arranged into a limited number of labor market segments. But this conclusion emerges from research on segmented labor markets that began in the 1960s with studies of urban labor markets by Barry Bluestone, David Gordon, Peter Doeringer and

* See R. Edwards, M. Reich, and D. Gordon (1975) and D. Gordon, M. Reich, and R. Edwards (forthcoming). This chapter owes much to that joint work. In describing different segments as separate markets, we are, of course, simultaneously specifying a certain level of analysis—that of the internal structure of the working class. Seen from a higher level of abstraction—the relation between working class and capitalist class, for example—the differences among the segments do not appear so great. For example, one of the central differences to emerge is the greater employment security of primary workers, especially independent primary workers, in contrast to secondary workers. Yet in capitalist society *all* workers are dependent upon capital for their employment, and while some workers have relatively greater guarantees than others of not being fired, no workers have complete job security, a truth some highly paid managers learned in the last recession when they lost their jobs. The analysis that follows, then, is aimed at understanding the composition and development of the working class and its sources of heterogeneity, rather than at suggesting the emergence of new classes.

Michael Piore, and others, who observed that urban blacks and other working poor people appeared to be operating in a labor market distinct from that of urban white males.[2] It was not just that blacks and others in what was labeled the "secondary labor market" were paid less; the labor market itself seemed to work differently for them. Education, for example, seemed to provide very little return for secondary workers, whereas it provided a substantial return in the other segment, the "primary market." Similarly, jobs in the secondary market did not seem to lead to better jobs, unlike the primary market where each job was potentially a stepping-stone to a better position. Observers could point to many other differences as well in the way the markets operated.

However, such observations remained largely unverified until David Gordon devised an empirical test. Taking some forty-seven measures of employment characteristics, Gordon used a statistical procedure that clearly revealed distinct clusters of jobs, with very different labor market outcomes (wage rates, frequency of unemployment, and so on) associated with each.[3] In short, his analysis provided support for the theory of segmented labor markets.

Several subsequent studies have further strengthened the case for the segmented market approach. In general, these studies not only show that the market *outcomes* are different by segment, but more importantly they provide evidence that the market *processes* also differ by segment.[4] But this research has suggested some reformulations in the original "dual market" theory. For one thing, because it is less riveted to the problems of poor and minority workers, the new research has argued persuasively for distinctions among not two but three labor market segments—the "secondary" market, the "subordinate primary" market, and the "independent primary" market. Moreover, while the earlier work emphasized a very small, "abnormal" secondary market, it now seems clear that the three segments are of about equal size. Widely varying estimates suggest that each represents between a quarter and a third of the total labor force, the remaining portion being accounted for by self-employed persons, employers, and high-level managers.[5]

Unlike the earlier work, which tended to focus on differences among workers, subsequent analysis has also suggested that the fundamental differences are not so much among the workers as among the jobs that workers hold. At any point in time, of course, differences do exist in both the workers and their jobs. Yet the research seems to say that if we are to understand the historical forces that established and maintain the divisions, we must look to the job structure.

One problem that has not been solved by recent research is precisely how to define the segments. Anecdotal observation like Doeringer and Piore's and empirical forays like Gordon's suggested that the segments should be defined as a cluster of characteristics, with no single characteristic being fundamental or invariably decisive.[6] What cluster of characteristics, then, defines a secondary job, a subordinate-primary job, or an independent-primary job? Research continues on this issue, but the main dimensions of the answer are already apparent, and probably only minor modification will be added by more precise quantitative criteria. Accepting the hazards of anticipating ongoing research, then, we can suggest the main differences distinguishing the segments.

The Secondary Market

One segment, the secondary market, is the preserve of casual labor—"casual," that is, not in the sweat required of the workers but rather in the lack of any worker rights or elaborate employer-imposed work structures. Here labor power comes closest to being treated simply as a commodity unfettered and unencumbered by any job structure, union, or other institutional constraints.

The secondary market includes many different types of jobs, and spans both production and nonproduction work. Low-skill jobs in small, nonunion manufacturing concerns constitute one part of this market. "Service" employment—the jobs of janitors, waiters and waitresses, hospital orderlies, deliverymen and messengers, attendants, guards, personal care workers, and others—represents a second major component. Another group consists of the lower-level positions in retail and wholesale trade: slots filled by sales clerks, order-takers, check-out clerks, inventory stockers, and so forth. The secondary market also includes increasing numbers of the lowest-level clerical jobs, those typing, filing, key-punching, and other positions that have become part of the large typing (or records-filing and retrieval or key-punching) pools. Finally, we must add migrant agricultural labor, seasonal employment required for the peak periods of planting and especially harvesting. Although other jobs such as part-time teaching or textile work in the South also fall into the secondary-market segment, the above categories contain the mass of secondary employment. Maureen Agnati's job, described in the first chapter, falls into the secondary market.

What marks these jobs as secondary is the casual nature of the employment. The work almost never requires previous training or education beyond basic literacy. Few skills are required and few can be learned. Such jobs offer low pay and virtually no job security. They are, in other words, typically dead-end jobs, with few prospects for advancement and little reward for seniority in the form of either higher pay or a better job. With little incentive to stay, workers may move frequently, and turnover in these jobs tends to be high. The only thing that a worker brings to a secondary job is labor power; the worker is treated and paid accordingly.

From the research that has been done, it is possible to give some indication of the characteristics of secondary employment and of the order of magnitude of the differences between segments. All the studies whose results are reported below were based on samples of male workers, so caution is required if we are to generalize. Moreover, the studies employed quite different techniques for categorizing into segments, and the samples reflect quite different underlying populations. Nonetheless, the results seem impressively similar. Consider pay, for example. In Paul Osterman's study, secondary workers' annual earnings in 1967 averaged only 69 percent of the average earnings of primary workers. Martin Carnoy and Russell Rumberger found that secondary workers' annual earnings ($5,690 in 1970) averaged 70 percent of the mean annual earnings of independent primary workers. Samuel Rosenberg found that the average hourly wage in secondary jobs ranged from 78 to 84 percent of the average hourly wage in primary jobs, while average annual income of secondary workers fell between 74 to 80 percent of the average for primary workers. In David Gordon's original study, hourly pay and annual incomes in the secondary market averaged 86 percent of pay and income in the primary market. Robert Buchele, in what is probably the most careful study to date, did not use pay as a criterion for categorizing jobs; instead he looked at intrinsic characteristics of the work itself. He found that among white middle-aged males, secondary workers' annual earnings averaged 81 percent of the earnings of subordinate primary workers and between 53 and 76 percent of the earnings of independent primary workers.[7]

From all these studies it appears that the wages associated with secondary work range from two-thirds to four-fifths of the wages for primary jobs. The finding that secondary workers earn less than primary workers is hardly news, since having a low wage was frequently among the criteria defining secondary status in the first place. What this research does do, however, is indicate the extent of the wages differential, one of the job characteristics included in the cluster that defines the segment.

Similarly, we can consider job tenure. One way of measuring tenure differences is to compare job tenure rates among groups heavily represented in the primary market (essentially white males) with those in the secondary markets (teenagers, black males, black females, all females over 25). Leaving aside the necessarily low job tenure among all categories of teenagers, we find that white males starting at age 25 have consistently longer job tenure than members of any of the other groups and that the absolute gap increases with age. In 1968 among workers 50 to 54 years old, for example, white males had occupied their current jobs for 12.8 years, compared to only 6.2 years for women and 10.1 years for nonwhite males.[8] But this test is only indirect, since demographically defined groups must be used as proxies for market-segmented categories. A more direct test can be inferred from data reported by David Gordon, since his analysis places workers in primary or secondary jobs. Both first-job tenure and present-job tenure were significantly higher for primary than for secondary workers in his samples. In Robert Buchele's sample of middle-aged white males, workers in secondary jobs were found to have significantly lower tenure (11.3 years) than either subordinate primary workers (13.8 years) or independent primary supervisory workers (15.2 years).[9] Gordon's analysis of other measures of employment stability—weeks worked per year, whether or not the worker looked for work during the year, and several stability-related personal background variables (such as marital status, whether the worker was a head of household, years in labor force, and so on)—further supports the idea that employment stability constitutes a significant difference between segments. Similarly, Samuel Rosenberg found that when occupations were classified into secondary and primary markets, workers in primary jobs had greater seniority than secondary workers in all four of the cities he studied. These results offer confirmation of the results obtained from looking at tenure differences among demographically defined groups; secondary employment seems to be associated with much more frequent job changes.[10]

Yet, as Samuel Rosenberg has also argued, the average tenure even for secondary workers is several years, suggesting that at least some secondary workers stay at their jobs for relatively long periods and are not perpetual job-changers. Robert Buchele also found that secondary workers had relatively high tenure. These findings reinforce the view that it is the lack of job security and the ever-present possibility of immediate replacement by others from the reserve army that marks a secondary job. If some secondary workers (especially those studied by Doeringer and Piore) respond to this situation by choosing to change jobs frequently, others (those studied by Rosenberg and Buchele) assess their chances differently and remain at a single job. All secondary workers, however, experience the lack of job protection and the immediate possibility of replacement.[11]

Recent research has also helped flesh out other aspects of secondary employment. For example, Carnoy and Rumberger found definite evidence that secondary jobs are dead-end employment in the sense that additional experience does not lead to higher earnings. Thus, in their sample the age-wage profile—the curve showing how much wages rise with increasing age—is flat, showing no wage increase for black secondary workers from the worker's late twenties until about sixty years of age, and for white secondary workers until about fifty years of age (thereafter wages tend to fall); in contrast, primary workers' wages tend to rise substantially with age. This finding is reproduced in both Buchele's and Osterman's studies, where labor force experience (or age) contributes so little to earnings that it is statistically insignificant. And David Gordon found that among black males in the secondary market, the age-wage profile is entirely flat, while among primary workers, wages rise with age.[12]

Another characteristic of secondary jobs that is well supported in these studies is the small return to education. Buchele found that for workers with less than a high school education, there was a slight benefit for each year of schooling achieved, but secondary workers got no additional return for any further schooling, although occupational training did help. In Osterman's sample, the effect of education in increasing earnings was four to six times greater for primary workers than for secondary workers; in fact, the return that secondary workers obtained from an extra year of education was so slight that statistically we cannot be sure it is different from zero, and the findings applied to all secondary males, whether white or black. Similar results, though stronger for black secondary workers, were obtained by Gordon and by Carnoy and Rumberger.[13]

Thus, labor market research seems to bear out the conclusion that the secondary market is indeed a distinct market, characterized both by different market outcomes and different market processes. It contains low-paying jobs of casual labor, jobs that provide little employment security or stability and for which the links between one job a worker may hold and the next are slight. These are dead-end jobs offering little opportunity for advancement, requiring few skills, and promoting relatively high voluntary turnover. Neither seniority nor education seems to pay off. And since employers have little investment in matching workers and their jobs, they feel free to replace or dismiss workers as their labor needs change.

The Subordinate Primary Market

In contrast to the secondary jobs, primary jobs offer some job security, relatively stable employment, higher wages, and extensive linkages between successive jobs that the typical worker holds. While the particular mechanisms providing security and stability and the nature of the actual linkages differ between the two tiers of the primary market, all primary jobs share the characteristic of offering well-defined occupations, with established paths for advancement.

The subordinate and independent jobs diverge, however, because of other characteristics, and again no single dimension emerges from labor market behavior as the defining criterion. The subordinate primary market has within it both production and nonproduction jobs.[14] The biggest group includes the jobs of the traditional industrial working class—production jobs in the unionized mass-production industries: plant jobs in auto assembly, steelmaking, rubber and tire manufacturing, electrical products construction, farm implements production, machinery manufacture, metal fabrication, camera and other consumer products assembly, home appliance manufacture, and the like. The other large group of subordinate primary jobs includes the positions of unionized workers in lower-level sales, clerical, and administrative work, found mostly in the major retailing, utilities, and manufacturing corporations. Other subordinate primary jobs include the production-type positions in core firms in transportation (railroad engineers, interurban and transit system bus drivers, and airline maintenance personnel), in retailing and wholesaling (warehousemen) and in utilities and other sectors of the core economy.

These jobs are distinguished from the casual-labor jobs of the secondary market most fundamentally (though not invariably) by the presence of unions. The jobs are better-paying than secondary employment, and they generally involve long-term, stable work with prospects for advancement and some job guarantees. In the case of unionized workers, the steps for advancement and the employment guarantees are contained in union seniority clauses; for nonunionized workers, both the promotional paths and the guarantees are less clear and are based only on employer practices, but they do exist. These are permanent, rather than temporary or casual, jobs.

A recent study by Lawrence Kahn makes clear the role of unions in the subordinate primary market. Kahn studied longshoremen in San Francisco (where a militant union was established in the mid-1930s) and in New York (where no union existed). He found that the labor processes in New York and in San Francisco prior to the formation of the union were basically similar. The volume of work fluctuated with the more or less random arrival of ships to be unloaded and loaded; the work tasks themselves required great effort but little skill; and job conditions were often hazardous. Not surprisingly, a system of casual labor prevailed, with low wages, arbitrary hiring procedures that encouraged favoritism, and not only no job security but also the need to be rehired every day in the daily "shape-up." These secondary-market conditions persisted into the 1950s in New York, but in San Francisco they did not survive the 1930s. The International Longshoremen's Association led a series of strikes and job actions from 1934 to 1936 that effectively ended the old system by instituting a union-run hiring hall, preferential hiring for union members, regular hours, grievance machinery, substantially higher wages, and regulation of the work load. In short, the union forced the establishment of the subordinate primary pattern. This settlement became the model when workers organized elsewhere (New York in the 1950s).[15]

On the other side, subordinate primary jobs are distinguished from independent primary jobs in that their work tasks are repetitive, routinized, and subject to machine pacing. The skills required are learned rather quickly (within a few days or weeks), and they are often acquired on the job. The jobs provide little opportunity for workers to have any control over their own jobs.

The job ladders that link one job with subsequent ones in the same occupation may derive either from the employing firm (as is generally the case with nonproduction jobs) of from industrial union rules (for production jobs), but in either case they tend to be firm-specific. That is, the path for advancement almost always depends on seniority within the firm, and indeed such seniority becomes, in this internal labor market, the necessary admission ticket to the better-paying positions higher on the job ladder. Workers have a big incentive to remain with one employer, and they show markedly lower turnover rates than secondary workers.

This picture of subordinate primary employment has been substantially confirmed in some detailed research. In addition to the evidence already cited in our discussion of the secondary market (which shows the higher pay and greater tenure of primary workers), we also have evidence more particularly focused on subordinate primary jobs. Consider, for example, the economic return to age or experience—which is a statistical way to determine whether jobs are dead ends or whether they are part of a "career ladder." In the secondary market, as we saw, the lack of any return to age or experience meant that little advancement was possible within a job and that experience did not qualify the worker for a better job. But in subordinate primary employment, all this changes.

Subordinate primary jobs offer substantial returns to age and experience. According to Paul Osterman's results, for example, workers thirty-one years old earned about $1,150 less per year than those who were forty-one; in other words, the extra decade's experience raised the older workers' wages by roughly 18 percent. (By contrast, the average secondary worker would get only $218 more than a secondary worker with ten years' less experience, roughly a 4 percent raise.) Other studies have also reported large returns to experience.[16]

Similarly, schooling (at least through high school and the first few years of college), also seems to pay off for subordinate primary workers. Osterman found that each year of schooling gives the average subordinate primary worker a bonus of $459 per year, or more than a 6 percent raise. (Again, the best estimate of the return for a secondary worker is $76, a mere 1½ percent increase.) Buchele found that each of the first three years of college returned over $1,000 per year in higher income, although after that the return seems to fall off. Large returns to schooling for subordinate primary workers at least through high school, and for white males even beyond, were also reported by Carnoy and Rumberger.[17]

Subordinate primary jobs may carry with them substantial risks of unemployment, but the risks are of a quite different sort from those present in secondary jobs. Secondary workers face dismissal even during boom times for disciplinary or other arbitrary reasons, but subordinate primary workers usually enjoy at least some employment protection against such firings, most importantly through unions.[18] The main danger for subordinate primary workers comes from business depressions, since these workers have little protection against being laid off or furloughed when production exceeds demand. High rates of unemployment may prevail, as the experience of the 1970s demonstrates, but even in these circumstances subordinate primary workers face prospects different from those facing secondary workers. Subordinate primary workers are generally laid off in order of least seniority, so high seniority may insulate a worker from all but the most severe layoffs. Unlike secondary workers, who are simply dismissed and cut adrift when business gets bad, subordinate primary workers usually continue some association with their union, perhaps receive union-negotiated supplemental unemployment benefits, and can be called back to work in order of seniority when business picks up. A worker laid off at the auto plants remains an (unemployed) auto worker, rather than simply joining the ranks of the anonymous unemployed.

The subordinate primary market, then, contains the jobs of the old industrial working class, reinforced by the lower-level jobs of unionized clerical employees. In these routinized, typically machine-operative positions, workers find that by staying on the job ladder they can progress to significantly higher wages and perhaps to better jobs. Schooling also pays off, especially, it appears, at the level of high school and the first few years of college. Cyclical unemployment is a not-uncommon feature in subordinate primary work, particularly in production or blue-collar positions; but even during spells of layoffs, subordinate primary positions display their distinctiveness from secondary work by the continuing connections between laid-off workers and their jobs.

The Independent Primary Market

Jobs in the independent primary market, like jobs in the subordinate primary market, offer stable employment with considerable job security, established patterns of career progression, and relatively high pay. But they differ from subordinate primary jobs in that they typically involve general, rather than firm-specific, skills; they may have career ladders that imply movements between firms; they are not centered on operating machinery; they typically require skills obtained in advanced or specialized schooling; they often demand educational credentials; they are likely to have occupational or professional standards for performance; and they are likely to require independent initiative or self-pacing.

Three groups of jobs dominate the independent primary market.[19] The first fills the middle layers of the firm's employment structure and consists of jobs for long-term clerical, sales, and technical staff, foremen, bookkeepers, personal and specialized secretaries, supervisors, and so on. A second group of independent primary jobs grows out of craft work that employs electricians, carpenters, plumbers, steam-fitters, and machinists. A third large group of independent primary jobs includes the professional positions—accountants, research scientists, engineers, registered nurses and doctors, lawyers and tax specialists, and others. As the jobs in these three groups indicate, the independent primary market, like the other segments, spans both blue-collar and white-collar work.[20]

Another characteristic of the independent primary market is the greater role played by the public sector. For professional and technical workers in particular, the state's share of employment has steadily advanced over the last three decades, to the point where the state now employs between 35 and 45 percent of all professional and technical workers. Teachers, social welfare workers, nurses, doctors, other health professionals, accountants, lawyers, engineers, and others have been hired in great numbers to carry out the state's permanent new functions in welfare, warfare, and regulation. Overall, the state sector appears to account for between a fifth and a third of all independent primary employment.[21]

The average level of pay in independent primary jobs is, of course, significantly higher than in the other segments. In Robert Buchele's study, for example, mean annual earnings ranged from 106 percent to 152 percent of subordinate primary earnings. Paul Osterman's estimate, again for average annual earnings, was 172 percent. Martin Carnoy and Russell Rumberger found independent primary earnings to be 132 percent of subordinate primary earnings.[22]

Moreover, earnings in independent primary jobs show much greater increases in response to experience or age than in the other segments, confirming the existence of important promotional or career ladders linking prior employment with subsequent jobs. In Paul Osterman's study, workers thirty-two years old earned roughly $9,550 on average; workers identical in other characteristics but having the additional experience, seniority, or whatever is implied by being ten years older, received $12,808—a whopping $3,258 or 34 percent raise, as compared to 4 percent and 18 percent respectively for secondary and subordinate primary workers. Carnoy and Rumberger also found greater returns on age for this segment than for the other segments, especially for white males, and the seniority bonus extended longer—right up to the retirement age, in fact.[23]

Similarly, formal education plays a much greater role in independent primary jobs. In Paul Osterman's study, each year of schooling boosted the average workers' annual earnings by $1,224, nearly a 10 percent raise (compared to 1½ percent and 6 percent increases in secondary and subordinate primary workers' incomes). Large returns to schooling for independent primary workers show up in other studies as well; Buchele found that each year of schooling after college provided supervisory workers with an extra $3,000 in income. Large returns were present at other levels (especially college) as well, and for all categories of independent primary workers. Carnoy and Rumberger found equally large returns for educational attainment.[24]

Despite these similarities, independent primary jobs also differ from each other, and the differences are especially pronounced in the patterns of unemployment and in movement up the job ladder. For supervisory and other administrative employees, the future lies in sticking with the company; they have the highest "tenure in present jobs" of all workers, the lowest overall unemployment rate, the fewest spells of unemployment, the lowest probability of having quit their jobs, the lowest number of jobs held during a given year, the highest probability of having received company training, and a very low probability (second only to that of professional workers) of having been laid off. Moreover, they are the only workers for whom having more than thirty years' experience contributes positively to earnings. In short, supervisory work fosters long tenure and little voluntary turnover, and it carries slight risks of unemployment. Once in a supervisory job, a worker tends to stay.[25]

Professional and craft employment, on the other hand, tends to establish promotional paths through professional or craft standards as well as through employer-imposed job structures. The result is a pattern of job movement that, measured in terms of the number of moves, more clearly resembles the secondary market. For example, in Buchele's study, the "years of tenure in present job" for professional and craft workers (11.7 and 11.6 respectively) was comparable to that for secondary workers (11.3) and much less than that for either subordinate primary workers (13.8) or independent primary supervisory workers (15.2). Similarly, the probability of having quit in any year and the average number of jobs held during the year were considerably higher for professional and craft workers than for other independent primary workers or for subordinate primary workers, and closest to statistics for secondary workers.[26]

But while the extent of job switching in professional and craft work approaches that in secondary jobs, its meaning is quite different. When workers change jobs in the secondary market, their moves generally do not lead to any advancement or any natural next jobs, and so secondary workers follow the random pattern of job switching described earlier. In professional or craft work, job changes mean movement from one employer to another but still within the occupational job ladders. The fact that professional workers earn a substantial return to experience through the first nineteen or so years of working, while secondary workers get no return, means that when professional workers move to new jobs and gain experience, they continue to increase their earnings.[27]

For craft workers, job switching does not imply progress (like secondary workers, craft workers get little return to greater experience), but it serves as a method for continuing employment in occupations that pay a premium (30 percent in Buchele's sample) over casual labor.

Increased voluntary turnover creates the statistical effect of higher unemployment rates, and so (in Buchele's study, for example) professional workers have a higher overall unemployment rate than supervisory workers, despite a *lower* probability of being laid off. In craft work, however, it is clear that involuntary unemployment looms much larger than in other independent primary jobs, or indeed in any other work. Craft workers suffer nearly as many spells of unemployment, a higher overall unemployment rate, and a much greater chance of being laid off than even secondary workers. Yet like subordinate primary workers (who, when unemployed, retain ties to their jobs, their unions, and their occupations while they wait to be recalled), craft workers have an even stronger bond to their occupation and, when laid off, remain (unemployed) craft workers rather than simply joining the ranks of those looking for any kind of work. Moreover, despite their higher unemployment rates, craft workers on average continue to earn substantially higher annual incomes than secondary workers.[28]

Independent primary jobs, then, constitute the third market segment.

Like other primary jobs, independent primary employment creates well-defined occupations with job ladders and established patterns of movement between jobs. The jobs in this segment are skilled jobs, requiring relatively high levels of schooling or advanced training. As Michael Piore has noted, formal education (or craft union membership or licensing) is an essential requisite for employment; while educational requirements are often not taken seriously in the other segments and are more or less rigorously enforced depending on how tight the labor market is, in independent primary jobs the credentials become nearly absolute requirements for entry. Large returns accrue to both additional schooling and experience. Independent primary jobs, especially the professional and craft positions, have professional or occupational standards that govern performance, and so mobility and turnover tend to be both high and associated with advancement. Except for craft work, these jobs carry slight overall chances of lay-offs. Most strikingly, all independent primary jobs foster occupational consciousness; that is, they provide the basis for job-holders to define their own identities in terms of their particular occupation.

Systems of Control and the Three Labor Markets

If, as this research suggests, the labor market is segmented into three parts, what forces account for the division? I have already suggested that market behavior itself cannot answer this question. After all, labor markets are but mechanisms bringing employers' needs for productive labor together with the available supplies of workers. Unless a high degree of market power exists (an implausible assumption for labor markets), labor markets constitute a means of mediation; they reflect the underlying forces in production and in the laboring population.

Racial and sexual discrimination provide one set of forces leading to labor market segmentation. Blacks and women were pushed into particular race- or sex-stereotyped jobs, jobs that were consistent with the broader social evaluation of each group. Blacks were hired into the dirtiest, most physically demanding, and lowest-skilled occupations, while women were pushed toward "helping" occupations, especially clerical work. Moreover, both groups, especially blacks, were intentionally recruited for particular occupations as a way for management to divide and thereby rule the firm's workforce. Blacks and women had little bargaining power and few alternate job possibilities, facts which ensured that their work would remain low-paying and with few job rights.

Intentional discrimination remains important, but increasingly it has been supplanted by institutional discrimination. And institutional discrimination, in addition to appearing in the form of segregated schooling and culturally biased tests, occurs through segmented labor markets. Thus, in probing the causes of segmented labor markets, we seek in part to understand how racial discrimination and sexual discrimination have become incorporated in the institutional processes of labor markets.

But the analysis of the preceding chapters provides yet another key to the origins of segmented labor markets; let me state it baldly before introducing the necessary qualifications. Labor markets are segmented because they express a historical segmentation of the labor process; specifically, a distinct system of control inside the firm underlies each of the three market segments. The secondary labor market is the market expression of workplaces organized according to simple control. The subordinate primary market contains those workplaces (workers and jobs) under the "mixed" system of technical control and unions. And the independent primary market reflects bureaucratically controlled labor processes. Thus, the fundamental basis for division into three segments is to be found in the workplace, not in the labor market; so to define the three market segments we now have a single criterion—the type of control system—rather than simply a cluster of market behavior characteristics.*

It should be clear that the relationship between types of control and labor market segments is not perfect or exhaustive. Anomalies appear and, more importantly, development occurs such that any static typology can never adequately capture all the transitional and developmental situations. The accompanying chart asserts that most jobs are concentrated in the

* The observation that each market segment seems to have a characteristic form of organizing work associated with it is not new. Michael Piore (1970, pp. 55, 57), for instance, has described discipline in secondary jobs as "harsh and often arbitrary" and has observed that,

> reward and punishment in the [secondary] workplace are continually based upon personal relationships between worker and supervisor.

Yet earlier observers focused only on markets and specifically on the pathology of secondary employment (in contrast to what was seen as the more normal patterns of primary work); as a result, the relationship between organization in the labor process and patterns in labor markets appeared to be *ad hoc*, and the emergence of the secondary market was without historical reasons or rationale. Arbitrary control became but one more of the characteristics in the cluster that defined the secondary market. Instead, as the analysis here shows, it is the primary markets that have emerged as new on the scene, and their appearance is a direct product of the internal transformation of the core firm.

System of Control / Market Segment (Jobs)	Simple Control	Technical Control	Bureaucratic Control
Secondary	I. • Small manufacturing jobs • Service jobs • Retail sales • Temporary and typing-pool office work	Southern textile jobs	Part-time academic jobs
Subordinate Primary	Unionized garment workers	II. • Jobs in auto and steel plants • Assembly-line production work • Machine-paced clerical work	Personal secretary jobs
Independent Primary	Jobs in small consulting firms	Technicians' jobs monitoring chemicals production	III. • Jobs at IBM, Polaroid • Craft work • Nonproduction staff jobs

The Correspondence Between Systems of Control and Labor Market Segments for Sample Jobs

diagonal cells (numbered I, II, and III) and that the off-diagonal cells are of minor importance. Yet certainly some jobs fall in the off-diagonal cells, and examples are listed in the chart. Nonetheless, the corresponding (diagonal) types of control and labor market segments appear to be poles of great magnetic force, attracting the majority of jobs.[29]

The system-of-control approach leads to a somewhat different understanding of the role of job skills, schooling, on-the-job training, experience, and other technical characteristics of labor. These characteristics are usually thought to create different types of labor (and so they do), and therefore to be the basis themselves of different treatment in the labor market. The relevance of these technical attributes, even their preeminence in certain cases, cannot be denied. However, the analysis presented here suggests that it is the system of control that creates the context within which experience, training, schooling, skills, and other attributes assume their importance. Rather than ignoring the technical relations of production, such an approach emphasizes that considerable choice surrounds the selection of any productive technique. In most industries, a range of techniques is already available. Even in those production processes where little choice exists, the decision whether to use high-skill or low-skill labor, for example, essentially depends on whether the firm finds it profitable to undertake the research and development necessary to convert high-skill production to low-skill production.[30] Whether it is profitable depends in turn not only on the relative wage costs but also on the rate at which labor power is transformed into labor—that is, on the organization of the labor process itself. Thus, the reason experience and schooling are unimportant for explaining secondary workers' incomes but are crucial for explaining subordinate primary workers' incomes derives not so much from invariant differences in the nature of the products being produced and in the accompanying inherent skill requirements as from the consistently different ways of organizing the labor process. Secondary work is organized so as to minimize the need for experience and schooling, whereas subordinate primary work is organized so as to build upon these factors. The technical processes of production place certain limits on the range of organizational possibilities, of course, but in practice these limits tend to provide considerable flexibility.[31]

This perspective, then, leads us to investigate the relationship between the labor process and labor markets. Indeed, structural forms of control (technical control and bureaucratic control) emerged out of the core firm's attempts to turn the tide of conflict on the shop and office floor decisively in its favor, and these efforts carried implications (not always foreseen) for the way the core firm's workforce would be recruited, paid, and reproduced.

Technical control at first seemed to require no alteration in the way the firm obtained its labor. Indeed, the early days of the Ford plants appeared to provide capitalists with that happy prospect of the unification of the potency of the reserve army outside the plant walls and the rigid internal discipline of technical control inside. Turnover was extremely high—certainly as high as in the secondary market today—and job security was nil.

Technical control united with secondary market-type casual labor lasted until the great CIO organizing drives of the 1930s. The success of the auto workers, steelworkers, electrical workers, rubberworkers, and others in building industrial unions doomed that combination and put in its place the configuration represented by cell II in the chart, technical control inside the firm matched with primary labor market-type job security, stability, and (through union seniority) promotional prospects. This configuration has characterized the traditional mass-production industries throughout the postwar period.

In effect, the agreement that was worked out amounted to the establishment of an internal labor market. An internal market is simply a set of procedures contained wholly within the firm for performing the functions of the external market: the allocation and pricing of labor. Unions, as at U.S. Steel, for example, won for their members the rights to fill vacancies based on seniority and to have outside hiring done only at lower-paying, entry-level jobs. Union scales governed each job's pay.

Technical control, then, does not directly require primary market job rights, and the relation between them is not invariable. Certainly, the advantages of technical control and casual labor markets have motivated the corporations' investments in Brazil, South Korea, and other repressive countries where workers cannot establish unions or win job rights. Similarly, the attempt by core firms (most conspicuously GM) to move production facilities to the South indicates that at least some employers think that old-time benefits of technical control and secondary labor are possible even within the United States. GM may have thought it could horn in on the turf of J. P. Stevens and other textile manufacturers, who long ago discovered that technical control and nonunion labor were possible because of the South's peculiar blend of antiunion law and local custom.

Yet what was possible for an isolated textile industry does not appear possible generally. GM has experienced its first successful union drive in its southern plants, and even J. P. Stevens is the target of a growing union struggle. The AFL-CIO has targeted the whole South as the arena for its first serious organizing efforts in many years. The unions have pushed labor law reform primarily to overcome the tactics of antiunion southern employers like Stevens. Local organizations, like those in North Carolina organized around the brown-lung dangers of the cotton mills, create incipient possibilities for militant resistance. Such efforts are still in their early stages and victory is by no means inevitable, yet they indicate that firms like GM and others will most likely be denied the advantages of technical control and secondary labor.

Technical control in the core firms brings unionization in its wake, and through unionization, the characteristics of primary-market employment.[32] Here seniority provisions and other union contract rules govern the allocation of workers to jobs, the wages to be paid, the relative vulnerability to layoff, and the protections and appeals from discipline and dismissal. The middle cell of the chart, then, must be understood as possessing the labor market characteristics that have emerged from a historic compromise—a bargain between core firms and industrial unions that leaves the management of the business in the employers' hands but guarantees to workers primary-market job rights.

Bureaucratic control also moved the firm out of secondary-market employment, not because of any compromise with workers but rather due to employers' efforts to avoid the need for such compromise. Bureaucratic control reversed the first-resort dependence on reserve-army discipline, and firms intentionally put in its place the greater job security, promotion prospects, and assumption of long-term employment that characterize primary-market jobs. But more than eliminating secondary employment, bureaucratic control pushed the firm specifically towards independent primary employment, with its emphasis on occupational or professional standards, incentives for identifying with the job, importance of schooling, and high return for experience. In the first place, bureaucratic control emerged out of those workplaces that tended to employ educated workers: the offices, shops, and labs of the white-collar staff, technical and professional workers, and so on. It was natural, then, that the new form of control, based on exploiting status differences among workers, should focus upon differences in the attainment of schooling and make them central to translating the workplace hierarchy into usable labor-market hiring criteria. This happy correspondence can be seen in the eagerness with which early employers seized upon educational credentials as convenient (and legitimizing) ways of screening workers, and the diligence with which educational reformers have sought to remold schools to fit the changing demands of work.[33]

More directly, the way bureaucratic control functions tends to require and reinforce independent primary patterns. For example, Polaroid, like other bureaucratically controlled firms, establishes promotion ladders and an internal market. New workers are recruited from the external labor market only for the bottom-rung jobs, the entry-level jobs within each skill category. Polaroid's job ladder for engineers is as follows:

Job Title	Years of Experience
Associate Engineer	0–2
Engineer	2–5
Senior Engineer	4–10
Principal Engineer	10–18
Senior Principal Engineer	over 15

When a vacancy occurs, Polaroid engineers can bid for the job. The actual decision is based in part on applicants' experience, which in practice means seniority gained while in Polaroid's employ. But, in addition, for all but the bottom-rung jobs on each ladder, the applicants' work records and recommendations from company supervisors, as well as formal training and skills, determine who gets promoted to the various openings.

Thus with regard to recruiting and reproducing the firm's workforce, bureaucratic organization operates as an internal labor market. As such, it must accommodate two quite different market processes: it must select, from among all workers, those who will be appropriate for bureaucratically controlled work; then it must allocate the selected workers, over the course of their careers, to higher-paying jobs through internal market mechanisms. In the context of bureaucratic control both of these tasks tend to foster independent primary employment patterns.[34]

Bureaucratic control, then, moves the firm towards independent primary employment patterns. It establishes the apparatus for the employer's model (rather than the compromise version) of the internal labor market, and it creates the incentives for high tenure, the importance of schooling, occupational consciousness, and the other characteristics of independent primary employment. The advantage for employers is simply the greater flexibility they enjoy in instituting productivity-enhancing internal market procedures.

If technical control leads to subordinate primary employment and bureaucratic control to an independent primary market, simple control results in secondary-type jobs; in this case, both the labor process and the accompanying labor market are distinguished by the *lack* of elaborate structural or institutional features. The essence of simple control, in either its entrepreneurial or hierarchical form, is the arbitrary power of foremen and supervisors to direct work, to monitor performance, and to discipline or reward workers. Almost by definition, the workers in such a system can have little job security. More subtly, the absence of a structurally based control system provides little avenue or incentive for worker promotion, so secondary jobs turn into dead ends.

Secondary employers generally do not have the scale, the volume of profits, or the stability to make the long-term commitments necessary to establish primary-market employment. For example, guarantees of employment security and benefits and privileges rising with seniority typically require contractual obligations extending considerably into the future.[35] Similarly, the administrative apparatus associated with formal periodic review of workers' performance, grievance appeals, and the like, requires a further long-term commitment of resources. The core firm, with its huge scale and extensive market power, plans for the long-term in all its operations, including the organization of its labor force; the periphery firm cannot.

The result of the great changes in work organization inside core firms, then, has been reflected in a corresponding change in labor markets. Systems of control in the core firms now differ from those in the firms of the competitive periphery, and in turn labor markets have become segmented. The different systems of control are not the only force pushing toward labor segmentation, but they surely are one of the most important.[36] This view of the aggregate job structure leads directly to an analysis of the labor force—that is, to the parts or fractions of the working class.

CHAPTER 10

Labor Redivided, Part II: The Fractions of the Working Class

THE DEVELOPMENT of twentiety-century American capitalism has fractured, rather than unified, the working class. Workers have been divided into separate groups, each with its distinct job experiences, distinct community cultures, and distinct consciousnesses. The inability of working class-based political movements to overcome these divisions has doomed all efforts at serious structural reform.

The mark of twentieth-century divisions in the working class is their enduring, deeply anchored, institutionalized nature. Employers have always attempted to exploit differences among workers, and their efforts often proved successful at crucial turning points in labor history.[1] But such efforts were transitory, requiring new outbursts of nativism or antiimmigrant bias or antiblack hatred or anti-Catholicism to renew the divisions. It is an unfortunate truth about the American past that new divisive campaigns were never long absent, but they still must be understood as political and ideological efforts rather than the products of economic structure. They were indeed rooted in real differences in the living conditions of the laboring populations, but nineteenth-century capitalism, much as it profited from these differences, was busy eroding them.

Not so in this century, where the divisions have been made more permanent because they were rooted in the normal, everyday operation of economic institutions, in particular in the differing systems of control in the firm and their associated labor market segments. In the last chapter, these divisions were described in terms of distinctions among jobs, and it is true that the clearest and (in terms of change) the most powerful divisions have evolved in the job structure. Yet sharp divisions between groups of jobs tend to create discrete populations of job-holders as well. The tendency of segmented markets to divide the working class is especially strong since the differences among market segments include distinct career mobility patterns; that is, job-holders tend to experience these differences not just in current jobs but over their entire lifetimes.*

Before turning directly to the fractions of the working class, we must choose some compromise in the problem of terminology. One set of terms—"lower class," "working class," and "middle class"—derives from the popular media and from bourgeois sociology. Although they have the advantage of being well known and simple, these terms also have many disadvantages. They are imprecise ("middle class" includes both those within capital's employ and those outside it); they focus too exclusively on income rankings; and by making different fractions of the working class into distinct classes, they mask the real relations we want them to reveal. Terminology from classical Marxism does not precisely fit the fractions described here either, and it has the added disadvantage that its usage in a substantial literature has left it with multiple and sometimes contradictory meanings.[2] In what follows, then, let us label the various fractions of the working class Fraction I, Fraction II, and Fraction III. Perhaps the closest descriptive titles for these respective segments would be the "working poor," the "traditional proletariat," and the "middle layers." These three groups roughly correspond to the three "classes" of bourgeois sociology, although it should be clear that they do not represent separate classes but instead are fractions of the working class; they are all composed of wage or salary workers dependent upon capital for employment.

Fraction I:
The Working Poor

American society in the 1960s rediscovered its poor. More, we learned poverty's distinctive social markings, and it became clear that the poor constitute an identifiable and enduring subpopulation of society. Two-thirds

*The evolution of economic life has tended to segment the working class, but the experience, "social practices," and political behavior of each fraction cannot be understood as simply an expression of these economic realities. Indeed, as recent historical scholarship has emphasized so well, the working class creates for itself a complex and multifaceted reality in which culture, family patterns, ethnicity, and tradition all play central parts. This holds for class fractions as well as for the working class as a whole. This chapter focuses on the fractions' economic existences, and it therefore represents an incomplete (and beginning) analysis.

of all poor persons in 1974 were either black, of Hispanic origin, elderly, or in families headed by women; some persons, of course, shared some or all of these characteristics. Whites comprise about 66 percent of all poor people, but the proportion of each population in poverty is much higher among blacks (31 percent) and Hispanics (23 percent) than among whites (9 percent). Similarly, slightly more than half of all poor persons come from families with a male present, but the proportion of female-headed households that are poor (31 percent) greatly exceeds those family groupings with a male present (8 percent). Most of the poor (86 percent) are less than sixty-five years of age, and indeed nearly half (42 percent) are younger than eighteen years old, but again the rate of poverty is higher among old people (16 percent) and the young (15 percent) than among those eighteen to sixty-five (9 percent).[3]

Moreover, poverty has a striking spatial dimension. Three-quarters of all poor people live either in rural areas or the central city, and the rates of poverty (14 percent for nonmetropolitan areas, 14 percent for the central city, 7 percent for the suburbs) reveal its geographical concentration. The rural poor are most likely to be residents of regions (such as Appalachia) where stagnating agriculture left a redundant population; the low density of settlement makes the social causes of poverty less immediately apparent. But in the cities, the poor are collected and pushed into highly visible, low-income ghettoes; more than a third of the urban poor live in the officially defined poverty areas—neighborhoods in which 20 percent or more of the inhabitants have poverty-level incomes.[4]

For all these reasons, the poor, and especially the urban poor, became a recognizable group. Yet if American society rediscovered its poor in the 1960s, it only belatedly recognized that its biggest poverty population is the *working* poor. In 1974, for example, slightly over half of those families with income below the officially defined poverty level had family heads who worked; in fact, for a fifth of poor families, the head of the household worked full time. In less than one-third of the officially defined poverty families there are no income earners, and the members of these families are primarily old people. For poor families with an adult male present, inability to find work is the third most important reason, after illness or disability and retirement, for the man's not working; for poor families headed by a female, inability to find work is again the third most important reason for unemployment, behind "keeping house" (two thirds of these families have two or more dependents) and illness or disability.[5] In short, most poor families are the working poor; the rest cannot work because of age, ill health, or the need to care for dependents, or because they cannot find work. And particularly among the able-bodied poor, the poor are poor because they are employed at low wages, are irregularly employed, or cannot find work at all.

The employment opportunities of the poor are sharply affected by the business cycle. Thus the boom of the 1960s produced increasing numbers of jobs and declining unemployment. Since the working poor also serve as a reserve army for better-paying jobs, being called to active duty when business booms and discharged when the action is over, the 1960s permitted some of the working poor to move into higher-wage jobs. The result was a steady decline in the number of persons officially counted as poor and some undoubted improvement in the real living situations of all low-wage workers. The darker side of the cycle has been observed during the stagnation of the 1970s, however, as low-wage workers have found sharply diminished job opportunities and the official poverty statistics have moved upward again.

Aside from cyclical variation, however, there is a deeper structural basis for the poverty of Fraction I; the working poor are in families where the principal wage-earner (male or female) or all wage-earners are employed in secondary-market jobs. The conditions of the secondary market (low wages, employment irregularity, lack of job security, and little benefit from greater seniority or education) establish the patterns for the employment experience of the working poor. The barriers to the primary markets—the lack of enough subordinate primary jobs; the craft restrictions, the educational requirements, and racial and sexual discrimination in independent primary jobs—set the limits for the employment possibilities of the working poor. Subject to secondary-market conditions and excluded (except toward the end of the boom) from primary markets, the working poor survive the ups and downs of the cycle as an enduring feature of American society.

The identity of Fraction I becomes clearer if we investigate the holders of secondary jobs. There seems little doubt that people who are black, Hispanic, female, teenage, or undocumented workers (illegal aliens) are heavily overrepresented. Again, caution is in order. Since the biggest single group in the labor force is white males, white males tend to show up in large numbers even in the secondary market. Nevertheless, several studies have documented the heavy overrepresentation of blacks. Similarly, Samuel Rosenberg's study of the low-income areas of four major cities found high proportions of Hispanic workers in secondary jobs.[6] But perhaps the most revealing estimates come from the very careful and useful study of low-wage employment by Barry Bluestone, William Murphy, and Mary Stevenson; more than three-quarters of all low-wage job-holders are black and/or female. Even here, however, the concentration among specific population groups is understated: Hispanics are not identified, the data come from census surveys that admittedly fail to count many black and brown workers, and undocumented workers are almost completely unrecorded.[7]

Proportion of Working Poor
By Sex-Race Groups

	Percent
White Males	22.4
White Females	26.3
Black Males	27.1
Black Females	24.2
	100.0

Source: Calculated from Barry Bluestone, William Murphy, and Mary Stevenson (1973), pp. 51, 215.

The newest source of secondary-market workers has been the flood of undocumented or illegal migrants from Mexico, the Caribbean, and elsewhere. Estimates on the size of this influx range from 5 to 10 million, and since most such workers are immediate job-seekers (children and old people having been left at home), it is clear that this group now constitutes a critical component of the total low-wage labor pool.[8] Fleeing phenomenal rates of unemployment and superexploitative wages in their home countries, undocumented workers arrive without rights or resources. They make ideal fodder for secondary-market employers, since their illegal status, the dangers of being discovered, and their inability to obtain unemployment compensation force them to become resigned to harsh discipline and low wages, with little or no protest. Thus are new recruits added to Fraction I.

We should note, however, that not all secondary workers can be properly analyzed as part of the working poor. Teenagers, for example, often accept secondary-market employment while still in school or on vacation. Many women are in low-wage jobs although, due to other family members' earnings, the family itself is not poor.[9] White males, before settling on a primary-market career, frequently begin by working in secondary-market jobs.[10] The nonwork environment of community, homelife, and culture distinguish these workers from the working poor.

But for the rest—the working poor with their principal wage-earners rooted in secondary employment—capitalism's segmentation of the labor force becomes manifested in enduring poverty. The working poor thus come to constitute a permanent fraction of the working class, a population for whom, even in good times, the chief concern must be survival.

Fraction II:
The Traditional Proletariat

The second fraction of the working class, the traditional proletariat, is that portion of the producing population employed in subordinate primary-market jobs. These are production workers who form the most familiar image of working-class life. The males tend to be manual workers in industrial plants, and they frequently are union members. The females tend to be homemakers, clerical workers, or factory operatives. Their incomes (at least in good times) are sufficiently above poverty levels to permit some to own their own homes and nearly all to enjoy the consumption benefits associated with high-wage factory labor.

Fraction II is properly labeled "traditional," not because it conforms to the working-class stereotype prevalent in popular films or mainstream sociology but because it (collectively) has the longest experience as wage labor. Fraction II workers are the descendants of the first large concentrations of industrial workers in the United States, the semiskilled and unskilled proletariat created by the upsurge of capitalism between the Civil War and the First World War. That original "triumph of capitalism" revolutionized the production of steel, electrical goods, processed foods, machinery, autos, and other industrial products and brought into existence the railroads, communications networks, utilities, and other infrastructures to serve the new order. In the process, capitalist development also gave birth to the first large industrial proletariat in the United States; the traditional proletariat today continues that employment.

In many cases these workers are not only descended from the earlier factory proletariat in some collective sense; they can also individually trace their own ancestors. Thus, the major concentrations of ethnic workers today—Italians, Poles, Hungarians, Germans, Greeks, Irish, Slavs, and others—represent a continuing link to the great migrations that provided the first factory populations. Large numbers of these workers live in the blue-collar communities that either uneasily coexist with low-income ghettoes and luxury-housing enclaves or that have increasingly invaded the residential areas outside the central cities. These communities are too prosperous to be accurately labeled "ghettoes" (though they once served as such), and they now function as stable ethnic neighborhoods. More generally, the traditional proletariat lives in what have come to be (meaningfully) referred to as "working-class neighborhoods."

If this second fraction of the working class survives as the lineal descendant of nineteenth-century workers, it has nonetheless undergone extensive change. For one thing, blacks have entered subordinate primary employment in large numbers. In both the First and Second World Wars, rural blacks migrating to industrial employment found that wartime labor shortages opened job opportunities that had been firmly closed to them. In the postwar period, their foothold has been secured on a more permanent basis. So, for example, Martin Carnoy and Russell Rumberger found that nearly half (47.3 percent) of the employed black males in their 1970 sample were subordinate primary workers. Similarly, Samuel Rosenberg found that between 60 and 74 percent of black males from four major cities were primary-market workers. Paul Osterman found that the proportion of black males in the subordinate primary market closely paralleled the representation of black males in his entire sample. If Osterman's sample can be taken as representative of the national male labor force—which it was weighted to be—then it would appear that blacks comprise some 8 to 10 percent of this segment. Whereas at one time blacks found industrial employment only during wars and strikes, they have now become a central and continuing source of factory labor.[11]

A second change concerns females. Most of the segmented-market studies have used samples consisting solely of male workers, so we are left with little solid information about the employment of women in subordinate primary jobs. It seems apparent, however, that some women workers have themselves moved into production or blue-collar subordinate primary jobs. This is part of the general increase in female industrial employment. Between 1959 and 1974, for example, the number of female workers on manufacturing payrolls jumped by nearly a million, an increase of over 55 percent. But female manufacturing workers are more likely to be employed as secondary workers than as subordinate primary workers (nearly 60 percent of all women in manufacturing are employed in textiles or related products, where secondary-market patterns prevail), so the increase in female manufacturing workers overstates the move into subordinate primary-type production jobs. Much more significant numerically for women is nonproduction or white-collar employment—comprising the other large group of subordinate primary workers. Female clerical and sales workers numbered less than half a million in 1900; by 1940 this group had increased to about 3½ million. Between 1940 and 1974 employment of women in sales and clerical work added another 10 million to the total. Much of this increase, like the increase in female production workers, undoubtedly took place in secondary-type jobs, but a substantial amount (much of the nonproduction personnel added by the core firms) has been in subordinate primary jobs.[12] Thus, just as the subordinate primary market has incorporated blacks, so has it come to embrace ever-larger numbers of women.

The increase in female subordinate primary workers—indeed, the increase in employment for both subordinate primary- and secondary-market women—has worked a substantial change in the typical family of Fraction II. The most representative traditional proletariat family is fast coming to depend upon two income earners: the husband is a blue-collar machine operative in the subordinate primary market, while the wife works as a clerical or operative herself, either in the subordinate primary market or (more likely) in the secondary market.[13] Their combined income is what decisively lifts them out of poverty status, and especially for younger families, the loss of either job threatens to move them back to the margin of poverty.

Unionization constitutes the third great change in the move from the nineteenth-century industrial proletariat to the Fraction II of today. Most industrial workers before the 1930s had few job protections; employed as casual labor, they experienced conditions much like secondary workers today. Unionization, however, brought the establishment of seniority protections, pensions, internal job bidding, and other job rights, that is, precisely those characteristics that changed the employment pattern to subordinate primary.

Thus, the traditional proletariat has come to form the second distinct fraction of the working class. It has attained a relatively high standard of living because of high and (with seniority) rising wages for unionized males and because of most families' reliance on having two income earners. In boom times such as the 1960s, the job security and good wages, combined with the routinized, machine-paced nature of subordinate primary work, tend to lead to increasing conflict on the shop or office floor, as workers seek relief from degraded work. In hard times like the 1970s, the precariousness of Fraction II's prosperity reasserts itself, and blue-collar families must again battle the dangers of unemployment and inflation. Uncertain and eroding real income again becomes a central concern.

Fraction III: The Middle Layers

Independent primary work supplies the jobs of the middle layers of employment, those workers who stand between all lower-level administrative and production workers, on the one side, and capitalists and the various echelons of high management, on the other. This group includes craft workers, technical and professional employees, and supervisors and middle-level administrative staff; public-sector employment constitutes a significant share.

Fraction III tends to be the preserve of white males. More than 70 percent of all independent primary workers are white males, and among craft workers (87 percent white males) and supervisory workers (79 percent white males), women and nonwhites are excluded almost altogether. Blacks hold less than 7 percent of these jobs; the only large instrusion into this segment has been achieved by white women in professional and technical jobs such as teaching, social work, and nursing. White males in independent primary jobs account for 48 percent of all white male workers.[14]

Wages tend to be considerably higher among independent primary workers than among workers in the other two market segments, and higher incomes undoubtedly help create the many notable differences in life style. Fewer wives of independent primary males work, although, as for other segments, the proportion is rapidly rising; and more Fraction III families live either in the suburban rings around major cities or, when in the city, in neighborhoods isolated from the poor.[15]

Fraction III thus gives rise to the "new middle class" that has appeared during the last three decades or so. This group has replenished the badly depleted ranks of the old middle class and has usually been interpreted as simply its extension. But as several have observed, the new middle class is unlike the old in some fundamental respects. The old middle class (or petty bourgeoisie) achieved its position by remaining outside the accumulation process, that is, outside the relations of employment between capitalists and workers; shopkeepers, tradesmen, petty commodity producers, independent professionals, and other middle-class elements retained their autonomy, some even rising to the status of small-scale employers. But today's middle-layer workers have been transformed into employees (even if privileged ones) of capital, made crucial to continued accumulation given the present organization of industry, and hence they were brought within the relations of employment as workers. The typical Fraction III worker can continue to dream of being "one's own boss," but the real basis for any significant numbers of them being able to achieve that dream has evaporated.

The contrast between old and new could hardly be greater. Where the members of the old middle class were necessarily risk-takers, attempting to calculate the possible returns of one course of action versus those of another, middle-layer workers today find employment within large institutions, experiencing risk-taking as a corporate (not an individual) phenomenon, and seeing the gains and losses from risk accrue to the organization, not to the individual. Where the old middle class always confronted the prospect of ruin and dreamed of the chance of big success, middle-layer workers today face a range of possibilities limited downward by the employment guarantees of independent primary employment and upward by the inherent constraints of working for someone else's profit. Where the old middle class had command over its immediate conditions of work (often, as J. K. Galbraith has noted, choosing to exploit itself through exceptionally long hours), today's Fraction III work is organized and governed by the highly structured apparatus of bureaucratic control. Where members of the old middle class were constantly making decisions based on their own interests, middle-layer workers today are perpetually applying preestablished rules or other work criteria. The old middle-class situation produced the shrewd, petty, calculating, opportunistic, independent-minded, politically conservative but personally bold small entrepreneur, but today's Fraction III employment produces the organization person. As we saw in a previous chapter, the outstanding characteristics reinforced in bureaucratic employment are rules orientation, habits of predictability and dependability, and internalization of the enterprise's goals and values.

For middle-layer workers today, then, the loss of control over the labor process has been as complete as for other fractions of the working class. The new control imposed upon Fraction III workers takes a different form from that imposed on other workers, and Fraction III workers superficially have more autonomy. But their situation fails the test of true autonomy, since such workers cannot decide anything about either the product of their work or their labor process; control over these fundamentals passed out of their hands when they became wage (or salary) workers. Instead, bureaucratic methods foster indirect control or "self-control," for they function in the interest not of the worker but of his or her employer.

Thus the middle layers of employment have come to constitute the third fraction of the working class. Relatively high wages, secure employment, and a low rate of unemployment make the issue of survival less crucial, although in the 1970s this concern has become less remote than before. Specific groups have been threatened by depression in the stock brokerage business, the cancellation of military contracts (such as that for the B-1 bomber), and the decline in school enrollments, and all groups have been made more nervous by the deep recession starting in 1974. Despite these occasional reminders of their lack of independence, the concerns of Fraction III workers focus instead on inflation and taxes—threats to affluence developing from outside the workers' own employment situations.

The Continuing Divisions of Race and Sex

Writing in *The Communist Manifesto,* Marx and Engels thought that the logic of capitalist accumulation would lead to the progressive erosion of all precapitalist distinctions among workers. Milton Friedman, in numerous forums with titles such as "Capitalism: The Cure to Racism," has propounded a similar thesis. Yet anyone familiar with the recent history of the American working class can but acknowledge the continuing reality of racial and sexual divisions.

How are we to account for such divisions? In part, of course, our analysis already provides an explanation for the positions of these groups. Blacks, Hispanics, and women entered the wage-labor force during the regime of monopoly capitalism. In contrast to nineteenth-century immigrants, who were pushed into direct competition with native white workers and often served as the unskilled phalanx that smashed the skills of native whites, the later groups entered during a period when developmental forces were pushing toward a segmented, rather than a homogeneous, workforce. They moved into secondary jobs because direct discrimination at the time of hiring prevented them from obtaining primary-market jobs. In addition, discrimination in schooling and other preemployment institutions further hindered their efforts to obtain entry to better jobs. As these and other forces produced segmented markets, segmented markets in turn tended to reproduce discrimination. Thus, blacks, Hispanics, and women are disadvantaged because they are crowded into the secondary-labor market. In this way, our analysis of market segmentation already accounts for part of the racial and sexual differences in income, unemployment, and other labor market outcomes.

Yet just as market segmentation partly explains racial and sexual divisions, so does it fail to explain them fully. Blacks and other minorities and women come to constitute yet further fractions of the working class, because racial and sexual relations continue to develop according to distinct processes of development or "separate dialectics." These various groups face very different circumstances, of course, and for most purposes to consider them together is misleading. They do, however, share the characteristic of having separate dialectics. Whereas the first set of fractions—the market-segment fractions—were derived from an analysis concerned solely with the capitalist accumulation process, such a procedure cannot be followed for blacks and females. The histories of racism and sexism, intimately linked though they are to that of capitalism, are not subsets of the latter. Accordingly, the dynamics of racial and sexual divisions require separate analyses.[16]

Such analyses will not be attempted here, but it is useful to outline four main consequences of the continuing divisions of race and sex for the division of the working class. First, racial and sexual divisions overlap but also transcend market segments, as is evident from the facts that discrimination occurs *within* each segment and that not all racial or sexual differences are reducible to segment differences.[17] In analysis of labor markets, then, the dimensions of race and sex are neither identical with nor othogonal to the market segments; they represent cross-cutting lines of division. In understanding the divisions within the working class, this point can be translated to mean that secondary- and primary-market blacks share real interests, as do secondary- and primary-market females. Racism and sexism themselves, and not just the inferior position of blacks and women in the labor force, become real material forces in society.

Second, continuing discrimination results in a surplus labor force whose chief characteristic is its employment at low wages. This point might seem obvious, but it is often confused.[18] Employers are concerned not only with low wages but also with high productivity; that is, they are concerned with low *unit costs*, which are not identical to low wages. From the increasingly homogeneous labor force of the nineteenth century, two different types of segmentations arose. One, the emergence of the primary workforces, resulted from the capitalists' compromise of paying higher wages, providing employment guarantees, and so on, in order to achieve higher productivity; that is, lower unit costs were to be achieved through a reorganization of work in which increased wages would be more than offset by increased productivity. In the subordinate primary market, as we have seen, this compromise was forced upon capitalists by unions; in the independent primary market, employers sought to forestall unions by introducing the reorganization on their own terms.

The other type of segmentation involved blacks and women, and its result was lower, not higher, wages. Discrimination was not forced upon employers; in contrast, the lack of any effective bargaining strength among blacks and women made discrimination possible. As blacks were driven out of southern agriculture and women left housework, racism and sexism prevented them from being able to enter the wage-labor force on equal terms with white males. Their increasing numbers relative to the jobs open to them necessarily implied low wages and, especially for blacks, high unemployment. The consequence is what has been labeled "superexploitation."

Third, race and sex provide the most visible and most powerful differences for employers to play upon in creating divisions among their workers. Race and sex are powerful dividers, no doubt, precisely because employers can call upon the separate dialectics associated with each; that is, racism and sexism blur the distinctions between employer and employees and introduce different lines of identification. Historically, race has been interjected during crisis periods, whereas sex has served as a more long-run divisive force. Black strike-breakers, for example, have frequently been imported by employers to stir racial hatred and undermine strike solidarity. Female labor, on the other hand, provided the basis for the separation (though "feminization") of clerical work from the mass blue-collar occupations.[19] Together, employers' manipulations of race and sex divisions have proved to be a powerful weapon for creating working-class disunity.

The impact of such divisions can be seen clearly in Michael Reich's work on racism. Reich reasoned that the impact of racism on black workers was relatively unambiguous (black workers lose), but that the effect on white workers was less clear. He therefore directed his attention to the distribution of income among whites and attempted to measure how racism influenced this distribution. His finding: greater racism means greater inequality among whites. The most straightforward way of interpreting this result is that racism strengthens employers (most of whom are white), divides the working class, and thereby weakens the ability of white (and black) workers to obtain higher wages.[20]

Finally the impressive and growing research on the roles of women and blacks in capitalist society suggests one central conclusion: change in their situations has occurred mostly in response to the interaction of the dialectics of race and sex with that of capitalist development. Heidi Hartmann, for example, has shown that women's work in the home has been considerably altered by the penetration of commodities into the traditional family realm. Both household appliances and purchased goods previously produced at home changed the mix of household tasks that women performed, and to a certain extent the introduction of these commodities left women with more time and fewer responsibilities crucial to the family's survival. Yet the particular form that the changes took is not easily explained. Appeals to technology seem inadequate. "Labor-saving" appliances, for example, turn out to require as much time as hand methods. Appeals to capitalist competition as such are not persuasive either. In the case of laundry, which Hartmann studies in detail, capitalist-sector production in power laundries provided laundry service as cheaply or more cheaply than did home laundry service; yet in this case household production triumphed over market production. Moreover, when extra time did become available to women, rather than using it for leisure or for wage-labor, they tended to raise their standards; nutrition, stimulative childcare, and hygiene replaced cooking, taking care of children, and cleaning. Hartmann suggests that the changes in women's work in the home can only be explained by a complicated interaction between capitalist production and what she and others have called the "patriarchal family system." Corollary examples for blacks and racism could be adduced as well. But the general point is that for both blacks and women, the separate dialectics of race and sex condition their participation in the capitalist economy.[21]

Blacks and women, then, came to constitute further fractions of the working class. For blacks, slavery, sharecropping, expulsion from the rural South, continuing discrimination, and residence in Harlem, Watts, the South Side, and other ghettoes—that is, the historical legacy and everyday manifestations of racism—shape a separate consciousness. For women, the double workload of wife-mother and worker, the demands and dangers of sexual objectification (from harassment to rape), the special responsibilities for children, the conflict between competence at home and ambition at work—in short, the consequences of sexism—also shape a separate consciousness. For members of both groups, their daily existence as workers is always conditioned by their special status.

The rise of technical and bureaucratic control inside the core corporations altered the way in which core firms recruit, direct, evaluate, motivate, and discipline their workforces. These two forms of control, and the residual simple control in firms of the competitive periphery, all give rise to distinct labor market processes; indeed, when combined with the economic manifestations of racism and sexism, these forces have led historically to the segmentation of labor markets. The institutionalization of these various forces in the operation of segmented labor markets has in turn created the material basis for enduring divisions or fractions within the working class. This process has created, as distinct elements, the working poor, the traditional proletariat, and the middle layers. Enduring divisions by race and sex create further and overlapping fractions of black workers and female workers. Each of these groups remains subject to the yoke of capitalist employment, yet each also experiences that employment under different concrete conditions. Since these differences have been institutionalized in the economic structure of society, and more fundamentally since they serve the needs of capital accumulation, they persist.

Thus goes the analysis. It has focused on the job structures underlying the various working-class fractions, yet it should be clear that such a narrow perspective can provide only the starting point for understanding each fraction's *social* existence. Without this preliminary analysis, we cannot reject false theories nor properly begin the construction of better ones. But in order to move beyond a description of class fractions to probe their dynamics, we must broaden our scope.

People do not act only or even mostly in response to their immediate economic situation; instead, their actions are always filtered by their perceptions of the world, perceptions of what is real and what is possible. At each step in the logic of these last two chapters—from distinct systems of control in the labor process to segmented markets, and from segmented markets to class fractions—other forces than those deriving from the organization of the workplace come into play. In the first step, these other forces range from unionization to the cultural legacy legitimizing racial and sexual discrimination to employers' conscious attempts to fragment their workforces to class forces in schooling and family structure to the constraints of technology. In the second step, among the forces that enter into play are the patterns of ethnic residence and culture and the impacts of popular media, ideology, and political participation. As the diversity of these influences emphasizes, the analysis of this chapter can only suggest an avenue whereby the labor process makes itself felt in redividing the working class; it cannot be the entire explanation.

Indeed, to comprehend the making of the American working class we must go far beyond the labor process to understand the total experience of American workers. Only a few years ago such a task seemed hopeless, yet today some impressive strides in this direction have already been taken. For example, Samuel Bowles and Herbert Gintis have studied the ways in which schooling helps both to reproduce class structures and to give rise to contradictions that challenge class society. Less self-conscious studies by Mira Komarovsky, Melvin Kohn, and others enrich the insights of Bowles and Gintis by extending the analysis to child rearing and home life. Studies of life at work by Katherine Stone, Studs Terkel, Barbara Garson, Ann Bookman, and others extend this concern to the culture of the workplace. Work by David Montgomery, Herbert Gutman, Alice and Staughton Lynd, Jeremy Brecher, and other historians of the American working class begin to provide a usable past, so long denied by the lack of a Marxist historical tradition. Michael Piore has attempted to link the economics of class fractions with wider sociological evidence, and Stanley Aronowitz has provided a highly ambitious (even if less than completely successful) synthesis of all these aspects of working-class life.[22] This work and that of others promise much for understanding—and changing—our society.

Finally, it should be noted that while this chapter has focused on class divisions, class unities exist as well. The stagnation of the 1970s—still a largely unanalyzed phenomenon—provides one reminder of these unities. The continuing irrationality of capitalist production provides another. Still a third is taken up in the next chapter: the struggle for democracy.

CHAPTER 11

Capitalism or Democracy? The Contradictions of Modern Control

THE RISE of structural control has both strengthened capitalist rule and laid the basis for a more fundamental challenge to it. For capitalists, structural control turned the conflict within the firm decisively in their favor and contributed to those forces that have divided the working class. But it has also tended to shift conflict to the political (state policy) arena, and there it has generated new forms of struggle. The chief result of this politicization of the class dynamic has been a growing tension between capitalist economy and democratic government. The tension explains important aspects of recent American political history, and understanding it is essential for rebuilding the workers' movement.

Since the 1930s or 1948 at the latest, the American working class has failed to mount a serious challenge for political power; but on the eve of World War II, workers appeared poised to play a central role in American politics. Armed insurrection, whose necessity so frequently monopolized left-wing conceptions of revolution, was never a serious possibility, but growing class consciousness did appear ready to transform "interest-group" politics into a politics of class confrontation. It seemed likely that the dominant issues would be defined along class dimensions—as has happened in Italy and France in recent years and to a lesser extent (but for a longer time) in Great Britain.

The period from the mass upsurge in the 1870s to the sit-downs of the late 1930s had been years of turbulent industrial conflict, and by the end of the thirties class-conscious activists had achieved one of their most long-sought goals: the mass organization of basic manufacturing workers into industrial unions. The labor movement in general had matured, leaving behind the nostalgic schemes for "workingmen's cooperation" that had been so popular in the nineteenth century, and instead focusing on methods of reforming and revolutionizing industrial employment. Compared to earlier decades, ethnic rivalries had greatly declined, especially as the use of English became more widespread among immigrants and their children. For the first time both black workers and female workers were included in the mainline labor organizations. Divisions within the working class were waning, organizations that were potentially class-wide were on the rise. There was a growing class consciousness among American workers, even if that growth was torturously slow and often detoured.

On a more explicitly political level, the Communist Party played a central role in the labor movement, and it had gained a considerable following in the universities, the artistic community, and the media. By postwar standards the party was big—with perhaps sixty thousand to one hundred thousand members—and the devotion and discipline of its people, combined with widespread popular sympathy for its everyday struggles for workers and farmers, ensured that its political influence extended far beyond its membership. The non-Communist left also displayed considerable vitality. Norman Thomas' Socialists attracted a wide audience; Upton Sinclair, a major leftist figure, captured the 1934 California democratic gubernatorial nomination; and in Minnesota the Farmer-Labor Party eclipsed the Democrats. The left even played a growing role in the traditional two-party system; as Roosevelt's 1936 campaign dependence indicated, organized labor was the centerpiece of the New Deal coalition in the mid-1930s. The Democratic Party appeared ready to be transformed into the (electoral) party of the working class. And the working class appeared ready to be a serious contender for power in the state.

That potential was never realized, of course, and in the postwar period the American working class has not mounted any serious challenge to capitalist rule. The working class today lacks political leadership, having no political party to represent its interests. In the absence of such a party, the unions represent the only pretenders to working class-wide organization. But nothing is more dismal than the state of the union movement. Most unions have ceased to press for reforms that would be in the general interests of workers. Instead, the labor hierarchies lobby for the particular interests of workers in their own industries. Their orientation to this more narrow constituency was evident in their long support of the Vietnam War, their lack of interest in organizing the unorganized, their opposition to much environmental legislation, and their inability to formulate any economic alternative to continuing high unemployment, high inflation, and erosion of real wages.

The unions' material losses have been as grievous as their ideological ones. Union membership as a proportion of the workforce is in a long slide; the unions have slipped nearly every year, from their peak in 1953 when union members constituted over 25 percent of the total workforce to the present, when they account for less than 20 percent. Even in their traditional manufacturing-sector base, unions have declined from over 50 percent of workers in 1956 to around 45 percent today.[1] As a result of both ideological and membership losses, the electoral power of the union movement, although long overestimated, is now definitely confined to the status of swing bloc in otherwise close elections. So we see the modern American working class, leaderless and without a sense of its own interests or goals.

The left's inability to build a strong movement during the past three decades or so grows out of many factors; yet surely the most fundamental one must be the real disunity of the working class itself. This chapter investigates the consequences for American politics of structural control and the fractionalizing of the working class. The argument can be summarized as two related points. First, while the redivision of the working class has weakened workers sufficiently to prevent conflict based on the open confrontation of classes, it has simultaneously reconstituted politics on a new basis. Conflict rooted in class relations continues in the form of what can be called "pseudo-pluralist" or "class-fraction" politics.

Second, the whole trend of modern capitalist development has tended to make capitalist control over state policy both more essential and more uncertain: more essential, because capital needs the state to direct the accumulation process; more uncertain, because working-class fractions have significant impact on the formulation of state policy. In response, the business community has attempted to restrict democratic forces within government and the political system, in effect continuing to support the form while abandoning the content of modern democratic government.

For the working-class fractions, however, democratic control over the state remains a necessary condition for pursuit of their interests. Split in the sphere of production, the working class is potentially reunited in the political arena around the defense and extension of democracy. Whether socialists can or will develop a program that is both socialist and democratic is uncertain, and whether such a program could chart a successful transition is a further imponderable. But these questions are not trivial; the future of democracy now appears to lie with the working class and with socialism.

The Rise of Class-Fraction Politics

The American working class has failed to assert itself as a class in the way that its long development before World War II seemed to promise. Of course, it cannot be denied that in the postwar period there have been some impressive victories by essentially working class-based groups, notably blacks, women, farmworkers, and public employees. Moreover, the reasons for this decline in class politics are complex, ranging from ideological factors (leadership decimation and public distrust resulting from McCarthyism and anti-communism during the entire postwar period) to the U.S. working class's (relatively) privileged position within the imperialist world system. Yet when all these factors have been accounted for, the essential point remains: over three decades, the organized strength of the working class has steadily eroded. Why?

The analysis in this book suggests an answer. The working class has been unable to challenge capitalist hegemony because it has been split into fractions. Each of these fractions has different immediate interests and has pursued these separate interests in the political arena. The result has been the demise of "class" issues and the rise of "fraction" issues.

We can see how paramount these issues have become by looking at the political priorities of each fraction. Consider, for example, Fraction II, the traditional proletariat. Its interests are now advanced as the special interest of the blue-collar constituency. The fraction is represented in the political arena by the major labor unions, particularly the AFL-CIO, and by the Democratic Party. Yet in the Democratic Party the labor vote is but one element among many that exist in coalition, and party officials allied with organized labor have difficulty obtaining party approval for even the highest labor priorities. Public jobs bills, labor law reform, repeal of the Taft-Hartley Section 14-B, a high minimum wage, national health insurance, common situs picketing, and other demands of organized labor have encountered strong resistance even within the Democratic Party in recent years.

Similarly, organized labor's efforts in the economic sphere have also increasingly assumed the role of fraction-specific pleas. The impact on other workers (and especially on nonunion workers) of a high-wage settlement in any industry has become at least ambiguous, as price increases now follow quickly upon the settlement of most major union contracts.* Other union

* In the strike wave of 1946, the United Auto Workers (UAW) assumed a class perspective in its bargaining: it demanded wage increases with no corresponding (automobile) price

concerns such as guaranteed annual wages, lifetime job security, and extensive pensions also reflect fraction-based interests, since, while all workers would unquestionably desire these benefits, in the present context they are possible only for workers of the monopolized core. Thus, the large labor unions increasingly act for a class fraction rather than for a class-wide constituency.

What is true for organized labor holds even more strongly for the other fractions. The 1960s constituted one of the few times when Fraction I—the working poor—made its presence felt as a coherent political force. The National Welfare Rights Organization, the Southern Christian Leadership Conference, community action, model cities, and local community and ghetto groups, as well as other "poor people's" lobbyists (including big-city mayors, after the urban riots), all pushed for expansion of services to the poor. Their efforts in fact succeeded in obtaining medicaid, public housing and rent subsidies, food stamps, higher welfare benefits, aid to poverty-area schools, and other benefits. Once again, however, the gains were largely addressed to class-fraction, not class-wide, concerns.

The demands of Fraction III can be seen as class-fraction concerns as well. Serious opposition to the Vietnam War appeared when the draft began calling the sons of middle-layer families. So, too, consumer activism, the pressure for expanding public higher education, demands for student power, the environmental movement, and most recently the "taxpayer's revolt" all largely derived from this fraction and expressed concerns most intensely felt by it. In many cases, these issues are inherently general, yet even so the politics have been those of class fraction rather than of class.

Finally, blacks and women have also contributed to fraction-based politics by struggling to end discrimination in hiring, work, and pay, to obtain affirmative action, and to protect their 1960s gains in the harsher times of the 1970s. The special concerns of these groups overlap the interests of other groups (many secondary workers are black and/or female), but an additional dimension is added because of the special status of blacks and women. In addition to work-related issues, black victories in the integration of public accommodations, housing, and schools, for example, and women's struggles to change sex roles in the family, to obtain birth control and abortion rights, and to achieve legal equality through the Equal Rights Amendment (ERA) have tended to focus on areas of working-class life beyond work.

The reality of class fractions has led to the political expression of

---

increases. Had the UAW won and had this model been followed in other industries, employers could not have shifted the burden of higher wages to consumers through inflation, and instead wage gains would have come directly from a declining profit share in national income.

fractional, not class-wide, interests. The point here is not that these fractions have "betrayed" the class cause. Far from it; they have acted upon class-rooted oppression as that oppression has been specifically experienced by each fraction. To expect any other behavior would be utopian, since political behavior is rarely and only irresolutely motivated by altruism. But class politics *has* assumed a new form.

The new form is one in which each working-class fraction presses upon the state its political priorities, and capitalists, from a more entrenched position, do likewise. But the underlying material (class) relations ensure that the interests of each working-class fraction come into conflict primarily with the interests of capitalists, and so the chief adversary of each class fraction is not another fraction within the working class but rather the business community. It is the various employers' groups that largely fund, give leadership to, and lobby for the defeat of any class fraction's demands.

Indeed, the principal combatants in virtually all postwar political battles have been one or more of the working-class fractions arrayed against the business interest. This formulation appears consistent with the bitter domestic conflicts in the late 1940s over the Cold War, the rights of the U.S. Communist Party, and Taft-Hartley. It also fits the 1950s' debates over McCarthyism and domestic economic policy and the 1960s' struggles concerning poverty, consumer issues, the Vietnam War, and (more complexly) the civil rights of blacks. And it holds for the 1970s issues of stagflation, women's rights, concern for the environment, and federal tax reform.[2]

This perspective does not require that no conflicts occur between working-class fractions, and it is possible to point to some that have already taken place. The news media often remind us that blacks and women pushing affirmative action have sometimes been opposed by unions defending seniority rules, that the working poor's demands for more public services have encountered some opposition due to the middle layer's desire for tax relief, that the environmentalists' successes in obtaining pollution restrictions can threaten the traditional proletariat's jobs in polluting plants, and so on. The logical possibility of such conflicts is a necessary corollary of a theory of class fractions, since the fractions have different (and to some extent potentially conflicting) interests. Yet the existence of these conflicts should not steer us away from the main point: most political battles have been fought *across* class lines, and these struggles have involved the most bitter and enduring political opponents.

Let us consider more closely the proposition that each fraction's chief adversary is the capitalist class, rather than other fractions in the working class. For Fraction I, for example, the principal barriers to expansion of social services—which, alongside jobs, is the most frequent articulated demand of the working poor—appear to be threefold. First, for all social services financed by state and local taxes, the competition among the states and cities for capitalist investment places a limit on social spending; New York City, Massachusetts, and other jurisdictions where benefits are high have allegedly taxed themselves out of employers' favor, and spending limits are needed to restore a "positive business climate." This factor also operates to some extent on the national level, where the threat of runaway shops is frequently invoked to curtail social spending. Second, expanded social services frequently compete directly with services provided by capitalists. Third, and perhaps most fundamentally, employers resist expanded social services because they fear that such services will interfere with the work ethic and with the position of the poor as a reserve army of potential workers. The widespread attention given to welfare fraud and to denying benefits to able-bodied, working-age adults; the concern over whether unemployment compensation makes the jobless too "choosy"; and the fierce hostility to having the government act as employer of last resort all testify to the real constraints facing the working poor. When the working poor operate in the political arena to struggle for their survival, they confront capitalists, not other workers.[3]

Fraction II, in pursuing its interests, also struggles primarily against employers. The traditional proletariat's chief struggles in recent years have been aimed at maintaining real wages, protecting jobs, eliminating occupational hazards, obtaining guaranteed annual wages, and improving medical benefits and pensions. In all of these cases, Fraction II demands spending that may directly impinge on corporate profits. Its immediate adversary, firm by firm and industry by industry, has been its employers; moreover, at the national level its efforts to achieve a full-employment policy, pension reform, organizing rights, national health insurance, and strict job-safety enforcement have all been opposed chiefly by capitalist groups such as the Business Roundtable, the Chamber of Commerce, and special ad hoc business lobbying groups.

Even for Fraction III, the chief opponent to expressed political priorities has been the business community. When students and their middle-layer parents demanded an end to the Vietnam War, opposition to their demand came from several sectors of society, yet business approval remained critical for the Nixon-Kissinger policy. Consumer regulations directly reduce corporate profitability. Environmental laws have necessitated large so-called unproductive (nonprofit-producing) investments. Even the drive to "reform" the federal tax code so as to reduce the tax burden on middle-income families follows directly from the declining role of the corporate profits tax in financing the federal government, combined with the proliferation of business-sponsored deductions and other loopholes. On social spending, Fraction III is split, since social services require tax revenues but also provide large numbers of jobs to middle-layer workers.

Finally, it is mostly (though not completely) true for blacks and women that their principal adversary has also been business. In the civil rights struggle and in attempts to desegregate unions and schools, blacks fought not just business uses of racism but also the manifestations of pervasive racism in all segments of society. Similarly, the feminist attack on male chauvinism (for example, the demand for abortion rights) has perforce been focused on more than sexism in the service of profits. In these ways, the separate dialectics of race and sex make no simple argument possible.[4] Yet in most of the battles, especially in the struggles for equal pay for equal work, an end to racial and sexual stereotyping of jobs, elimination of discrimination in promotion policies, and affirmative action and restitution for past discrimination, blacks and women have attempted to limit the prerogatives of management and end superexploitation. The next phase of antidiscrimination enforcement is likely to be the development of standards of comparative worth, by which to judge whether employers are illegally discriminating in the pay awarded for *unequal* or *dissimilar* jobs; in this, disadvantaged groups will directly infringe upon the employer's right to set wage rates. Moreover, the increasingly desperate plight for unemployed youth in black urban ghettoes has forced blacks into intensifying conflict with the business lobbies in state capitals and Washington over public job bills. The political program of blacks and women is thus clearly countered by business opposition.

Superficially, postwar politics appear to conform to the "pluralist" model, but in fact this is not so.* The pluralist vision relies on the absence of any single social cleavage, thereby establishing the political process as a continually changing and cross-cutting set of coalitions and interest groups. But the old special-interest politics was based on a diversity of social groups inherent in a society with several competing modes of production. Not only

* "Pluralism" is the dominant (capitalist) theory of the state that identifies the brokering and politicking of special-interest groups as the principal political process of western democracies. These groups are seen as having cross-cutting and overlapping memberships such that policy outcomes reflect a constantly shifting set of coalitions. While groups are not necessarily equal in terms of power, no particular group is dominant; democratic government becomes the arena in which coalitions are formed, and politicians perform the social function of creating (electoral) coalitions in their attempts to achieve public office. Governments in power must respond to the diverse pressures (through lobbying, threats to form rival coalitions, appeals to "public opinion") of such coalitions. Democracy thus reflects the interest of society at large, as those interests are articulated by the special-interest groups, and the state is neutral, standing outside or "above" the class relations.

capitalists and workers but farmers, shopkeepers, landowners, self-employed tradesmen, independent craftworkers, and others represented significant constituencies within the polity. The triumph of capitalism has largely eliminated the political importance of these groups, leaving a society increasingly dominated by two classes: capitalists (the business community) and workers, the latter having become an overwhelming majority of the labor force.[5] So the real basis for pluralist politics has been destroyed, and class increasingly creates a single social cleavage.

The reason why class fractions create "pseudo-pluralist" rather than real pluralist politics—that is, why independent struggles by less-than-working-class-wide groups do not conform to the pluralist model—is quite simple. Despite the disunity of the working class, the central dialectic in the political arena remains the clash of class interests, not the conflict of special group interests. Instead of the shifting alliances and cross-cutting groups posited by pluralist theory, the old class lines of cleavage continue to exert their force, only now they do so within the context of class fraction politics.

Thus, within the regime of monopoly capitalism, class conflict continues, and there is mounting evidence that class-fraction politics do indeed impose real costs on capital. The working class has been able to shift much of the distributional conflict from the marketplace to the state arena, and there it has been successful in raising its share. There has, for instance, been a steady decline in the portion of personal income going to propertyholders—from 29 percent in 1949, to 23 percent in 1969, to 19 percent in 1976. Through the 1950s and 1960s, the wage share rose; but in the 1970s, when the wage share fell, the gap was taken up not by profits but rather by government transfer payments (unemployment benefits and social security). Taxes, transfers, and governmental expenditures have on balance diminished income inequality during the postwar period; moreover, the trend appears to be strongly in the direction of an increasingly large redistributive effect.[6] Perhaps most important of all is the ability of the working class to place real limits on what constitutes a politically feasible macroeconomic policy, that is, on how much unemployment and how long high unemployment will be endured as an anti-inflation measure.

None of these working-class victories is unmitigated. Political pressure to reduce the high 1970s unemployment surely meant that fewer workers lost their jobs in the war on inflation; it also meant, however, continuing stagflation. Again, while workers' bargaining during the 1960s effectively reduced the profit rate, the crisis of the 1970s revealed the inherent power that remains with capitalists as a result of their control over investment. These cases show the *systemic* limits on the workers' power. Nonetheless, the gains of working-class fractions have indeed come at some significant cost to capital, and these gains are likely to intensify the contradictions within capitalism.

Fractionalizing the working class has not recreated pluralist politics; instead, the form of class politics has changed. In the post-1945 period, working-class fractions have struggled for their separate interests against the capitalist class. The absence of a working-class party has prevented the conjoining of all fractions' demands into a class agenda, and the divisions among workers have opened great possibilities for capitalists to play one fraction off against another.[7] Nonetheless, the underlying material conflict—between capitalists and all workers—continues to assert itself.

The Capitalists Abandon Democracy*

In the United States, capitalism and political democracy have developed together. Their symbiosis is by no means a necessary relationship, as the many capitalist and undemocratic regimes in the world remind us. Even in the democratic countries, the capitalist class's virtual monopoly on political resources has ensured that democratic rule is consistent with bourgeois hegemony. Capitalism's credit for fostering democratic rule is further qualified by the observation that the "lower orders" of society, in seeking to advance their position, have constituted the chief force pressing for the extension of democracy. In the United States, for example, nonpropertyholders, blacks, and women extended the franchise because they struggled for their own rights. Nonetheless, one cannot avoid the conclusion. The United States and the other nations that have sustained democratic rule (however imperfect) have been capitalist societies. In addition to the accumulated wealth that Marx saw as an essential prerequisite to socialism, capitalism has thus bequeathed us a second valuable legacy: democratic political traditions.

The central problem for our time is whether this relationship will continue. The historical association between capitalism and democracy cannot be presumed to persist automatically, any more than we can expect capitalism's future to be like its past. Indeed, the real question now is whether the marriage between capitalism and political democracy was made in

* This argument is based on joint work with Michael Reich; see Richard Edwards and Michael Reich (1978).

heaven and will therefore be eternal, or whether it is merely a marriage of convenience to be soon discarded. Capitalist ideology asserts that it is the former; twentieth-century political history (and even more, the events of the postwar period) suggest that the latter is true.

Throughout U.S. history and especially in this century, the relationship between capitalist economy and democratic government has been altered by two unfolding processes. One is the capitalists' increasing dependence upon the state to regulate, direct, and stimulate the economy. The other is the changing composition of the electorate, as the population becomes more dominated by the working class and suffrage has been won by women and blacks. The result is that while control over the state has become more essential for capitalists, it has also become more uncertain, and the further development of capitalism throws the future of democracy in doubt.

The first process of change is the growing economic role of government. In some cases capitalists have been forced to accept state intervention, in other cases they have independently sought it, but in all cases the state has been needed to resolve the contradictions of monopoly capitalism. In the transition to the new regime, anticorporate forces demanded regulation of the trusts, while corporate capitalists saw in regulation the possible means to police shared monopoly. During World War I, businessmen obtained first-hand knowledge of the largesse available through large-scale government planning. In the 1930s, labor turned to the state to recognize and enforce its right to organize, while capitalists (not without some internal opposition) began to rely on the state to stimulate and maintain the macroeconomy. In the postwar years, these groups have pushed upon the state responsibility for educating and training the labor force, providing subsidies to specific industries, supporting research and development, monitoring workplace health and safety, financing the basic social insurance schemes, and arbitrating the bargaining disputes between capital and labor. In addition, the state collects an increasing proportion of national income through taxes and provides an increasing percentage of final demand through military contracts, social service spending, and so forth. Finally, a substantial portion of the total wage bill takes the form of a social wage, distributed as income and benefits paid by the state. In all these ways, the accumulation process has become increasingly politicized and the prospects for successful accumulation increasingly depend on state policies.[8]

At the same time, the character of the democratic electorate has been changing. For one thing, the old middle classes—small-propertied groups like petty employers, self-employed persons, farmers, merchants, and independent craftsmen and tradesmen, who used to encompass a significant population and count even more heavily in political matters—have disappeared; at the turn of the century such groups represented about 30 percent of the labor force, but today they account for less than 10 percent. Correspondingly, there has been a steady expansion of the working class, from roughly 60 percent in 1900, to 75 percent in 1950, to 85 percent in 1975.[9] Equally important, excluded groups have won the vote; property restrictions for voting have been eliminated, and women and blacks have successfully struggled to achieve the franchise. These new groups share one characteristic; almost uniformly they are wage or salary workers, and they do not own property that contributes critically to their way of earning a living. Thus the electorate has increasingly come to reflect the growing working-class majority in society.

These developments have brought the forces for capitalism and those for democracy into long-run conflict, and the conflict has been particularly intensified by the dynamics of class-fraction politics. By diverting working-class struggles from the economic sphere and increasingly focusing them in the state arena, the new form of politics makes control of government policy crucial. As the working poor achieve better social service benefits, an additional "social drag" on profits is imposed and the reserve army support for workplace discipline is weakened. As the traditional proletariat demands greater job security, better pensions, medical benefits, and occupational health and safety measures, employers lose prerogatives and possibilities for profit. As the middle layers demand consumer and environmental protection, they impose further costs on capitalists' operations. As blacks and women achieve antidiscrimination and affirmative action rights, they reduce employers' ability to divide and rule their labor forces. All this imposes increasingly severe strains and constraints on the profitability of capitalists' investment.

For capitalists, controlling the state has become both more essential and more precarious. It is understandable, then, that they should search for ways to restrict the democratic content of politics. They have not been unsuccessful; the central lesson of recent U.S. political history is that, as suffrage has been extended, the impact of elections on state policy has been reduced. Elected and democratically accountable government institutions have, in real power terms, been weakened throughout this century. The basic process at work here is the substitution of administrative power for power derived from the electorate. As a result, party politics, citizen voting, and the entire electoral process have come to have less and less effect on government policy.

In part, this shift is reflected in the dramatic decline of the Congress as a real governing body; even internally, with its committee system based on seniority, the Congress insulates itself from popular will. The shift is also seen in the rapidly growing power of the bureaucracies, public authorities, regulatory bodies, permanent commissions, courts, "expert" or "professional" bodies, and so on. As the Federal Reserve Board, National Security Council, and the various great federal departments impose their will, they erode democratic power by replacing it with administrative power. Choices are removed from the political sphere, where they can be seen as products of clashing material interests, and instead are placed in the hands of administrators and technocrats, who can make decisions on the basis of technical or administrative criteria. The distinction is apparent even in their manner of selection: the Congress is popularly elected, of course, while the bureaucracy and court positions are appointive. Moreover, while officials in popularly accountable bodies tend to serve fairly short terms (two, four, or six years), the nonaccountable agencies are run by officials enjoying, as an additional protection from popular will, extremely long terms (five, seven, or ten years, or even life).

The shift to administrative power also grows out of the expansion of executive power. Although the president is elected, executive power has been increasingly institutionalized and insulated from popular influence. There have been several significant steps on this path in the twentieth century, including the Executive Branch's capture of the process of drafting legislation, its creation and expansion of the Executive Offices, and the establishment of the national security apparatus. These changes called for experts and bureaucrats to be in charge, with little or no provision for popular participation or accountability.

As with the federal government, so in state and local governments power and decision making have been transferred out of popularly accountable institutions (legislatures, city councils, town meetings) and into other institutions that retain only the most formal ties to democratic content. State bureaucracies, special bodies such as the New York Port Authority, regulatory and licensing commissions, and social welfare bureaucracies have become the antidemocratic form of modern state government.

In these developments we see the *substance* of democratic government being gutted, while the *form* is maintained. It is as though capitalists have applied to the state the lessons they learned in the workplace: institutionalized authority replaces more direct—and more directly challenged—rule. Until recently, one needed to infer this strategy from persuasive but nonetheless indirect evidence. However, the Trilateral Commission—that Rockefeller-financed international citizens' group claiming Jimmy Carter and Walter Mondale among its members—finally stated the obvious. In its report, *The Crisis of Democracy*, it warned of the social dangers deriving from what it perceived to be a growing "excess" of democracy. Too much democracy does not serve capital.[10]

Except in a political crisis, the danger to democracy comes not from the coup, then, but from the incessant pressure to make democratic rule more modern, more efficient, more based on professional expertise, that is, more insulated from the demands of the working-class majority. Capitalists here, like "capitalist-roaders" in China, seek to put expertise instead of politics in command.

This analysis is no lament for some golden age of democracy; nineteenth-century democracy's great failure, aside from excluding blacks and women and others, was that it was restricted to a narrowly defined political sphere. Rather, the analysis challenges the mindless assertion that as capitalism develops, so does democracy. The marriage may have been over for some time, even though we, its children, are the last to know of it.

Socialists in Defense of Democracy?

If capitalism and democracy have increasingly come into conflict, the best hope for democracy's survival appears to lie with socialism. But will (or can) the working class and socialists defend and extend democracy?

This question admits of no easy answer. For one thing, the American working class does not share a commitment to socialism. Decades of anticommunist propaganda and mistakes made by socialists have taken their toll, and explicitly socialist parties enjoy little support. Yet, while the name remains anathema, the social programs put forward by progressive groups enjoy considerable support. Moreover, there has been a growing interest among workers, especially those in "rank-and-file" movements, in self-consciously socialist politics.

More directly relevant to the question is the fact that the so-called socialist countries have made little progress toward installing real democracy. And in the West, the left as a whole carries a terrible burden of antidemocratic theory and practice, deriving from the twin disillusionments of the Second International and contemporary Social Democratic parties. This collective past creates a presumptive and almost reflexlike bias against the "sham" of bourgeois democracy; more, it tends to give rise to a devaluation of the merits of democracy itself.

The problem is still more serious. No left party has constructed a satisfactory transition strategy that both defends (and utilizes) democratic government *and* provides for a transition to socialism. The difficulty is plain: as soon as a socialist party or coalition of parties nears power, a disastrous decline in "business confidence" sets in. Capitalists, who during the period when socialists are building an electoral majority still control investments, naturally stop investing, fearing expropriation. The fall-off in investment creates economic chaos, as foreign exchange reserves plummet, unemployment rises, inflation spurts up, capital flees, and hoarding begins. Socialist electoral victories thus tend to generate economic crisis, and as socialists succeed in the democratic arena, they are foiled by the capitalists' continuing economic power. Socialists then are confronted with an impossible choice: either back off from taking power or reassure capitalists that the socialist victory will not harm capital. In either event, the continuing extrademocratic power of capitalists defeats the democratic transition strategy.

These problems of history and strategy do not provide an auspicious background for the linking of socialism and democracy. Yet just as the relation between capitalism and democracy is undergoing change, so is the relation between socialists' program and democracy being revised. Most socialists acknowledge that previous formulations of strategy have failed to create revolution (or even strong revolutionary movements) anywhere in the advanced capitalist world, and increasing numbers see that their failure stems directly from the failure to take democracy seriously. So we find that in the most recent period, considerable progress has been made in reunifying the vision of industrial and political democracy. The commitment by the Western European Communist Parties—French, Italian, Spanish, and others—to a democratic program means that theoretical ideas will achieve their most severe and appropriate testing in the real practice of attempting a democratic transition. In the United States, a commitment to democracy by at least a significant share of the American left opens the way for new theory and practice here. The determination of these groups to find a program that is both democratic and thoroughly socialist promises much.

By such efforts, both the meaning and scope of democracy are being redefined, so the struggle involves extending democracy as well as retaining current democratic processes. The new programs declare that democracy must incorporate more than the choice of leaders through quadrennial or even biennial voting. Elections are not unimportant, but the content as well as the form of the political process must be democratized to expand popular participation; that is, to increase the extent to which decision-making processes allow for and encourage widespread discussion of issues, mobilizing of support, and expression of interests. From this perspective, democratic politics becomes not merely a device for recording preferences but also an organic process in which people can discuss and *formulate* their own attitudes and priorities. So too, the government must be more immediately responsible, to ensure that state policy is kept in line with the expressed real interests of the citizenry. More, democratic decision making must be extended to the range of social decisions currently beyond the reach of democratic rule, particularly those of economic and social life. Wide participation and close accountability would seem to require decentralization wherever possible.

Whether this ambitious agenda can be accomplished remains uncertain, but there are at least some strong reasons to hope. Most importantly, the renewed interest in democracy among socialists rests not just on the ideas of socialists; instead, it builds upon more powerful forces operating in society. In particular, the division of the working class into class fractions and the shifting of class conflict into the political sphere imply two corollaries. First, there can be no immediate economic or social demands that unify the entire class; rather, a common program would necessarily incorporate a variety of such demands, each appropriate to the specific circumstances of one or other of the fractions. Second, just as the class is divided in the sphere of production, so the defense and extension of democracy potentially reunites the class in the political sphere; after all, the interests of all the fractions, as the overwhelming majority in society, can only be safeguarded in a system where majority rule is realized. The defense and extension of democracy thus becomes a *class* demand, and the taking up of this demand by socialists offers an avenue for reuniting the working class.

Interest in democracy is already evident in the struggle to democratize the large unions. Rank-and-file groups have waged courageous campaigns to open up the Steelworkers Union, to reclaim the Teamsters, to institute local initiative in the United Mine Workers, and to return power to the memberships in numerous other unions. These efforts suggest that broad segments of the working class appear ready to participate in the emerging struggle for democratic rule.

The defense of democracy thus entails a demand for its application at all levels and in all spheres of society. This is a crucial point, for here emerges the central theme of all socialist programs: the defense of political democracy is simply the logical corollary to the demand for democracy at the workplace and social control of the production process. Once workers raise a challenge to the existing system of control in the firm, they will through their experience be led to see the common content of these struggles. The defense and extension of democracy may ultimately rest, then, on the working class's effort to take possession of the means of production and to organize, through democratic rule, society's material resources for the benefit of all in society. Democracy thus becomes the rallying cry not only to unite various fractions of the working class, but also to unite the political and economic struggles of that class.

Whether a socialist and democratic society (and not just a democratic socialist program) can be constructed remains a further imponderable. Certainly our highly concentrated and increasingly undemocratic capitalism grows more intolerable daily. So, too, it seems inevitable that democratic socialism cannot be realized unless progressive forces everywhere struggle for both democracy and socialism. To do less shortchanges our future.

APPENDIX

It is possible to use the classic study of economies of scale by Joe S. Bain to evaluate the turn-of-the-century mergers. Bain (1956, Chapter 3) compared the actual average size of the four largest firms in each of twenty industries in 1947 to the estimated technologically optimal plant size. Firms in nineteen of twenty industries exceeded the optimal scale, often being many times greater than that necessary for maximum efficiency. We can usefully combine Bain's estimates of optimal plant size with the concentration estimates for the period 1895–1904 provided by G. Warren Nutter (1951). These data provide a way of evaluating the economies of scale that the turn-of-the-century consolidations were likely to achieve.

There are eleven industries for which both Bain and Nutter give data. Columns 1 and 2 of Table A-1 present the two sets of estimates. Column 3 indicates that the proportions controlled were far in excess of the proportion that Bain found to be necessary for efficiency in 1947. The figures in Column 3 contain some biases associated with the different years involved, however.

TABLE A-1

Relation to Concentration in 1895–1904 to Size Required to Achieve Optimal-Sale Plant, 11 Industries

Industry or product	1 Percent of 1947 national market required for Optimal Scale (Bain)[a]	2 Percent of 1895–1904 national market controlled by each industry's largest firm (Nutter)[b]	3 Ratio of actual size of 1895–1904 firms to estimated optimal size (2÷1)	4 Ratio of industry value added in 1900 to value added in 1947, constant dollars[c]	5 Corrected ratio of actual size of 1895–1904 firms to estimated optimal size (3×4)
Copper refining	10.0	30 (64 for four firms)	3.0	1.55	4.7
Cigarettes	5.5	75 (90)	13.6	1.12	15.2
Gypsum products	2.5	80	32.0	0.72[d,e]	23.0
Typewriters	20.0	75	3.8	0.13[d]	0.5
Metal containers	1.166	65 to 75	55.8	0.61[f]	34.0
Distilled liquor	1.5	80 to 95	53.3	0.52	27.7
Steel	1.75	61	34.9	0.44[g]	15.4
Meatpacking	2.25	50 (for four firms)	5.6	1.90	10.6
Petroleum refining	1.75	84 (86)	48.0	0.20	9.6
Farm machinery	1.25	70 (85)	56.0	0.39	21.8
Canned fruits and vegetables	0.375	40	106.7	0.16	17.1

[a] Taken from Joe S. Bain (1956), Table VIII. Of the twenty industries studied by Bain, nine (including automobile manufacture and rayon production) were excluded because, for obvious reasons, Nutter provided no 1895–1904 concentration data.

[b] Taken from G. Warren Nutter (1951), Table 6. Alternate estimates given by Nutter appear in parentheses.

[c] Data for 1900 are "net value of product" from U.S. Census Office (1902), Tables LX and 1; data for 1947 are "value added" from U.S. Bureau of the Census (1949), Table 2; prices used to deflate current dollar data given in U.S. Bureau of the Census (1959), Table E13–24.

[d] 1900 datum is calculated as value of products less cost of material used from Table 1.

[e] 1900 figure is for lime and cement.

[f] 1900 figure is for tinsmithing, and so on.

[g] 1900 figure is for iron and steel.

First, the production technology changed between 1895–1904 and 1947; but assuming that technological change either was scale-neutral or tended to increase the minimal scale of the optimal plant, Column 3 would tend to understate the excess of actual size over optimal size. Second, economic growth between the two periods would imply that a given percentage of the 1895–1904 national market would represent a smaller absolute scale than the same percentage in 1947; consequently, the optimal scale expressed as a percent of the national market would be different. We can correct for this bias by multiplying Column 3 by a correction ratio for each industry; the ratio would be the (constant dollar) 1900 value-added divided by the 1947 value-added. The new figures are the ratios of the actual size of the leading firm of each industry to the estimated optimal size, now corrected to reflect the same absolute scale of production in 1900 as was assumed by Bain in 1947. The corrected figures are given in Column 5.

The results indicate that in ten of the eleven industries the turn-of-the-century consolidations extended far beyond what was required to achieve technical efficiency. (In both Table A-1 and in Bain's original study, only typewriters failed to be produced in larger-than-optimal plants.) While these arguments do not offer proof, they do tend to undermine the interpretation of consolidation as resulting from largely technological factors.

It is also possible to combine studies by Shaw Livermore (1935) and John Moody (1904) to demonstrate the effect of market power on the success or failure of the mergers. Livermore, in a study of the successes and failures of industrial consolidations around the turn of the century, provided a list of 155 mergers that he considered to be of "economic importance." After studying their subsequent fates, he divided them into six categories: early failures, later failures, "limping" or marginal firms, "rejuvenations now successful," successes, and outstanding successes. Here they are regrouped into definite failures ("early" and "late") and successes ("rejuvenations," "successes," and "outstanding successes"); the "limping" firms have been omitted as ambiguous. In all, 138 firms remain. Of these 138, fifty-five were listed by John Moody in his *Truth about the Trusts* as having monopoly control of 50 percent or more of their markets.

This test suffers from several sources of error. Livermore's list itself was partly based on market power, thus confounding the results somewhat. We cannot be sure that firms listed by Livermore but not listed by Moody did not in fact control 50 percent or more of the market. On the other hand, it seems doubtful that any important monopoly would have escaped Moody's attention. The markets Moody listed as being controlled varied widely by degree of aggregation. Finally, Moody's estimates, though qualitatively correct, cannot be interpreted as quantitatively precise ("more than 50 percent" probably is best interpreted as "significant market control"). However, while these problems make the test not very precise, they do not introduce any obvious bias in either direction.

TABLE A-2

Success and Failure of Consolidations Listed by Livermore, According to Moody's Estimate of Monopoly Power

(n = 138)

	Percent of Failures[a]	Percent of Successes[a]	Total Percent
Firms listed as controlling 50 percent or more of market[b]	13	27	40
Firms not listed or listed as controlling less than 50 percent of market	33	27	60
Total	46	54	100

[a] As listed by Shaw Livermore (1935).
[b] As listed by John Moody (1904).

Table A-2 presents the cross-tabulation. The chi-square difference is easily significant at the .05 level, supporting the conclusion that control of the market apparently had a significant impact on success or failure. In addition to investigating statistical significance, we can evaluate the effect of market power by looking at the *magnitude* of the effect: in Table A-2, market power increased the chances of success by about a half: 67 percent of the monopoly firms succeeded versus 46 percent of the others; however, a large portion of the firms controlling more than 50 percent of their markets still failed.

The estimate of the size of the core given in Table A-3 can be taken only as a very crude indicator. As argued in Chapter 5, the core should be conceived of as being based on firms (capitals) as the unit of observation rather than on industries. Thus the core is defined as firms that both are large and enjoy extensive market power. However, no statistics are available that would permit an easy calculation of the size of the core. See Joseph Bowring (1979) for more precise specification.

TABLE A-3

National Income Originating in Monopolistic Industries, 1963 (Billions of Dollars)[a]

Sector	1 Income from Industries with "Substantial Market Power"	2 Total Sector Income
Agriculture	—	18.6
Mining	2.3	5.9
Construction	16.0	24.1
Manufacturing	69.2	(143.8)
Transportation and utilities	31.9	39.9
Wholesale trade	3.2	26.7
Retail trade	8.8	46.6
Finance, insurance and real estate	20.0	53.2
Services	20.2	54.1
Total	171.6	412.9
Percent Monopoly (column 1 divided by column 2)	41.6	

[a] Adapted from William Shepherd (1970), Appendix Table 14.

TABLE A-4

Growth in the Number of Large Firms[a]

	1919[b] (Firms with assets in excess of $50 million)	1969[c] (Firms with assets in excess of $75 million)
Transportation and utilities	103[d]	292
Industrial	60	856
Merchandising	3	110
	1919[b]	1969[e]
	(Firms with assets in excess of $1 billion)	(Firms with assets in excess of $1.5 billion)
Transportation and utilities	4	30
Industrial	1 or 2	62
Merchandising	0	2

[a] "Large" firms defined in two (arbitrary) categories; see Richard Edwards (1975a), Table VI, for prices used to convert 1919 asset levels to 1969 equivalents.

[b] Data for 1919 are taken from Richard Edwards (1975a), Table V.

[c] Data in U.S. Bureau of the Census (1972), p. 480; calculated on the assumption that half of the firms in size category $50.0 million to $99.9 million had assets in excess of $75 million.

[d] Estimated.

[e] Data from *Fortune*, May, 1970.

The powerful tendency toward centralization of capital is given in Table A-5. Because the federal government conducts periodic surveys of manufacturing but does not systematically collect data for the other sectors, the most reliable figures cover manufacturing. As the first part of Table A-5 shows, the concentration of manufacturing assets in the largest corporations is a persistent process observable as far back as the data go. The increasing importance of these very large firms is also revealed in the powerful trend in sales data, as the bottom panel in Table A-5 shows.

TABLE A-5
Increasing Importance of Large Firms in the Economy

a) The Percentage of All Manufacturing Assets Held by the Largest Manufacturing Firms[a]

	Top 100	Top 200
1925	35.1	
1931	42.3	
1939	42.4	
1948	40.1	48.2
1955	43.8	53.1
1960	46.0	56.3
1965	47.6	56.7
1970	48.5	60.4
1973[b]	47.6	60.3

b) Sales of the 500 Largest Industrial Corporations as a Percentage of GNP[c]

1955	40.4
1960	40.5
1965	43.3
1970	47.2
1975	57.1

[a] Studies by the Staff of the Cabinet Committee on Price Stability (1969), pp. 45, 92; U.S. Bureau of the Census (1976a), p. 502; David Penn (1976), Table 1.

[b] Data for years after 1972 incorporate statistical revisions that make them noncomparable to prior years; see David Penn (1976) for overlap.

[c] *Fortune*, May issues, 1956, 1961, 1966, 1971, 1976; U.S. President (1977), Table B-1. Note that the sales of the corporations include intermediate sales (sales to other producers) and final sales (sales to final users), whereas GNP includes only final sales.

Table A-6 charts the post-World War I fates of 1919's largest corporations. The second column shows the number of firms included; for example, the table shows that for manufacturing and mining there were 110 firms that could be identified as having assets in 1919 equal to or greater than $50 million. The succeeding columns tell what happened between 1919 and 1969. The third column lists firms that are unambiguously successful, that is, those that have increased their assets (in constant dollars) over the period. The next column, mergers and acquisitions, represents an uncertain fate: mergers may result from a firm's weakness (and hence a susceptibility to takeover), its strength (making its earnings attractive to the acquiring firm), or simply a consolidation. Thus the category "merged or acquired firms" reflects both strong and weak companies, and little can be concluded about whether they are successful or unsuccessful firms. On the other hand, the final three columns in Table A-6 measure what are clearly failures: firms that were unable to reproduce their assets, that went bankrupt, or that disappeared for other reasons.

Consider first the aggregates given in the subtotal row; it is obvious that firms that were large in 1919 have been extremely successful in avoiding failure. Compared to the fates of medium-sized firms over the same period, or even to the experience of big companies in the first two decades of this century, the large corporations in the monopoly capitalist period have been remarkably adept at avoiding failure. (These comparisons and the associated analysis appear in Richard C. Edwards, 1975a.) Urban transit companies were the only ones to experience a substantial failure rate.

TABLE A-6

The Survival of Large Firms, 1919–1969[a]

	1919	Fate by 1969				
	Number of Large Firms[b]	Successful Firms[c]	Merged or Acquired Firms	Unsuccessful but Still Independent Firms[d]	Liquidated Firms	Other
Manufacturing and mining	110	70	30	2	8	0
Utilities	36	25	8	0	1	2[g]
Railroads	22	12	4	5	1	0
Life insurance[e] and banking[f]	34	27	6	0	1	0
Merchandising	8	8	0	0	0	0
Subtotal	210	142	48	7	11	2
Urban Transit	15	0	0	2	10	3[h]
Total	225	142	48	9	21	5

[a] Adapted from Richard Edwards (1975a), Tables 3,4, and Appendix Table III.

[b] For manufacturing and mining, utilities, life insurance, and urban transit, large firms are defined as those with assets equal to or greater than $50 million; for railroads, assets equal to or greater than $300 million; for banking, deposits equal to or greater than $200 million; for merchandising, assets equal to or greater than $20 million.

[c] Firms whose 1969 assets were greater than or equal to 1919 assets in constant dollars.

[d] Firms whose 1969 assets were less than their 1919 assets in constant dollars.

[e] Period covered is 1917 to 1967.

[f] Period covered is 1922 to 1967.

[g] Dissolved by court orders.

[h] Purchased by municipal governments, usually after liquidation proceedings had begun.

Table A-7 shows the increasing importance of nonproduction workers in large establishments.

TABLE A-7
The Ratio of Nonproductive Workers (N) to Production Workers (P) by Size of Establishment[a]

Size of Establishment (Number of employees)	N/P × 100 In 1954	N/P × 100 In 1972
1–499	23.0 to 24.7	31.5
500–2499	26.2 to 26.4	33.5
2500 and over	36.3	43.8

[a] Source: George Delehanty (1968) p. 149; U.S. Bureau of the Census (1975b), Table 8. The 1972 figures were calculated according to description given by Delehanty.

TABLE A-8

The Rising Ratio of Nonproduction Workers (N) to Production Workers (P), by Industry[a]

	N/P × 100			
Industry or Product	In 1947	In 1955	In 1965	In 1975
All manufacturing	19.5	26.8	34.4	40.6
Tobacco	7.3	9.0	16.1	23.5
Chemicals	32.2	48.4	66.4	78.3
Petroleum and coal	29.9	45.5	61.8	56.1
Rubber	22.7	26.6	28.5	30.9
Primary metals	14.6	18.4	22.4	28.9
Fabricated metals	18.9	24.1	29.1	34.2
Nonelectrical machinery	26.2	35.1	42.9	54.4
Electrical machinery	30.0	36.7	45.9	55.6
Transportation equipment	21.7	30.2	40.2	42.9

[a] Source: George Delehanty (1968), Appendix Table A-5; U.S. Bureau of Labor Statistics (1976), Table B-2. Figures for 1975 are calculated according to description given by Delehanty.

TABLE A-9

Rising Ratio of Nonproduction Workers (N) to Production Workers (P) in Two Core Corporations

American Telephone and Telegraph			
	1958	1967	1976
Production Workers[a]	349,049	354,130	382,499
Nonproduction Workers[b]	250,779	302,039	377,362
N/P × 100	71.8	85.3	98.7
Polaroid			
	1961	1977	
Production Workers	1,612	4,879	
Nonproduction Workers[c]	1,707	6,032	
N/P × 100	105.9	123.6	

[a] Telephone operators plus plant craft employees.
[b] Managerial, professional, business office, sales, and supervisory employees.
[c] Office and all exempt (salaried) employees.
Source: Private communications from AT&T and Polaroid.

NOTES*

Chapter 1

1. This account is taken from Ann Bookman (1977); Bookman's work presents an exceptionally insightful description of supervision, control, and conflict at Digitex. Both the name of this firm and the names and personal details of all the workers have been changed to protect them.

2. Karl Marx (1867), Vol. I, pp. 175–176.

3. "By labor-power or capacity for labor is to be understood the aggregate of those mental and physical capabilities existing in a human being, which he exercises whenever he produces a use-value of any description." Ibid., p. 167.

4. S. B. Mathewson (1931), pp. 16–17.

5. Stanley Aronowitz (1973), pp. 22–23.

6. Karl Marx (1852), p. 457.

7. As Marx (1867, Vol. I, pp. 330–331) put it: "All combined labor on a large scale requires, more or less, a directing authority, in order to secure the harmonious working of the individual activities, and to perform the general functions that have their origin in the action of its separate organs. A single violin player is his own conductor; an orchestra requires a separate one." See also S. A. Marglin (1974), F. Roosevelt (1975), and Theodore Anderson and Seymour Warkov (1961).

8. Again we may quote Marx (1867, Vol. I, p. 331): "As the number of the cooperating laborers increases, so too does their resistance to the domination of capital, and with it, the necessity for capital to overcome this resistance by counter-pressure. The control exercised by the capitalist is not only a special function, due to the nature of the social labor-process, and peculiar to that process, but it is, at the same time, a function of the exploitation of a social labor-process, and is consequently rooted in the unavoidable antagonism between the exploiter and the living and laboring raw material he exploits."

Chapter 2

1. Thomas Cochran (1948), pp. 56, 272; Robert Ozanne (1967), p. 3; William Hutchinson (1930) Vol. I, pp. 271, 308; Stanley Buder (1967), pp. 10, 17.

2. Thomas Navin and Marion Sears (1955).

3. Alfred Chandler (1959), p. 3.

4. See David Gordon, Michael Reich, and Richard Edwards (forthcoming), Chapters 2 and 3.

5. Stephen Hymer (1972).

6. Harold Passer (1952), p. 379.

* Complete publication information for these notes may be found by locating the author and date in the bibliography.

7. William Hutchinson (1930) Vol. I, p. 308; Robert Ozanne (1967), pp. 7–9; Thomas Cochran (1948).

8. Robert Ozanne (1967), pp. 3, 36; William Hutchinson (1930), Vol. II, p. 402; Harold Passer (1952), p. 382; Stanley Buder (1967), p. 17; Almont Lindsey (1964), p. 24.

9. Robert Layer (1955); Alfred Chandler (1965), p. 19.

10. U.S. Bureau of the Census (1902), Part I, page lxxii; Daniel Nelson (1975), pp. 7–9.

11. Alfred Chandler (1965), p. 38; Harold Passer (1952), p. 379.

12. Quoted in William Carwardine (1894), p. 86; Stanley Buder (1967), p. 144.

13. Allan Nevins and F.E. Hill (1962) especially Chapters II and III.

14. Alfred Chandler (1965), p. 24.

15. Ibid., p. 21.

16. See Katherine Stone (1975) and David Brody (1960).

17. Interchurch World Movement (1920), p. 128.

18. Daniel Nelson (1975), chapter 3.

19. Quoted in Alfred Chandler (1965), pp. 27 (emphasis in original); 25; and 29.

20. See U.S. Strike Commission (1895), p. 442–444; William Carwardine (1894), p. 103; Daniel Nelson (1975), pp. 36–38 and chapter 5 provides a useful discussion.

21. Alfred Chandler (1965), p. 33.

22. Ann Bookman (1977), p. 129.

23. Ibid., pp. 144–45.

Chapter 3

1. See David Gordon, Michael Reich, and Richard Edwards (forthcoming), Chapters 4 and 5.

2. See, for example, Eliot Jones (1921), pp. 186–189; William Hogan (1971), pp. 236–7.

3. Quoted in Victor Clark (1949), Vol. II, pp. 174–5.

4. Eliot Jones (1921), p. 201.

5. The average wholesale price index (1910–1914 = 100) for 1886–1890 was only 53.3 percent of the average index for 1866–1870. Abstracting from cyclical fluctuations, the price index indicated a fairly steady decline throughout the period (see U.S. Bureau of Census (1959), p. 115).

6. Karl Marx (1867), Vol. I, p. 626; see the whole discussion on this process in Chapter XXV, "The General Law of Capitalist Accumulation."

7. "The world would still be without railways if it had had to wait until accumulation had got a few individual capitals far enough to be adequate for the construction of a railway. Centralization, on the contrary, accomplished this in the twinkling of an eye, by means of joint stock companies." Karl Marx (1867), Vol. I, p. 628. See also Thomas Navin and Marion Sears (1955).

8. Eliot Jones (1921), pp. 321–2.

9. Harold Passer (1952).

10. Harry Laidler (1931), p. 48; Eliot Jones (1921), Chapter IX; White and Kemble (1903).

11. Ralph Nelson (1959, p. 37), gives the following figures:

Merger Capitalizations	(Millions of $)
1897	120
1898	651
1899	2,263
1900	442
1901	2,053
1902	911
1903	298

These capitalizations should be judged against an aggregate figure of roughly $10 billion to $15 billion for the entire United States manufacturing capital stock; calculated from Daniel Creamer (1954), Table 2; the data were corrected to reflect 1900 prices. The merger data given above include double-counting (mergers of previous mergers), some inflation of assets due to overcapitalization, and some categories (such as mining) not covered by the estimate of aggregate manufacturing capital. Hence the comparison of merger capitalizations to aggregate manufacturing capital is useful to establish orders of magnitude but not for more precise calculations. John Moody (1904).

12. For a full discussion of data resources, methodological issues, and results involved in analyzing the success (or failure) of the largest corporations, see Richard Edwards (1975a).

13. See Karl Marx (1867, Vol. I, p. 626): "The battle of competition is fought by cheapening of commodities. The cheapness of commodities depends, *ceteris paribus*, on the productiveness of labor, and this again on the scale of production"; see also Karl Marx (1849), pp. 43–44. Carnegie quote in text above.

14. Comparison of successive years of *Moody's Industrials* manuals supports this assertion; see also Eliot Jones (1921), Chapter XIX.

15. G. Warren Nutter (1951, p. 50) provides one quite conservative assessment of "enterprise monopoly" in 1899. He reports the following estimates of the relative extent of monopoly (as measured by the percentage of income originating in each division accounted for by monopolistic industries):

Public utilities	100
Transportation and communication	92
Mining	40
Manufacturing	32
Finance	22

16. See, for example, J. W. Jenks, 1900; W. L. Thorp, 1924; U.S. Industrial Commission, 1902; Eliot Jones, 1921; and H. B. Summers, 1931.

17. L. W. Weiss (1971), p. 371.

18. The failure of the trusts to achieve complete monopoly—with a few notable exceptions—did not imply that the new firms were without significant power. The lack of exclusive control over broad industry categories (the 85 percent control International Harvester was conceded to have over the farm implements industry) sometimes concealed much greater control over special products or particular regions, for example, I-H's control of harvesters in the Midwest. Similarly, less than complete consolidation often still left the biggest firm with sufficient strength relative to other producers to be able to dictate market shares or prices; U.S. Steel, controlling 60 percent of the steel rail business, was generally understood to be able to set the price without challenge. Eliot Jones (1921), p. 214.

19. Eliot Jones (1921), p. 486.

Chapter 4

1. John Commons, et. al., (1935), Vol. IV, p. 97.

2. David Brody (1960), Chapter III. Brody (1960, p. 68) notes that after a lifetime of conflict, T.J. Shaeffer, president of the Amalgamated Association, lectured convention delegates in 1905: "I enter my most vigorous protest against any strike which does not emanate from the employer." Unnecessary belligerence would mark a "union as unreflecting, jejune, and vicious." The steel union thereafter trusted its fate to a policy of submissiveness to U.S. Steel.

3. Thus, centralization in the steel industry was seen to imply that strikes increasingly

assumed an industry-wide character, since any action against U.S. Steel, for example, was necessarily an action against over half the industry.

4. Robert Ozanne (1971); Daniel Nelson (1975), chapter 1; Harold Passer (1952), p. 382; Charles Gulick (1924), p. 57.

5. Daniel Nelson (1975), Chapter 1.

6. This was the problem that so obsessed Frederick Taylor (1903) and set him off on his "scientific management" experiments.

7. In the modern firm, capitalists have striven diligently to restore positive incentives, though on an entirely different basis from what was undertaken in the entrepreneurial firm. See below, Chapter 8. Capitalists in the nineteenth century also perceived the problem, and this probably explains their enduring efforts—from Lowell to Pullman—to establish "model" work communities, in which workers would live harmoniously with their employers in a sanitized environment free of the polluting effects of cities, workers in other industries, and so on. See Norman Ware (1924) and Stanley Buder (1967). It also helps explain their interest in primary education; see Samuel Bowles and Herbert Gintis (1975).

8. Based on prorating industry data (of which U.S. Steel comprised about half); U.S. Census Office (1912), Vol. IV, p. 338.

9. Harold Passer (1952), pp. 383-387.

10. Of course, a tiny percentage of the population owned stock: "People's Capitalism" was and is a myth. But ownership of the stock of one (consolidated) corporation was less frequently held by one individual or family, and each (capitalist) individual or family came more frequently to own stock in several corporations. In this way, the capitalist class, as individuals *but not as a class*, diversified their holdings.

11. Harold Passer (1952), p. 385.

12. Joseph Litterer (1963).

13. John Commons, et.al. (1935), Volume IV, Chapter 4.

14. Robert Ozanne (1967), Chapter 3.

15. See, for example, the testimony of workers in Interchurch World Movement (1920), Chapter V; Almont Lindsey (1942), p. 95; Joseph Litterer (1963), p. 373.

16. David Montgomery (1974) includes strikes to gain union recognition in his measure of control struggles. This procedure might be challenged for other periods, since it could well be argued that union recognition has most often resulted in collective bargaining over wages and benefits rather than establishing any control over workers. However, for the period in question, this method is quite appropriate. In hierarchical control, where foremen's power is nearly unlimited by work rules or effective supervision from higher managers, the presence of union shop stewards would effectively constrain that power. Hence, the context of union recognition would determine the extent to which recognition is a "control" issue; see especially pp. 13–16 and Table One.

17. Testimony of George Pullman in U.S. Strike Commission (1895), p. 529.

18. Richard Ely (1885), p. 463.

19. Wages were reduced an average of 25 percent, but the cuts were unevenly distributed and some wages were slashed up to 41 percent; see Almont Lindsey (1942), pp. 98–99. The confrontation, the immediate cause of the walkout, is subject to several interpretations, but it appears likely that precipitate action by a foreman and his supervisor, without the approval of higher-ups, triggered the strike; see. U.S. Strike Commission (1895), p. 7.

20. Cited in William Carwardine (1894), p. 77.

21. Ibid., p. 103.

22. U.S. Strike Commission (1895), p. 432. See the testimony of Thomas Heathcoate, Theodore Rhodie, Merritt Brown, and Myrtle Webb in U.S. Strike Commission (1895). Several workers (e.g., B.B. Ray) testified to the blacklisting before the U.S. Strike Commission (1895); see also Thomas Carwardine (1894), Chapter IX.

23. Stanley Buder (1967), p. 155; William Carwardine (1894), p. 71.

24. Cited in William Carwardine (1894), pp. 77–78.

25. Ibid., p. 79; italics in original; Almont Lindsey (1942), p. 29.

26. U.S. Strike Commission (1895), p. 110.

27. Ibid., p. 112.

28. David Brody (1965), p. 17.

29. Ibid.

30. David Montgomery (1974), p. 13; Interchurch World Movement (1920), p. 44; the latter figure is calculated by interpolation from Paul Douglas (1930), pp. 94, 114.

31. The figures are: average hourly earnings in steel, 65.3 cents; in Douglas' seven other industries, 38.5 cents; average full-time weekly earnings in steel, $43.16; in the other seven, $20.55. Calculated by interpolation or taken from Paul Douglas (1930), p. 94 and Tables 21, 34, and 36; Interchurch World Movement (1920), p. 85; italics in original. The same investigators declared (p. 85) that "over one-third of all productive iron and steel workers were . . . below . . . the level set by government experts as the minimum of *subsistence* standard for families of five" (italics in original). From data given elsewhere in the report (p. 99), it appears that despite an extraordinarily large proportion of unmarried men among foreign workers, average family size was still just slightly less than five.

32. Interchurch World Movement (1920), pp. 121, 219–221. U.S. Senate (1919), Vol. I, p. 242.

33. U. S. Senate (1919), Vol. II, pp. 496, 524, 525, 674–677, 992; Interchurch World Movement (1920), pp. 138–142.

34. "In normal times, the Steel Corporation had no adequate means of learning the conditions of life and work and the desires of its employees. Company officers admitted that they had no real way of reaching, or of keeping in touch with, the mass of workers." Interchurch World Movement (1920), p. 22.

35. U.S. Senate (1919), Vol. II, p. 559.

36. Ibid., p. 496.

37. Ibid., p. 524.

38. Ibid., pp. 551, 601.

39. Gabriel Kolko (1963); David Cohen and Marvin Lazerson (1972).

40. Gabriel Kolko (1963), Chapter 5; Eliot Jones (1921), Chapters XVII and XVIII.

41. Ida Tarbell (1926), pp. 57–8.

42. V.R. Berghahn (1973) is one example; similar but less convincing arguments have been made for Italy and Britain.

43. Murray Rothbard (1972), p. 72.

44. U.S. Steel, *Annual Reports,* various dates; see also Robert Cuff (1973); James Weinstein (1968).

45. James Weinstein (1968), chapter 8.

46. John Commons et al., (1935), Vol. IV, p. 32; see also William Preston (1963).

47. See James O'Connor (1973); Michael Best and William Connolly (1976); and Gabriel Kolko (1963).

Chapter 5

1. J. K. Galbraith (1973) describes these as two distinct business "systems," but Paul Sweezy (1973) properly points out that neither represents a system, and that ascribing systematic relations between them in this manner suggests a degree of planning or coordination that is misleading. Others who have written about the dual economy are James O'Connor (1972), Robert Averitt (1968), and Joseph Bowring (forthcoming).

2. Many writers have focused on a different (alleged) change: the demise of capitalists and the rise of an independent managerial class. The substitution of managers for capitalists, if true, would not change the argument to follow. There is, however, accumulating evidence casting doubt on the independence of managers; see especially Michel DeVroey (1975), Maurice Zeitlin (1975), Lawrence Pedersen and William Tabb (1976), David Kotz (1978), and Philip Burch (1972).

3. Robert Averitt (1968).

4. Economists identify these two aspects of investment with the mean and variance of the distribution of expected returns; see Harry Markowitz (1959). The assertion in the text then

amounts to saying that the large firm, for any given expected rate of return (mean), faces a lower risk (variance).

5. For more precise estimates of the continuing importance of large firms in industries that had already been highly concentrated by 1919, see Richard C. Edwards (1975a), especially Appendix Table II.

6. William Shepherd (1970), p. 118, Appendix Table 9. "Significant" change was defined as a 10 percentage point rise or fall in the four-firm industry concentration ratio.

7. SIC industries 2062 (cane sugar refining) and 2274 (hard-surface floor coverings) were excluded due to major changes in coverage, leaving 33 industries for the period 1947-1972. Industries were then grouped as follows (with 1972 SIC identification in parentheses if different from 1947 code):

Declining four-firm share		Increasing four-firm share	
2826 (28921)	Explosives	2043	Cereal breakfast foods
2841	Soap and glycerine	2771	Greeting cards
2898 (28991)	Salt	3333	Primary zinc
3331	Primary copper	3521 (35231)	Tractors
3411	Tin cans	3581 (3633)	Domestic laundry equipment
3641 (3621)	Electrical engine equipment	3717 (3711, 3714)	Motor vehicles
3615 (3612)	Transformers	3871 (3873)	Matches and clocks
		13861	Photographic equipment

Each of the remaining eighteen of Shepherd's "consensus oligopolies" had less than a 10-point shift in its four-firm concentration ratio; see William Shepherd (1970) pp. 117–119 and 268–296; U.S. Bureau of the Census (1975a), Tables 5 and 6.

8. Antitrust laws, to the minimal extent that they have been enforced since 1920, are almost always directed against cases of monopoly or near-monopoly (IBM, AT&T) rather than of stable oligopoly. So GM has invested heavily in other industries—it is dominant in some forty-odd industries *other than* autos—rather than pushing for total control over autos.

9. William Shepherd (1970), p. 155; John Blair (1972, p. 22) comes to much the same conclusion based on 1967 data; Willard Mueller and Larry Hamm (1974) concluded that concentration was steadily increasing during 1947-1970.

10. G. Warren Nutter (1951); George Stigler (1949).

11. From this perspective monopoly power can be seen in part as firm size *relative* to market size.

12. For extended discussions of these points, see Robert Averitt (1968), Chapters 4 and 6, and J. K. Galbraith (1967). Stanley Ornstein (1976) suggests that advertising is more associated with scale than with market power; see also William Comanor and T. Wilson (1969).

13. See Richard Edwards, Michael Reich, and Thomas Weisskopf (1978), Chapter 6.

14. Michael Gort (1962, Chapter 8) found that limited growth prospects, especially those derived from shared monopoly, were the most important motive propelling firms to diversify; similarly, Theodore Moran (1973) links oligopoly in the home market to the firm's decision to invest abroad.

15. Cited in John Blair (1972), p. 33; *Iron Age* quotation from September 21, 1944.

16. U.S. Senate, (1965) testimony of Dixon and Oxenfeldt; see also John Blair (1972), Chapter 2.

17. *Studies by the Staff of the Cabinet Committee on Price Stability* (1969), p. 77.

18. In William Shepherd (1970), p. 141; for an even earlier study documenting extensive diversification, see Willard Thorp (1924). Michael Gort (1962, Chapter 3) also suggests that diversification has been a long-established trend.

19. *Studies by the Staff of the Cabinet Committee on Price Stability* (1969), pp. 75, 79.

20. More serious battles loom when technical developments erode the boundaries between

industries; the fights between AT&T and IBM over long-distance hookups of computers and between IBM and Xerox over office machinery are cases in point.

21. William Shepherd (1970), pp. 142-3.

22. The profits from diversification have been the subject of considerable but so far contradictory study; see, for example, S. A. Rhoades (1973, 1974); Ronald Melicher and David Rush (1973); and J. Fred Weston and Surenda Mansinghka (1971). Diversification reduces risk rather quickly if the expected returns from the different activities are not correlated, so some observers feel that the mixed success of the 1960s' conglomerates is due to their overdiversification (relative to what is required to reduce risk).

23. Data taken from Richard Edwards, Michael Reich, and Thomas Weisskopf (1978), Tables 13-A and 13-B; Chapter 13 presents an extended treatment of the issues reviewed here.

24. Theodore Moran (1973) presents the oligopoly argument in the context of the "product cycle" theory; see also Arthur MacEwan (1978). On scale effects, see Thomas Horst (1972), p. 261; Raymond Vernon (1971, Chapter 1) takes the same view, and Bernard Wolf (1975) provides further though not unambiguous support.

25. U.S. Department of Commerce (1970), p. 1, as cited in Raymond Vernon (1971).

26. One assessment of the tax advantages of transfer pricing is given in Glenn Jenkins and Brian Wright (1975).

27. Richard Edwards, Michael Reich, and Thomas Weisskopf (1978), Statistical Appendix to the Introduction to Chapter 13. Confirming evidence is provided by Bernard Wolf (1975) based on a broad sample of large U.S. corporations for 1962 and 1966. Wolf found that firms that invest abroad had higher profit rates than "primarily domestic firms": 9.73 percent versus 7.18 percent in 1962, 11.44 percent versus 9.22 percent in 1966. Moreover, the same result held when foreign-investing versus primarily domestic firms *within* each industry were compared: in 1962, the multinationals outperformed the domestics in 17 out of the 22 industries studied, in 1966 in 16 out of 21 industries.

28. After-tax profits computed as net income divided by total firm assets. Market power criterion based on four-firm concentration ratio for industry shipments (CR4) of firm's principal product. Competitive industry defined as industries with CR4<40; monopoly industries defined as industries with CR4≥ 40. Size criterion based on total firm assets. Small firms defined as firms with total assets less than $100 million; large firms defined as firms with total assets equal to or greater than $100 million. SOURCE: U.S. Internal Revenue Service *(Source Book of Statistics of Income)* and U.S. Bureau of the Census *(Enterprise Statistics)*. Data sets were linked by the Research Program in Competition and Business Policy (J. Fred Weston, Director), University of California, Los Angeles, who generously made them available. Full documentation upon request.

29. The results cited in the text are evidently not due to the particular criteria for classification used. For example, virtually the same results can be extracted from a 3 by 3 matrix, where firms are divided into small (less than $25 million in assets), medium (assets between $25 and $100 million), and large (assets greater than or equal to $100 million) categories; and industries are divided into competitive (CR4< 20), mixed (CR4 between 20 and 40), and monopoly (CR4≥ 40) groups. Once again, only the large monopoly firms do substantially better. See also Bradley Gale (1972).

30. See H. O. Stekler (1964) and George Stigler (1963), p. 48. These earlier studies cannot be brought up to date by the data underlying the figure in the text, because (unfortunately) the Census and IRS data are grouped, making it impossible to calculate the variances for each cell for each year. For the years 1958–1969, the secular variance in the mean for each cell supports the findings of Stekler and Stigler; the coefficient of variation is smallest for "large firm-monopoly industry" category. For the 1970s, however, a reversal appears to have occurred. For possible reasons why, see Chapter 8. See also Joseph Bowring (1979).

31. The social and technical change referred to is, of course, the advent of automobiles and suburbs. Bradford Snell (U.S. Senate, 1974) provides one version of how this change came about. It seems that in the late 1920s and early 1930s the auto manufacturers, and especially GM, found their car markets reaching saturation, so GM devised a plan to ruin the (primarily rail) urban transit lines and thereby expand the market for buses (and cars). The plan was to buy control of urban transit companies, convert the rail lines to bus transport, tear out the (now unused) tracks to make going back to rail lines impossibly costly, and then resell the companies to provide funds for the next "conversion" operation. Initial attempts (Kalamazoo; Springfield, Ohio) were successful but quite crude and provoked criticism; subsequently auto makers worked through

dummy corporations and had a much broader impact, including quite possibly changing the operations of some of the big-city lines listed as failures in Table A-6. If this account is true (and Snell provides impressive documentation), it would suggest that the transit companies' rate of bankruptcy, in such remarkable contrast to that of other large firms in Table A-6, is explained not by bad luck in investments or unmanageably great "social and technical change," but rather by the conspiracy of capitalists with much bigger resources.

32. Stephen Hymer (1972).

33. Richard Edwards, Michael Reich, and Thomas Weisskopf (1978), Table 5-C; U.S. President (1976), Table A-15.

34. Harold Passer (1952); see also Alfred Chandler (1962), pp. 31-32.

35. Harry Braverman (1974). See also Chapter 1, note 8.

36. Seymour Melman (1951) provides evidence for rising N/P ratios in industry from 1899. His evidence and, even more, his analysis of the data are persuasively criticized by George Delehanty (1968). The figures in Table A-7 are for officially-defined "establishments," not firms. There has been much discussion of whether or not there exist economies of scale in administration. The evidence in Table A-7 suggests either that there are not or that such economies get swamped by the *new* functions added to administration in the large firm. In either case there are optimistic conclusions for the possible decentralization of industry.

37. U.S. Bureau of Labor Statistics (1976), Table B-2.

38. Margery Davies (1975, p. 281; and forthcoming).

Chapter 6

1. Stuart Brandes (1976), p. 48. For general treatments of welfare capitalism see Brandes, James Weinstein (1968), and David Brody (1968).

2. Discussion of welfarism at McCormick/International Harvester is based on Robert Ozanne (1967), Chapters 2, 3, 4; and International Harvester, (n.d., circa 1920), pp. 57–60.

3. Quoted in Robert Ozanne (1967), p. 83.

4. Ibid., pp. 83–84.

5. Ibid., p. 77.

6. Stuart Brandes (1976), p. 32 reaches this conclusion as well.

7. Both quotes from Joseph Husband and J. S. Runnells (1916), p. 49.

8. Machine and Allied Products Institute (1962), p. 3; Charles M. Ripley (1919) describes from the company's perspective the full range of programs.

9. United States Steel, Bureau of Safety, Relief, Sanitation, and Welfare, Bulletin No. 3 (August 1912), p. 7. Much of the following discussion is based on the reports of this Bureau.

10. Quoted in David Brody (1960), p. 154.

11. Douglas Fisher (1951), p. 81; U. S. Steel, Bureau of Safety, Relief, Sanitation, and Welfare, Bulletin No. 7, (December 1918), p. 14.

12. Quoted in James Weinstein (1968), p. 47.

13. United States Bureau of Labor Statistics (1919), pp. 15, 73, 101, 108.

14. Stuart Brandes (1976), p. 28.

15. Robert Ozanne (1967), p. 104.

16. Ellis Morrow (1921), p. 5.

17. Interchurch World Movement (1920), p. 120.

18. Stuart Brandes (1976), Chapter X.

19. Histories of the scientific management movement, with their almost mandatory recounting of Taylor's famous "Schmidt" experiment, are common and have recently undergone yet another revival. See for example Lyndall Urwick and E.F.L. Brech (1945, 1946, 1948), Milton Nadworny (1955), Hugh Aitken (1960), and Harry Braverman (1974).

20. Harry Braverman (1974), p. 87. Peter Drucker (1954, p. 280) makes virtually the same statement, completing the left-to-right consensus.

21. Harry Braverman (1974, p. 89), citing Lyndall Urwick and E.F.L. Brech (1945), acknowledges that "Taylor was the culmination of a pre-existing trend," though he still credits Taylor with the innovation. David Brody (1968, p. 152) attributes welfarism to Taylor's inspiration, though there is little evidence for this other than Taylor's own claims.

22. F.W. Taylor (1911), p. 53.

23. Ibid., pp. 142–143.

24. Ibid., p. 135; see also Taylor (1912), p. 193.

25. Milton Nadworny (1955), pp. 27–28 and p. 11. See also David Nelson and Stuart Campbell (1972, p. 13) on the impatience and eventual alienation of the Bancroft management.

26. No comprehensive list of applications of scientific management is available.

27. Compare Robert Hoxie's (1915, pp. 3–4) list with the firms in Richard Edwards (1975a, Appendix Table V).

28. See Daniel Nelson and Stuart Campbell (1972).

29. Milton Nadworny (1955), p. 28. Daniel Nelson and Stuart Campbell (1972), pp. 12–13.

30. Watertown account based on Hugh Aitken (1960).

31. Hugh Aitken (1960), Chapter 4 and Milton Nadworny (1955), pp. 79–84.

32. C.B. Thompson (1915). See the discussion by Bryan Palmer (1975).

33. Harry Braverman (1974), Chapter 4.

34. Some earlier efforts had appeared, especially the Rockefeller Plan introduced at Colorado Fuel and Iron after the Ludlow Massacre; see Stuart Brandes (1976), Chapter 13.

35. National Industrial Conference Board (1933), pp. 6–16.

36. Ellis Morrow (1921).

37. Irving Bernstein (1970), pp. 603, 610–613. GE's attitude toward unionism was remarkably enlightened during the 1920s and 1930s under Swope's leadership. After the Second World War, however, under the labor relations strategy devised by the notorious Lemuel Boulware, GE turned viciously antiunion.

38. Robert Ozanne (1967), pp. 119–120.

39. Ibid., pp. 122, 131.

40. Ibid., Chapter 7.

41. Irving Bernstein (1972), p. 156; see also Stuart Brandes (1976), pp. 142–144 and David Brody (1968), pp. 162–178.

42. Stuart Brandes (1976), p. 122.

Chapter 7

1. Moses Brown, one of the earliest American textile manufacturers (whose fortune funded the university that bears his name) indicated how the factory had improved on the old putting-out system:

> We have 100 people now at weaving, but 100 looms in families will not weave so much cloth as 30, at least, constantly employed under the immediate inspection of a workman. (Quoted in Victor Clark [1949], p. 432.)

On the conflict between these Rhode Island–based manufacturers and the Boston industrialists, see Caroline Ware (1931) and Hannah Josephson (1949).

2. Norman Ware (1964), p. 106.

3. In addition to operating faster machinery, textile workers were forced to tend *more* machinery. Weaving room workers saw their workload increase from two looms in the 1830s to four or five looms by the 1870s; similarly, spindles per operative jumped from twenty-five in the 1830s to over seventy by the 1880s. Norman Ware (1924), pp. 121–122.

4. Norman Ware (1924), pp. 120–121; Herbert Gutman (1972).

5. For a more complete treatment of technology as a control device, see the excellent discussion in Harry Braverman (1974), especially Chapter 9.

6. *The Lancet* (Jan. 14, 1905), p. 120.

7. Ibid., p. 122 (emphasis added).

8. Francesca Maltese (1975).

9. H. L. Arnold and L. F. Faurote (1915), p. 41. Molders, of course, had been a highly skilled, highly organized craft in the nineteenth century. The same observers went on to note (pp. 41–42):

> As to machinists, old-time, all-around men, perish the thought! The Ford Company has no use for experience, in the working ranks anyway. It desires and prefers machine-tool operators who have nothing to unlearn, who have no theories of correct surface speeds for metal finishing and will simply do what they are told to do, over and over again, from bell-time to bell-time.

10. Henry Ford (1926). Ford's other "principles" stressed "orderly progression" of work and the breaking of individual tasks into their simplest parts. The article was undoubtedly ghost-written for Ford, yet it nonetheless grew out of and reflected his experience. It is useful for demonstrating that Ford and his associates were acutely aware of the control consequences, as well as the technical efficiencies, of the line.

11. H.L. Arnold and L.F. Faurote (1915), p. 114.

12. Ibid., p. 245.

13. Ibid., pp. 6, 8 (emphasis added).

14. Ibid., pp. 2, 46. This ratio is all the more remarkable when it is remembered that nearly all the nonsupervisory employees were unskilled, so that the small number of supervisors is not hiding a craft organization of production.

15. Source: Private communication.

16. John Yanouzas (Fall, 1964), p. 247. Based on the activity descriptions provided in Charles Walker et al., (1956, pp. 154–156), I grouped Yanouzas' categories as follows:

Control Element 1: Work progress, equipment and tools, materials, production scheduling, work standards, and [one-half of] personnel administration.

Control element 2: Quality and [one-half of] employee job performance.

Control element 3: [One-half of] personnel administration and [one-half of] employee job performance.

17. Peter Blau and W.R. Scott (1962), p. 117.

18. Arnold and Faurote (1915), p. 247.

19. Ibid., p. 328.

20. Ibid., p. 46.

21. Charles Walker and Robert Guest (1952), pp. 72–73.

22. William Faunce (1958), pp. 401 ff.

23. As Harry Braverman (1974, p. 197 ff.) rightly argues, these control devices vastly reduce the skill required of the machinist.

24. Anthony Broy (November, 1972), p. 119.

25. "Minicomputers that Run the Factory," *Business Week* (December 8, 1973), p. 68.

26. "The Smart Machine Revolution," *Business Week* (July 5, 1976).

27. Ibid., p. 38 ff.

28. Gene Bylinsky (November, 1975), pp. 134 ff.

29. Vernon G. Converse III (November, 1974); "The Smart Machine Revolution," *Business Week* (July 5, 1976).

30. "A Price Monitor Keeps the Dough Rising," *Business Week* (December 7, 1974), p. 72; Anthony Broy, (November, 1973), pp. 179 ff.

31. This process is well described by Harry Braverman (1974).

32. Francesca Maltese (1975), p. 90.

33. A large number of blacks, perhaps 30,000 to 40,000, were imported into the steelyards during the 1919 strike. Here, however, the intent was not so much to create a permanent pool of surplus labor as it was to foster racial tensions and disrupt the strike. Many of the blacks stayed in the mills after the strike, however; see David Gordon, Richard Edwards, and Michael Reich (forthcoming); see also Edna Bonacich (1976).

34. Francesca Maltese (1975).

35. See especially Harry Braverman (1974) and Margery Davies (forthcoming).

36. Irving Bernstein (1970), pp. 524–525.

37. Of the many discussions of Lordstown, perhaps the best is Stanley Aronowitz (1972).

Chapter 8

1. On the other hand, at GE after 1946, the "master plan" was published as the multivolume set, *Professional Management in General Electric*.

2. Calculated or taken from Lance Davis et al. (1972), Table 6.8; U.S. Bureau of the Census (1954, pp. 16–19; 1963, pp. 17–21; and 1973, 17–22.)

3. All quotations on AT&T from Elinor Langer (1970).

4. Interview with "Fred Doyal" (1–5–78).

5. All Gouldner quotations from Alvin Gouldner (1954), pp. 162–165; emphasis in original.

6. General Electric (1959), pp. 278–279; emphasis in original.

7. Alvin Gouldner (1954), pp. 174–5; see also Robert Merton (1952).

8. The many sociological discussions and critiques of bureaucracy make it unnecessary to review this extensive literature here; see Max Weber (1946), A.M. Henderson and Talcott Parsons (1947), Peter Blau (1955), Richard Hall (1963), Michel Crozier (1964), and Melvin Kohn (1971).

9. Michel Crozier (1964), p. 158.

10. E.g. Melvin Kohn (1969); Fred Katz (1968).

11. The literature on workplace culture is vast, but good descriptions of this phenomenon are contained in Herbert Gutman (1972) and Studs Terkel (1975). The increasing imposition of bureaucratic control is the central point of Fred Katz's book (1968).

12. Polaroid quotations throughout this chapter are taken from unpublished documents made available by the company.

13. See Carl Gersuny (1973), pp. 87–88.

14. See Richard C. Edwards (1972; 1975b; 1976; 1977).

15. See, for example, Jacob Mincer (1974). Recent work by Paul Ryan (1977) persuasively counters the human capital interpretation on this point.

16. *Work in America* (1972), Chapter 1; for corroboration, see the studies reviewed in Harold Sheppard and Neal Herrick (1972).

17. Stanley Aronowitz (1973), Chapter 1.

18. David Jenkins (1973), especially Chapter 12.

19. Excellent reviews of these cases are contained in David Jenkins (1973) and Daniel Zwerdling (1979).

20. Thomas Fitzgerald (1971), p. 42 (emphasis added). For Fitzgerald, such problems mean that employers should abandon participation schemes and instead offer "monogrammed glasses, prizes, bonuses" and other material incentives. Unfortunately for GM, the company seems to have taken Fitzgerald's advice, causing great discontent among its workers; see Judson Gooding (1970).

21. Entire incident and quotations related in David Jenkins (1973), pp. 313–15.

22. See, for example, the controversy surrounding the Bullock Report, which proposed to Parliament that workers be granted equal representation on the governing boards of every large British corporation; *New York Times*, January 27, 1977, p. 3, and February 2, 1977, p. 3. An important French case is reported in *Cahiers de Mai* (1973). Juan Espinoza and Andrew Zimbalist (1978).

23. Other reasons for wages' becoming fixed costs exist as well. Some of the firm's commitments are legal: pension plans, medical benefits, severance pay, and the record-keeping for them frequently impose substantial costs for high turnover. The nature of the work itself, especially of the overhead component (sales, administration, personnel) that looms so large in the core firm's operations, makes frequent changes in the size of the workforce difficult. For all these reasons, the corporation's wage bill becomes increasingly inflexible.

24. Peter Vanderwicken (1975), pp. 176, 178; *New York Times*, October 1, 1977; October 26, 1977, pp. D1, D5; October 27, 1977, p. 16; November 6, 1977, Section 11 (Connecticut edition), p. 1; private communication from Polaroid; "How IBM Avoids Layoffs Through Retraining," *Business Week*, November 10, 1975, pp. 110–112.

25. For useful reviews, see Ralph Beals (1975) and Howard Wachtel (1976).

26. Ed McConville (1975).

Chapter 9

1. Neoclassical economists, especially human capital theorists, remain committed to their ideal of the individual as economic agent. They have not been able to square this view with the facts, however, and sex and race continue to be important explanations in wage or income analysis; see, for example, Zvi Griliches and William Mason (1972).

2. Michael Piore (1969); Barry Bluestone (1970); Barry Bluestone, et al. (1973); David Gordon (1971); Peter Doeringer and Michael Piore (1971). For a different argument making much the same point, see Paul Sweezy (1972).

3. David Gordon (1971), Chapter 4. The variables are quite diverse, including monetary and status measures, demographic variables, education and training indexes, employment stability measures, industry and job characteristics variables, migration measures, labor market search variables, occupational mobility variables, and attitudinal scales. Gordon's analysis was based on the two-segment or dual-market model.

4. Paul Osterman (1975, p. 513), for example, arbitrarily classified jobs as secondary if, as dual-market theory suggested, they were "characterized by low wages, instability of employment, and similar factors." By comparing the factors explaining wage variation *within* the secondary and primary segments, he was able to show that the "wage-setting process does differ substantially [between] the segments." Similarly, Martin Carnoy and Russell Rumberger (1975, p. 53) studied data for 1965 and 1970. After dividing jobs into market segments according to various dual-market characteristics (training required, job-holder's relation to other people during work, and so on), they compared the processes generating various market outcomes: mobility between and within segments, the return to education and seniority within segments, and so forth. Their research concluded that the relationships among education, work experience, earnings, and other variables differed significantly between segments. Robert Buchele (1975), in a careful study of middle-aged white males, discovered large differences between the market segments in annual earnings, likelihood of unemployment, and eight other labor market outcomes. More than that, however, he showed that a large proportion of each of these differences could not be explained by "human capital" variables (education, experience), and that the differences in fact resulted from segmented markets themselves. See, in addition to the essays cited above and in Note 2, Barry Bluestone (1974); David Gordon (1972a,b); Samuel Rosenberg (1975); Lawrence Kahn (1975); Francine Blau (1975); Michael Piore (1975); Martin Carnoy and Russell Rumberger (1975); Bennett Harrison (1972); and Edna Bonacich (1976). For dissenting views, see Paul Andrisani (1973), Michael Wachter (1974), and Glen Cain (1976).

5. The most careful estimates of the overall size of each segment in the national labor force will be published by David Gordon (forthcoming), and the one-quarter to one-third estimates given in the text for each segment are compatible with his preliminary results. Harry Braverman's (1974, pp. 379, 403–4) discussion can be interpreted as placing the combined secondary and subordinate primary workforce at two-thirds to three quarters and the independent primary at over 15 but less than 20 percent of the total labor force. Erik Wright (1976, p. 37) would seem to estimate the former (combined) group at 40 to 50 percent, the latter at 25 to 37 percent. Martin Carnoy and Russell Rumberger (1975, Tables 2 and 3) estimate the relative sizes (not allowing for self-employed) of the segments as secondary, 17 percent; subordinate primary, 47 percent; independent primary, 36 percent.

6. Analytically, it seemed essential to find clear differences among segments on one or two fundamental dimensions, in order to provide an objective and replicable method of determining market boundaries. Yet early attempts to develop such "definitional" dimensions (Richard C. Edwards, 1975b) fell short of the mark. Moreover, the ancedotal evidence suggested that such definition would be artificial and the resulting categories would not represent what was actually being observed. Below it is suggested that such a criterion does exist, but that it is a characteristic of the labor process, not of labor markets. This point has caused much confusion among those who have written on segmentation, because as they searched for a clean and decisive criterion for dividing occupations and/or workers, they have understandably come to different conclusions. Similarly, the critics of segmentation theory have criticized the approach for its failure to come

up with a market dimension as a clear means of division. But such a criterion is impossible, since the market segments but reflect divisions in the "sphere of production," and so we must look to the labor process for the roots of segmented markets. At the level of labor markets, then, the segments appear as clusters of characteristics, and *at the level of labor market analysis* we cannot choose any particular determining dimension.

7. Calculated from Paul Osterman (1975), p. 516. Martin Carnoy and Russell Rumberger (1975), Table 16. Calculated from Samuel Rosenberg (1975), Tables 3-11 and 3-12. The range for annual incomes was lower than the range for hourly wages because secondary workers on average are employed for fewer weeks per year. Calculated from David Gordon (1971), p. 385. Calculated from Robert Buchele (1976), Table 23. Whenever Buchele's results are reported below, his occupational classes 1 to 3 (professional, supervisory, and craft jobs) are cited as "independent-primary," his class 4 (subordinate) as "subordinate-primary," and his class 5 (menial) as "secondary." His sample is the National Longitudinal Survey Pre-Retirement Years data.

8. *Monthly Labor Review*, September, 1969, p. 18, Table 1.

9. Robert Buchele (1976), Table 22; occupational classes 1 (professional) and 3 (craft) had tenure rates comparable to secondary workers, as Michael Piore (1975), among others, had hypothesized.

10. David Gordon (1971), Samuel Rosenberg (1975), Table 3-10.

11. In Buchele's study, for example, the lower tenure rate among secondary workers *cannot* be attributed to less workforce experience or less education, since, after correcting for these factors, a large difference remains; Robert Buchele (1976), Table 22.

12. Martin Carnoy and Russell Rumberger (1975), pp. 40–41. Robert Buchele (1976), Table 23; Paul Osterman (1975), Tables 4, 5, and 6. David Gordon (1971), pp. 416–418. Gordon did find that among white secondary males there is a return on age, but he notes that this effect may well be due to younger whites moving out of the secondary market. This interpretation is strengthened by evidence that white males begin employment in the secondary market (during college and before deciding on a career.) but then move on to primary jobs with experience; see Samuel Rosenberg (1975), Table 5-1.

13. Robert Buchele (1976), Table 23. Paul Osterman (1975), Tables 4, 5, and 6. David Gordon (1971), Table V-6; Martin Carnoy and Russell Rumberger (1975), pp. 41–42.

14. Perhaps at one time "blue-collar" was an effective shorthand term for this market segment, but as many observers (David Gordon, 1972b; Paul Osterman, 1975; Harry Braverman, 1974) have noted, the blue- versus white-collar distinction has lost most of its persuasiveness. For one thing, many blue-collar jobs have achieved the pay, independence, mental labor components, and privileges formerly associated with white-collar status; more significantly, the machine-pacing, low pay, lack of privileges, and manual-labor job activities formerly thought to characterize only blue-collar employment have increasingly come to dominate at least the lower rungs of white-collar jobs. The old distinctions, which may well have been inaccurate for the past, become positively mystifying for the present, hence the need for new categories.

15. Lawrence Kahn (1975), Chapter III. In New York, organized-crime figures dominated the longshoremen's union, and the 1950s reorganization of work followed the (temporary) breaking of their corrupting grip.

16. Calculated from Paul Osterman (1975), Tables 2 and 4. The earnings-generating function in Osterman's study, as is usual, contains a single term for schooling but a quadratic term (age and age squared) for age or experience. This form implies that every year of schooling is of equal benefit to any other year, but that the return on age is different at different ages. Hence in calculating the age return, we must always specify a particular age interval (the intervals cited in the text are always for the mean-minus-ten-years to the mean age or experience. See also David Gordon (1971), Tables V-6 and V-7, especially for white males; Martin Carnoy and Russell Rumberger (1975), Tables 16 and 17 and pp. 41-44. Robert Buchele (1976, Table 23) did not find a significant experience return.

17. Calculated from Paul Osterman (1975), Tables 2 and 4; Robert Buchele (1976), Table 23; Martin Carnoy and Russell Rumberger (1975), Tables 16 and 17.

18. This characteristic shows up strongly in Robert Buchele's analysis (1976, Tables 6, 7, 9, 18, and 20) of the probability of having been laid off. Craft workers had the highest probability, but subordinate workers in Buchele's sample experienced a probability even higher than secondary workers. Similarly, craft workers and subordinate primary workers suffered a higher

overall unemployment rate than secondary workers. However, when the data are corrected for employment by core versus periphery firm (as should have been done in *defining* market segments), the secondary-market peripheral-firm worker has a substantially higher overall unemployment rate, frequency of unemployment, and probability of having been laid off than subordinate primary-market core-firm workers.

19. The relative size of these three occupational groups is subject to some dispute. For example, in Robert Buchele's (1976, Table 3) sample, craft work was the largest category; however, his inclusion of auto mechanics, repairmen, and electrical technicians—workers with few craft protections—inflates the size of his craft category.

20. Because a research focus on the primary market is more recent, less agreement exists as to who should be included in the independent primary segment. Michael Piore (1975), for example, leaves out craft workers; Robert Buchele (1976) treats professional, supervisory, and craft workers as three distinct "occupational classes."

21. Various estimates exist of the importance of public jobs in the independent primary market, and the only real point of consensus is that the biggest impact occurs in the professional occupations. Martin Carnoy and Russell Rumberger (1975), Tables 5 to 8, put the figure at slightly over 20 percent, an estimate that seems to coincide with that given by Robert Buchele (1975), Table 3.

22. Calculated from Robert Buchele (1976), Table 23; Paul Osterman (1975), Table 2; Martin Carnoy and Russell Rumberger (1975), Table 16.

23. Calculated from Paul Osterman (1975), Tables 2 and 4 and Martin Carnoy and Russell Rumberger (1975), Tables 16 and 17. For black males, the return to age may be greater in the subordinate primary sector, but their sample of black independent primary workers is very small. Robert Buchele (1975, Table 23) found a positive return for professional employees during the first nineteen years of experience, and a positive return for supervisory employers who had more than thirty years experience; other experience returns for independent primary workers were insignificantly different from zero.

24. Calculated from Paul Osterman (1975), Tables 2 and 4; Robert Buchele (1976), Table 23; Martin Carnoy and Russell Rumberger (1975), Tables 16 and 17.

25. Robert Buchele (1976), Tables 6, 7, 9 to 13, and 23; the coefficient—the best estimate—for "more than 30 years' experience" is positive but not statistically significantly different from zero. The coefficients for the other categories of independent workers are negative.

26. Robert Buchele (1976), Tables 6, 7 and 9 to 13.

27. Ibid., Table 23.

28. Ibid., Tables 6, 7, 9, and 23.

29. The secondary market includes periphery-sector manufacturing firms that have made increasing use of technical or mechanical methods of control, especially time and motion study and machine-pacing of individual jobs. These firms in general still retain simple control (arbitrary power of foremen and supervisors) as their basic organization of power, reinforced by these mechanical means; most revealingly, the enforcement of machine paces is achieved through bullying and other personal tactics aimed at the worker. Nonetheless, the peripheral sector (containing all enterprises except core firms) displays great diversity, and so do its workplaces.

30. For one interesting and persuasive study of the impact of type of organization on the importance of experience, see Paul Ryan's (1976) study of the welders at Quincy, Massachusetts shipyard. For an excellent description of the process of transforming high-skill production into low-skill production, drawing evidence from a broad range of industries, see Harry Braverman (1974), Parts II and IV.

31. In the human capital version, only the technical characteristics matter, and they do not give rise to distinct markets but rather simply to different market outcomes because of people's different endowments of human capital; see Jacob Mincer (1974). In the dual labor market version, general versus specific skills, on-the-job learning versus lack of it, and so on become the causes of market segmentation; see Peter Doeringer and Michael Piore (1971). The statement here is equivalent to saying that within the range of possible techniques, there is sufficient choice to permit selection based on compatability with different forms of work organization. The firm's choice cannot be described as "efficient," since this concept cannot be defined once we admit the distinction between labor and labor power but it certainly is the most profitable.

32. Note that the success of industrial unions in pushing mass-production core firms to

subordinate primary-employment patterns does not in general derive from their ability to exclude other workers; instead, the unions' power derives from their ability to mobilize all those in the industry. In this sense segmentation results from the struggle over control of the labor process rather than through market exclusion.

33. See Loren Baritz (1960); Ivar Berg (1971); and Samuel Bowles and Herbert Gintis (1975).

34. We can see how these two processes foster independent-primary employment from the results reported in the last chapter. Consider first the independent-primary characteristic of long tenure. Bureaucratic control relies on directing tasks by means of work criteria, and its incentive system is based on periodic evaluation and institutionalized rewards through promotion. All of these components presuppose lengthy employment for their functioning and their effect. At the lowest levels, employers try to screen out workers who show up for work irregularly, have high turnover, and manifest the other unstable work characteristics dysfunctional for bureaucratic employment. As reported in the last chapter, work at these levels is organized and controlled through explicit rules and well-developed and routinized procedures. Workers who do not follow the rules are penalized by no advancement and, perhaps, eventual dismissal. Central to this method of work direction is an incentive structure that rewards workers who obey these rules and who work reliably and dependably.

For new workers, explicit rules are the principal work criteria, and new workers are in a sense on probation, while they learn the rules and demonstrate that they have mastered proper rules orientation; hence, workers in low-level jobs find that learning to follow rules is a necessary trait for keeping one's job and for gaining the supervisor's approval.

The importance of rules orientation in predicting supervisors' ratings in the lower-level jobs seem to capture the importance of this trait in the first process (in distinguishing inappropriate or nonindependent primary-type workers); in this process the supervisor's evaluation is crucial. On the other hand, rules orientation was found to be insignificant in predicting pay differences in these jobs. This result is consistent with its insignificance in predicting either supervisor's ratings or pay in higher-level jobs: rules orientation is simply not important in the second internal-market process (allocating workers).

At higher levels in the hierarchy, the second process becomes the basis for the reward structure. The organization of work at these levels depends more on implicit rules, expectations, and self-motivation or self-control. Obeying rules by itself is insufficient here and is neither highly rewarded within a group nor used as the basis for advancement to or through the higher levels. Instead, access to and success in these levels is predicated on developing reliable and dependable work habits and (especially) an outlook similar to that of the higher-echlon management of the enterprise—in a sense, on becoming an "organization person." This conclusion is suggested by our finding that the trait "habits of dependability and predictability" was rewarded at middle levels and the "internalization of enterprise's goals" trait was most highly rewarded at higher levels. Importantly, the latter trait is the most significant one for achieving higher pay, the internationalization trait appears to be the path to advancement. Indeed, all three modes of compliance might well be interpreted as successively more sophisticated stages of accepting and internalizing the firm's goals.

The effect of this mode of control on job tenure should be clear. Consider the problem the firm has when hiring a worker who is new to that firm. The employer cannot easily determine whether or not this worker has those behavior traits they find important in their workers. Despite millions of dollars and forty years of research, no psychological test exists that can be given to new workers to predict job success reasonably well. So personnel managers use psychological tests that admittedly predict very little; they fall back on educational credentials as screening devices on the (not unwarranted but imprecise) assumption that diligence at work depends on the same characteristics as success in schooling (see Richard C. Edwards, 1977; Samuel Bowles, Herbert Gintis, and Peter Meyer, 1975; and Samuel Bowles and Herbert Gintis, 1973); and they rely heavily on recommendations from previous employers and on the applicant's work record, though it is usually difficult to evaluate the context of previous work experience. But in the final analysis, the firm can only learn whether a worker has the appropriate traits through a long process of actual experience with the worker on the job, and to do so it must keep workers long enough to make its assessment.

Similarly, when the firm attempts to fill its higher slots with workers who are predictable and dependable and have internalized the enterprise's goals, no simple tests, no demonstration or certification of skills can suffice. Again, the only sure test is the firm's own experience with the worker as its employee, the record of which is its file of supervisor's evaluations of the worker's performance. Bureaucratic control again fosters long tenure.

Another independent-primary characteristic that grows out of bureaucratic control is the "occupational consciousness" of independent primary workers. As indicated in the last chapter, bureaucratic control directly reinforces identifying with the job and internalizing the firm's goals. These behaviors among supervisors and middle-layer workers typically produce an overall identification with the firm itself, as the worker's occupation becomes indistinct from employment with the firm. Among craft or professional workers, with the reinforcing weight of craft tradition or professional association, the bureaucratic incentives typically produce a strong identification with the worker's occupation. In all three cases, bureaucratic control fosters the strong sense of identity with one's work.

35. Viewed from the worker's perspective, such obligations seem less permanent, since they can be jettisoned through bankruptcy proceedings or lost through company mergers, and many workers experience the loss of retirement benefits despite contractual rights. Nonetheless, for the small company, such measures, while eagerly accepted *in extremis*, are naturally not viewed as normal ways to run profitable business.

36. Other sources are racism and sexism, the conscious efforts of employers to split the working class, and more diverse "cultural" factors involving family structure and schooling. See David Gordon, Richard Edwards, and Michael Reich (forthcoming).

Chapter 10

1. The effort to use ethnic divisions in the steel plants (1880–1920) is one important sample; see Katherine Stone (1975).

2. Several Marxists (e.g., Harry Braverman, 1974; James O'Connor, 1975; Francesca Friedman, 1976) have focused on "productive" versus "unproductive" workers; others (e.g., Harry Braverman, 1974) have focused on the various elements (floating, stagnant, latent) of the reserve army, and at least one (Samuel Rosenberg, 1977) has identified the secondary market with the reserve army; still others (e.g., Erik Wright, 1976) have emphasized mental versus manual labor; others (e.g., Herbert Gintis, 1970) have described the differences between a new working class and the old working class. Barbara and John Ehrenreich (1977) propose a theory of the (new) "professional-managerial class," but their argument that this group constitutes a class is weak. None of these categorizations seems useful for describing the phenomenon discussed in the text.

Erik Wright (1976) has put forward the concept of "contradictory class positions," that is, class positions somehow between the proletariat, the bourgeoisie, and the petit bourgeoisie. This concept appears most akin to the schema suggested here. Wright's single category of proletariat would include what is here referred to as the working poor *and* the traditional proletariat. His categories of "bottom managers, foremen, and line supervisors" and "semi-autonomous employees" reflect what is here labeled the "middle layers." The latter term, incidentally, is Harry Braverman's.

3. U.S. Bureau of the Census (1976a), pp. 1, 2, 36, 38, and 89.

4. Ibid., pp. 36, 38, and 46.

5. Ibid., pp. 4, 92–94, and 108.

6. The number of white males tends to be overstated in studies by Samuel Rosenberg (1975), Robert Buchele (1976), and Martin Carnoy and Russell Rumberger (1975) because of the exclusion of females from their sample and (for Buchele and Carnoy and Rumberger) the inability to distinguish workers of Hispanic origin. In Rosenberg's sample (see his Table 3–4) white males accounted for between one quarter and one-third of male secondary workers. Higher estimates appear in the other studies, including Paul Osterman's (1975); see also David Gordon (1971).

7. The Bureau of the Census admitted that it had failed to locate 5.3 million persons in 1970, including 7.7 percent of the black population. For a discussion of this point, see Samuel Rosenberg (1975), p. 60.

8. For perhaps the earliest observation of this new migration, see Michael Piore (1974); a similar estimate is given in the *New York Times,* April 3, 1977, p. 1.

9. Among full-time, full-year workers in nonpoor families studied by Barry Bluestone, William Murphy, and Mary Stevenson (1973), more females (58 percent for white women, 73 percent for black women) had low wages than did males (20 percent for white men, 45 percent for black men).

10. In Samuel Rosenberg's (1975, Table 5–1) study, between one-half and three-quarters of all white males who began working in secondary-market jobs had moved to primary-market employment by 1969; for black, Hispanic, and "other" males, the mobility was also substantial but significantly less. The year 1969 marks the end of a boom period, thereby maximizing the measured movement due to reserve-army causes. Carnoy and Rumberger (1975, p. 15) reported the same phenomenon.

11. Martin Carnoy and Russell Rumberger (1975), Table 2; Samuel Rosenberg (1975), Table 3–4; Paul Osterman (1975), Table 2.

12. U.S. Dept. of Labor (1975a), Table 45; U.S. Bureau of the Census (1975c),

13. See footnote 9 above. The 1970 Census indicates that nearly half of all husbands in typical subordinate-primary occupations (operatives) had working wives, and that these females were about equally divided among clerical, operative, and other kinds of work; U.S. Bureau of the Census (1973a), Table 48. Other information indicates that if the husband and wife are both present and the husband is younger than 65 years old, the wife is more likely to work than not; indeed, the proportion of married women working is much greater than half for families in their 20s, 30s, and 40s. (See U.S. Bureau of the Census, 1976b, pp. 346–47.) Males who are subordinate primary workers are more likely than other male workers to have working wives; this can be seen from the following table, which shows that if the husband's income is approximately in the subordinate-primary range, the wife's labor force participation rate reaches a peak. The table, of course, includes families of all ages, not just those of working age. (See U.S. Dept. of Labor, 1975b, p. 23.)

Labor Force Participation Rates for Married Women by Income of Husbands, 1974

Husband's Income	Proportion of Wives Working
Under $3,000	35.5
$3,000–$4,999	35.8
$5,000–$6,999	43.3
$7,000–$9,999	49.3
$10,000 and over	43.4

14. Calculated from U.S. Dept. of Labor (1975a), Table 19, and U.S. Bureau of the Census (1973a), Table 2. This table does not separate self-employed professionals from salaried professionals; this imparts a bias to our estimates only if the proportion self-employed differs by race-sex group. Since white males seem more likely than others to be self-employed, the figures cited in the text may overstate the dominance of white males in independent primary jobs. On the other hand, the Census includes as "professionals" many lower-level workers (lab technicians, nonsupervisory nurses) who ought to be classified as subordinate-primary workers, and their inclusion here inflates the nonwhite male groups. These qualifications emphasize the need to interpret the figures as illustrating orders of magnitude rather than presenting precise measurements.

15. U.S. Bureau of the Census (1973a), Tables 29,48: U.S. Bureau of the Census (1973b), Table 4.

16. This point (for blacks) is made forcefully by Harold Baron (1971, 1975) and Michael Reich (forthcoming); for women, see Nancy Chodorow (1978) and Francine Blau (1975). The position of Hispanics has not been well analyzed and therefore remains unclear. A useful introduction to some of the vast literature on these topics is contained in Chapters 9 and 10 of Richard C. Edwards, Michael Reich, and Thomas Weisskopf (1978).

17. Martin Carnoy and Russell Rumberger (1975), Tables 16 and 17; Edna Bonacich (1976); David Gordon (1971), Tables V–6 and V–7.

18. For example, Harry Braverman (1974) appears not to recognize the distinction between low wages and low unit costs, despite his own emphasis on the labor-labor power distinction.

19. The 1919 steel strike was the most notable example, but as Edna Bonacich (1976, Table 5) documents, it was hardly atypical. For women, see Margery Davies (1975).

20. Michael Reich (forthcoming).

21. Heidi Hartmann (1975), Chapters 1, 5, and 6. The principal factor reducing the quantity of housework appears to be smaller family size, not labor-saving devices.

22. Samuel Bowles and Herbert Gintis (1975); Mira Komarovsky (1962); Melvin Kohn (1969); Katherine Stone (1975); Studs Terkel (1972); Barbara Garson (1975); Ann Bookman (1977); David Montgomery (1974); Herbert Gutman (1972); Alice and Stoughton Lynd (1973); Jeremy Brecher (1972); Michael Piore (1975); Stanley Aronowitz (1973).

Chapter 11

1. U.S. Department of Labor (1975a), pp. 106, 389, and 382-386; private communication from Bureau of Labor Statistics.

2. In concrete analysis of each of these cases, of course, more specific factors would need to be considered as well. For a detailed discussion of how this class dynamic works itself out in the competition between Democratic and Republican parties, see Richard Edwards and Michael Reich (1978).

3. For a discussion of the fiscal crisis limits on social spending, see James O'Connor (1973). For the general competition argument see Paul Baran and Paul Sweezy (1966); for a specific case, that of mass transit, see U.S. Senate (1974). For the work ethic limit on social spending, see Richard C. Edwards (1978).

4. The relationships between capitalism and racism and between capitalism and sexism are complex, and capitalism's responsibility for creating and sustaining racism (and to a lesser extent sexism) is far greater than the text suggests; for example, the appearance of capitalism as a world system created wage labor in the European countries and slave labor in the United States and Latin America. In many ways, world capitalism created modern racism; see Harold Baran (1971).

5. If we count as workers all those wage and salary earners (including the currently unemployed) except for salaried officials and managers, workers as a proportion of the total U.S. labor force constituted 84 percent in 1975; this is calculated from Michael Reich (1978), U.S. President (1976) and U.S. Bureau of the Census (1977). Several other definitions of the working class are possible, but this does not change the point made in the text; see Erik Wright (1976) for one useful discussion. Nicos Poulantzas (1975) provides one of the few analyses that would disagree with both the trend and the argument.

6. Shares calculated from U.S. President (1977), Table B-20. "Wage share" includes total wage and salary disbursements and other labor income. "Profits share" includes farm and nonfarm proprietors income, rental, dividend, and personal interest income. "Transfer share" includes total transfers minus personal contributions for social insurance. See also M. Reynolds and E. Smolensky (1975); see also Sheldon Dantziger and Robert Plotnick (1975) and S. Dantziger (1977). William Nordhaus (1975) has provided strong evidence on the decline in profit rates between 1948 and 1973. This evidence confirms the experience of other countries with large socialist or social democratic parties. For example, in the Organization for Economic Cooperation

and Development (OECD) countries, low growth countries are big social service spenders, and conversely. Also, the relationship between public social service spending and gross private fixed investment in the major capitalist countries is negative and greatly increasing in absolute magnitude. See Samuel Bowles and Herbert Gintis (1978) and Christine DiStefano (1977). Douglas Hibbs (1976) provides yet another (and impressive) analysis supporting the view that the working classes in the advanced capitalist countries have moved the distributional conflict into the political arena and been successful there.

7. The alleged trade-offs between the environment and jobs, between seniority and affirmative action, and between welfare and taxes are examples of attempts to get one fraction to oppose another. The trade-offs exist only in the context of private control over investment and the need to maintain business confidence.

8. Gabriel Kolko (1963); James Weinstein (1968); Ronald Radosh (1972); Murray Rothbard (1972); the general thesis has been argued most cogently by James O'Connor (1973).

9. See note 5 above.

10. Trilateral Commission (1975); see also Samuel Bowles (1977).

BIBLIOGRAPHY

Aitken, Hugh. *Taylorism at Watertown Arsenal*. Cambridge, Mass.: Harvard University Press, 1960.

Anderson, Theodore, R. and Warkov, Seymour. "Organizational Size and Functional Complexity." *American Sociological Review*. 1961.

Andrisani, Paul. *An Empirical Analysis of the Dual Labor Market Theory*. Unpublished Ph.D. thesis, Ohio State University, Columbus, 1973.

Arnold, H. L. and Faurote, L. F. *Ford Methods and the Ford Shops*. New York: The Engineering Magazine Company, 1915.

Aronowitz, Stanley. *False Promises: The Shaping of American Working-Class Consciousness*. New York: McGraw-Hill Co., 1973.

Averitt, Robert. *The Dual Economy*. New York: Norton, 1968.

Bain, Joe S. *Barriers to New Competition*. Cambridge, Mass.: Harvard University Press, 1956.

Baran, Paul and Sweezy, Paul. *Monopoly Capital*. New York: Monthly Review Press, 1966.

Baritz, Loren. *The Servants of Power*. Middletown, Conn.: Wesleyan University Press, 1960.

Baron, Harold. "The Demand for Black Labor." *Radical America*, March-April, 1971.

———. "Racial Domination in Advanced Capitalism: A Theory of Nationalism and Divisions in the Labor Market." In *Labor Market Segmentation*, edited by Richard Edwards, Michael Reich, and David Gordon. Lexington, Mass.: D. C. Heath, 1975.

Beals, Ralph. "Concentrated Industries, Administered Prices, and Inflation: A Survey of Recent Empirical Research." Unpublished paper, Amherst College, Amherst, May, 1975.

Berg, Ivar. *Education and Jobs: The Great Training Robbery*. Boston: Beacon Press, 1971.

Berghahn, V. R. *Germany and the Approach of War in 1914*. New York: St. Martin's Press, 1973.

Bernstein, Irving. *Turbulent Years: A History of the American Worker*, 1933–1941. Boston: Houghton Mifflin, 1970.

———. *The Lean Years*. Boston: Houghton Mifflin, 1972.

Best, Michael and Connolly, William. *The Politicized Economy*. Lexington, Mass.: D. C. Heath, Lexington Books, 1976.

Blair, John. *Economic Concentration*. New York: Harcourt Brace Jovanovich, 1972.

Blau, Francine. *Pay Differentials and Differences in the Distribution of Employment of Male and Female Office Workers*. Unpublished Ph.D. thesis, Harvard University, Cambridge, Mass., 1975.

Blau, Peter. *The Dynamics of Bureaucracy*. Chicago: University of Chicago Press, 1955.

———. and Scott, W. R. *Formal Organizations*. San Francisco: Chandler Publishing Company, 1962.

Bluestone, Barry. *The Tripartite Economy: Labor Markets and the Working Poor. Poverty and Human Resources*, July-August, 1970.

———. "The Personal Earnings Distribution: Individual and Institutional Determinants." Unpublished Ph.D. thesis, University of Michigan, Ann Arbor, 1974.

———. Murphy, William M.; and Stevenson, Mary. *Low Wages and the Working Poor*. Ann Arbor, Mich.: The Institute of Labor and Industrial Relations, 1973.

Bonacich, Edna. "Advanced Capitalism and Black/White Race Relations in the United States: A Split Labor Market Interpretation." *American Sociological Review*, 1976.

Bookman, Ann. *The Process of Political Socialization Among Women and Immigrant Workers: A Case Study of Unionization in the Electronics Industry*. Unpublished Ph.D. thesis, Harvard University, 1977.

Bowles, Samuel. "Have Capitalism and Democracy Come to a Parting of the Ways?" *The Progressive,* June, 1977.

———. "Liberal Democracy and the Accumulation Process." Unpublished paper, 1978.

———. and Gintis, Herbert. "I. Q. in the United States Class Structure." *Social Policy,* January-February, 1973.

———. *Schooling in Capitalist America.* New York: Basic Books, 1975.

———. "The Problem with Human Capital Theory." *American Economic Review,* May, 1976.

———. and Meyer, Peter. "Education and Personal Development: The Long Shadow of Work." *Berkeley Journal of Sociology,* Fall, 1975.

Bowring, Joseph. *The Dual Economy: Core and Periphery in the Accumulation Process.* Unpublished Ph.D. thesis, University of Massachusetts, Amherst, forthcoming.

Brandes, Stuart. *American Welfare Capitalism, 1880–1940.* Chicago: University of Chicago, 1976.

Braverman, Harry. *Labor and Monopoly Capital.* New York: Monthly Review Press, 1974.

Brecher, Jeremy. *Strike!* San Francisco: Straight Arrow Books, 1972.

Brody, David. *The Steelworkers in America: The Non-Union Era.* Cambridge, Mass.: Harvard University Press, 1960.

———. *Labor in Crisis: The Steel Strike of 1919.* New York: J. B. Lippincott, 1965.

———. "The Rise and Decline of Welfare Capitalism." In *Change and Continuity in Twentieth-Century America: The 1920s* edited by John Braeman et al. Columbus: Ohio State University Press, 1968.

Broy, Anthony. "Automation in High Gear." *Dun's,* November, 1972.

———. "The Revolution in Testing and Measurement," *Dun's,* November, 1973.

Buchele, Robert. *Jobs and Workers: A Labor Market Segmentation Perspective on the Work Experience of Middle-Aged Men.* Unpublished paper submitted to the Secretary of Labor's Conference on the National Longitudinal Survey of the Pre-Retirement Years, Boston, 1976.

Buder, Stanley. *Pullman.* New York: Oxford University Press, 1967.

Burch, Philip H. *The Managerial Revolution Reassessed.* Lexington, Mass.: D. C. Heath, Lexington Books, 1972.

Bylinsky, Gene. "Here Comes the Second Computer Revolution." *Fortune,* November, 1975.

Cahiers de Mai. "The Lip Watch Strike." *Radical America,* Nov.-Dec., 1973.

Cain, Glen. "The Challenge of Segmented Labor Market Theories to Orthodox Theory: A Survey." *Journal of Economic Literature,* December, 1976.

Carnoy, Martin and Rumberger, Russell. *Segmented Labor Markets: Some Empirical Forays.* Palo Alto, Calif.: Center for Economic Studies, 1975.

Carwardine, William. *The Pullman Strike.* New York: Arno Press, 1969. (First published in 1894.)

Chandler, Alfred. "The Beginnings of 'Big Business' in American Industry." *Business History Review,* Spring, 1959.

———. *Strategy and Structure: Chapters in the History of American Industrial Enterprise.* Cambridge, Mass.: MIT Press, 1962.

———. "The Railroads: Pioneers in Modern Corporate Management." *Business History Review,* Spring, 1965.

Chodorow, Nancy. *The Reproduction of Mothering.* Berkeley, Calif.: University of California Press, 1978.

Clark, Victor. *The History of Manufactures in the United States.* 3 vols. New York: Peter Smith, 1949.

Cochran, Thomas C. *The Pabst Brewing Company.* London: Oxford University Press, 1948.

Cohen, David, and Lazerson, Marvin. "Education and the Corporate Order." *Socialist Revolution,* May-June, 1971.

Comanor, William and Wilson, T. "Advertising and the Advantages of Size." *American Economic Review,* May, 1969.

Commons, John et al., *History of Labor in the United States.* 4 vols. New York: Macmillan, 1935.

Converse, Vernon G. "Selecting Handling Systems for Automatic Testing." *Automation,* November, 1974.

Creamer, Daniel. *Capital and Output Trends in Manufacturing Industries, 1880–1948.* Occasional Paper No. 41. New York: National Bureau of Economic Research, 1954.

Crozier, Michel. *The Bureaucratic Phenomenon.* Chicago: University of Chicago Press, 1964.

Cuff, Robert. *War Industries Board.* Baltimore: Johns Hopkins Press, 1973.

Dantziger, Sheldon, "The Distributional Effect of Government Transfers," paper presented at the Union for Radical Political Economics, 1977.

Dantziger, Sheldon and Plotnick, Robert. "Demographic Change, Government Transfers, and the Distribution of Income," Discussion Paper 274-75, Institute for Research on Poverty, Madison, 1975.

Davies, Margery. "Woman's Place Is at the Typewriter." In *Labor Market Segmentation,* edited by Richard C. Edwards, Michael Reich, and David Gordon. Lexington, Mass.: D. C. Heath, 1975.

———. *The Evolution of Job Structures in Three Female Occupations.* Unpublished Ph.D. thesis, Brandeis University, forthcoming.

Davis, Lance, et al. *American Economic Growth: An Economist's History of the United States.* New York: Harper and Row, 1972.

Delehanty, George. *Nonproduction Workers in U.S. Manufacturing.* Amsterdam: North Holland Pub. Co., 1968.

De Vroey, Michel. "The Separation of Ownership and Control in Large Corporations." *Review of Radical Political Economics,* Summer 1975.

Di Stefano, Christine. "Social Expenditures and Capitalist Growth: A Statistical Analysis," Unpublished paper, University of Massachusetts, 1977.

Doeringer, Peter and Piore, Michael. *Internal Labor Markets and Manpower Analysis.* Lexington, Mass.: D. C. Heath, Lexington Books, 1971.

———. et al. *Urban Manpower Programs and Low-Income Labor Markets: A Critical Assessment.* Report to the U. S. Department of Labor, 1972.

Douglas, Paul. *Real Wages in the United States, 1890–1926.* Boston: Houghton Mifflin, 1930.

Drucker, Peter. *The Practice of Management.* New York: Harper and Row, 1954.

Edwards, Richard C. *Alienation and Inequality: Capitalist Relations of Production in Bureaucratic Enterprise.* Unpublished Ph.D. thesis, Harvard University, 1972.

———. "Stages in Corporate Stability and the Risks of Corporate Failure." *Journal of Economic History,* June, 1975. [1975a].

———. "The Social Relations of Production in the Firm and Labor Market Structure." *Politics and Society,* 1975. [1975b].

———. "Individual Traits and Organizational Incentives: What Makes a 'Good' Worker?" *Journal of Human Resources,* Winter, 1976.

———. "Personal Traits and 'Success' in Schooling and Work." *Educational and Psychological Measurement,* Spring, 1977.

———. "Who Fares Well in the Welfare State?" In *The Capitalist System,* 2d ed., by Richard C. Edwards, Michael Reich, and Thomas Weisskopf. Englewood Cliffs, N.J.: Prentice-Hall, Inc., 1978.

———, Reich, Michael; and Gordon, David, eds. *Labor Market Segmentation.* Mass.: D. C. Heath, 1975.

———, Reich, Michael; and Weisskopf, Thomas. *The Capitalist System,* 2d ed. Englewood Cliffs, N.J.: Prentice-Hall, Inc., 1978.

———, Reich, Michael. "Political Parties and Class Conflict in the United States." *Socialist Review,* May-June, 1978.

Ehrenreich, Barbara and Ehrenreich, John. "The Professional-Managerial Class." *Radical America.* Part I, March-April, 1977; Part II, May-June, 1977.

Ely, Richard. "Pullman: A Social Study." *Harper's Monthly,* June, 1885.

Emmet, Boris and Jeuck, John. *Catalogues and Counters: A History of Sears, Roebuck and Company.* Chicago: University of Chicago Press, 1950.

Espinosa, Juan and Zimbalist, Andrew. *Economic Democracy.* New York: Academic Press, 1978.

Faunce, William. "Automation in the Automobile Industry." *American Sociological Review,* August, 1958.

Fisher, Douglas. *Steel Serves the Nation, 1901–1951.* New York: U.S. Steel Corporation, 1951.

Fitzgerald, Thomas. "Why Motivation Theory Doesn't Work." *Harvard Business Review,* July-August, 1971.

Ford, Henry. "Progressive Manufacture." *Encyclopedia Britannica*, 13th edition. New York: The Encyclopedia Britannica Co., 1926.

Friedman, Francesca. "The Internal Structure of the American Proletariat: A Marxist Analysis." *Socialist Revolution*, October-December, 1975.

Galbraith, John K. *The New Industrial State*. Boston: Houghton Mifflin, 1967.

———. *Economics and the Public Purpose*. Boston: Houghton Mifflin, 1973.

Gale, Bradley. "Market Share and Rate of Return." *Review of Economics and Statistics*, November, 1972.

Garson, Barbara. *All the Livelong Day*. Garden City, N.Y.: Doubleday, 1975.

General Electric Company. *Professional Management in General Electric*. 4 vols. 1953–1959.

Gersuny, Carl. *Punishment and Redress in a Modern Factory*. Lexington, Mass.: D. C. Heath, Lexington Books, 1973.

Gintis, Herbert. "New Working Class and Revolutionary Youth." *Socialist Revolution*, May-June, 1970.

Gooding, Judson. "Blue-Collar Blues on the Assembly Line." *Fortune*, July, 1970.

Gordon, David. *Class, Productivity, and the Ghetto: A Study of Labor Market Stratification*. Unpublished Ph.D. thesis, Harvard University, 1971.

———. *Theories of Poverty and Underemployment*. Lexington, Mass.: D. C. Heath, Lexington Books, 1972. [1972a].

———. "From Steam Whistles to Coffee Breaks." *Dissent*, Winter, 1972. [1972b].

———. "Methodological and Empirical Issues in the Theory of Labor Market Segmentation." Forthcoming.

———. Edwards, Richard C. and Reich, Michael. "Labor Market Segmentation in American Capitalism." Forthcoming.

Gort, Michael. *Diversification and Integration in American Industry*. Princeton, N.J.: Princeton University Press, 1962.

Gouldner, Alvin. *Patterns of Industrial Bureaucracy*. Glencoe, Ill.: The Free Press, 1954.

Griliches, Zvi and Mason, William. "Education, Income and Ability." *Journal of Political Economy*, May-June, 1972.

Gulick, Charles. *Labor Policy of the United States Steel Corporation*. New York: Columbia University Press, 1924.

Gutman, Herbert. *Work, Culture, and Society in Industrializing America, 1815–1919*. New York: Knopf, 1976.

Hall, Richard. "The Concept of Bureaucracy: An Empirical Assessment." *American Journal of Sociology*, July, 1963.

Harrison, Bennett. *Education, Training, and the Urban Ghetto*. Baltimore: Johns Hopkins Press, 1972.

Hartmann, Heidi. *Capitalism and Women's Work in the Home, 1900–1930*. Unpublished Ph.D. thesis, Yale University, 1975.

Henderson, A. M. and Parsons, Talcott, eds. *Max Weber: The Theory of Social and Economic Organization*. New York: Oxford University Press, 1947.

Hibbs, Douglas. "Long-Run Trends in Strike Activity in Comparative Perspective." Unpublished paper, Center for International Studies, Cambridge, 1976.

Hogan, William. *Economic History of the Iron and Steel Industry in the United States*. Lexington, Mass.: D. C. Heath, Lexington Books, 1971.

Horst, Thomas. "Firm and Industry Determinants of the Decision to Invest Abroad: An Empirical Study." *Review of Economics and Statistics*, August, 1972.

Hoxie, Robert F. *Scientific Management and Labor*. New York: D. Appleton and Company, 1915.

Husband, Joseph and Runnells, John S. *What a New System of Management Did for Us*. Pullman Company, 1916.

Hutchinson, William. *Cyrus Hall McCormick*. Vols. 1 and 2. New York: The Century Company, 1930.

Hymer, Stephen. "The Multinational Corporation and the Law of Uneven Development." In *Economics and World Order*, edited by J. Bhagwati. New York: Macmillan, 1972.

Interchurch World Movement. *Report on the Steel Strike of 1919*. New York: Harcourt, Brace, and Howe, 1920.

International Harvester Company. *McCormick Works*. Chicago: n.d. (circa 1920).

Jenkins, David. *Job Power: Blue and White Collar Democracy*. Garden City, N.Y.: Doubleday, 1973.

Jenkins, Glenn and Wright, Brian. "Taxation of Income of Multinational Corporations: The Case of the U. S. Petroleum Industry." *Review of Economics and Statistics*, February, 1975.

Jenks, J. W. *Trusts and Industrial Problems*. U. S. Department of Labor Bulletin No. 29. Washington, D. C.: U. S. Government Printing Office, 1900.

Jones, Eliot. *The Trust Problem in the United States*. New York: Macmillan, 1921.

Josephson, Hannah. *The Golden Threads: New England's Mill Girls and Magnates*. New York: Russell and Russell, 1949.

Kahn, Lawrence. *Unions and Labor Market Segmentation*. Unpublished Ph.D. thesis, University of California, Berkeley, 1975.

Kamarovsky, Mira. *Blue-Collar Marriage*. New York: Random House, 1962.

Katz, Fred E. *Autonomy and Organization: The Limits of Social Control*. New York: Random House, 1968.

Kohn, Melvin. *Class and Conformity*. Homewood, Ill.: Dorsey Press, 1969.

Kolko, Gabriel. *The Triumph of Conservatism*. Chicago: Quadrangle Books, 1963.

Kotz, David. "Finance Capital and Corporate Control." In *The Capitalist System*, 2d ed. edited by Richard C. Edwards, Michael Reich, and Thomas Weisskopf. Englewood Cliffs, N.J.: Prentice-Hall, Inc., 1978.

Laidler, Harry. *Concentration of Control in American Industry*. New York: Thomas Crowell Company, 1931.

Langer, Elinor. "The Women of the Telephone Company." *New York Review of Books*, March 12, 1970 and March 26, 1970.

Layer, Robert. *Wages, Earnings, and Output in Four Cotton Textile Companies in New England, 1825–1860*. Unpublished Ph.D. thesis, Harvard University, Cambridge, 1952.

Lindsey, Almont. *The Pullman Strike*. Chicago: University of Chicago Press, 1964. (First published in 1942.)

Litterer, Joseph. "Systematic Management: Design for Organizational Recoupling in American Manufacturing Firms." *Business History Review*, Winter, 1963.

Livermore, Shaw. "The Success of Industrial Mergers." *Quarterly Journal of Economics*, 1935.

Lynd, Alice and Lynd, Staughton. *Rank and File*. Boston: Beacon Press, 1973.

MacEwan, Arthur. "Capitalist Expansion and the Sources of Imperialism." In *The Capitalist System*, 2d ed., by Richard C. Edwards, Michael Reich, and Thomas Weisskopf. Englewood Cliffs, N.J.: Prentice Hall, Inc., 1978.

Machinery and Allied Products Institute. *The G. E. Approach to Industrial Relations*. Washington, D. C., 1962.

Maltese, Francesca. "Notes for a Study of the Automobile Industry." In *Labor Market Segmentation*, by Richard C. Edwards, Michael Reich, and David Gordon. Lexington, Mass.: D. C. Heath, 1975.

Marglin, Stephen. "What Do Bosses Do? The Origins and Functions of Hierarchy in Capitalist Production." *Review of Radical Political Economics*, Summer, 1974.

Markowitz, Harry. *Portfolio Selection*. New York: John Wiley and Sons, 1959.

Marx, Karl. *Capital*. Volumes I, II, and III. New York: International Publishers, 1967. (Volume I first published in 1867.)

———. "The Eighteen Brumarie of Louis Bonaparte." In *The Marx-Engels Reader*, by Robert C. Tucker. New York: W. W. Norton, 1972. (First published in 1852.)

Mathewson, S. B. *Restriction of Output Among Unorganized Workers*. Carbondale, Ill.: Southern Illinois University Press, 1969. (First published in 1931.)

McConville, Ed. "How 7,041 Got Fired." *The Nation*, October, 1975.

Melicher, Ronald and Rush, David. "The Performance of Conglomerate Firms: Recent Risk and Return Experience." *Journal of Finance*, May, 1973.

Melman, Seymour. "The Rise of Administrative Overhead in the Manufacturing Industries of the United States, 1899–1947." *Oxford Economic Papers*, 1951.

Merton, Robert et al. *Reader in Bureaucracy*. New York: The Free Press, 1952.

Mincer, Jacob. *Schooling, Experience, and Earnings*. New York: Columbia University Press, 1974.

Montgomery, David. "The 'New Unionism' and the Transformation of Workers' Consciousness in America, 1909–1922. *Journal of Social History*, Summer, 1974.

Moody, John. *The Truth About the Trusts*. New York: Moody Publishing Company, 1904.

Moran, Theodore. "Foreign Expansion as an 'Institutional Necessity' for U. S. Corporate Capitalism." *World Politics*, April, 1973.

Morrow, Ellis. *The Lynn Plan of Representation*. Lynn, Mass.: The General Electric Company, 1921.

Mueller, Willard and Hamm, Larry. "Trends in Industrial Market Concentration, 1947–1970." *Review of Economics and Statistics*, November, 1974.

Nadworny, Milton. *Scientific Management and the Unions, 1900–1932*. Cambridge, Mass.: Harvard University Press, 1955.

National Industrial Conference Board. *Collective Bargaining Through Employee Representation*. New York: National Industrial Conference Board, 1933.

Navin, Thomas and Sears, Marion. "The Rise of a Market for Industrial Securities." *Business History Review*, June, 1955.

Nelson, Daniel. *Managers and Workers: Origins of the New Factory System in the United States, 1880–1920*. Madison: University of Wisconsin Press, 1975.

———, and Campbell, Stuart. "Taylorism Versus Welfare Work in American Industry: H. L. Gantt and the Bancrofts." *Business History Review*, Spring, 1972.

Nelson, Ralph. *Merger Movements in American Industry, 1895–1956*. Princeton, N.J.: Princeton University Press, 1959.

Nevins, Allan and Hill, F. E. *Ford: Decline and Rebirth, 1933–1962*. New York: Scribner, 1963.

Nordhaus, William. "The Falling Share of Profits." *Brookings Papers in Economic Activity*, No. 1, 1974.

Nutter, G. Warren. *The Extent of Enterprise Monopoly in the United States, 1899–1939*. Chicago: University of Chicago Press, 1951.

O'Connor, James. *The Fiscal Crisis of the State*. New York: St. Martins's Press, 1973.

———. "Productive vs. Unproductive Labor." *Politics and Society*, Vol. 5, No. 3, 1975.

Ornstein, Stanley. "The Advertising-Concentration Controversy." *Southern Economic Journal*, July, 1976.

Osterman, Paul. "An Empirical Study of Labor Market Segmentation." *Journal of Industrial and Labor Relations*, 1975.

Ozanne, Robert. *A Century of Labor-Management Relations at McCormick and International Harvester*. Madison: University of Wisconsin Press, 1967.

———. *Wages in Theory and Practice*. Madison: University of Wisconsin Press, 1971.

Passer, Harold. "The Development of Large-Scale Organization: Electrical Manufacturing Around 1900." *Journal of Economic History*, Autumn, 1952.

Palmer, Bryan. "Class, Conception and Conflict: The Thrust for Efficiency, Managerial Views of Labor, and the Working Class Rebellion, 1903–1922." *Review of Radical Political Economics*, 1975.

Pedersen, Lawrence and Tabb, William. "Ownership and Control of Large Corporations Revisited." *Antitrust Bulletin*, 1976.

Penn, David W. "Aggregate Concentration: A Statistical Note." *Antitrust Bulletin*, 1976.

Piore, Michael. "On-the-Job Training in the Dual Labor Market." In *Public-Private Manpower Policies* by Arnold Weber et al. Madison, Wisc.: Industrial Relations Research Association, 1969.

———. "Manpower Policy." In *The State and the Poor*, by S. Beer and R. Barringer. Cambridge, Mass.: Winthrop Publishing Company, 1970.

———. "The 'New Immigration' and the Presumptions of Social Policy." *Industrial Relations Research Association Series, Proceedings of the IRRA Meetings*, December, 1974.

———. "Notes for a Theory of Labor Market Stratification." In *Labor Market Segmentation*, by Richard C. Edwards, Michael Reich, and David Gordon. Lexington, Mass.: D. C. Heath, 1975.

Poulantzas, Nicos. *Classes in Contemporary Capitalism*. London: NLB, 1975.

Preston, William. *Aliens and Dissenters: Federal Suppression of Radicals, 1903-1933*. Cambridge, Mass.: Harvard University Press, 1963.

Radosh, Ronald. "The Myth of the New Deal." In *A New History of Leviathan*, edited by Ronald Radosh and Murray Rothbard. New York: Dutton, 1972.

Reich, Michael. "The Evolution of the United States Labor Force." In *The Capitalist System*, 2d ed., by Richard C. Edwards, Michael Reich, and T. Weisskopf. Englewood Cliffs, N.J.: Prentice-Hall, Inc., 1978.

———. *Racial Discrimination: White Gains, White Losses*. Forthcoming.

Reynolds, Morgan and Smolensky, Eugene, eds. *Public Expenditures, Taxes, and the Distribution of Income*. New York: Academic Press, 1977.

Rhoades, S. A. "The Effect of Diversification on Industry Profit Performance in 241 Manufacturing Industries: 1963." *Review of Economics and Statistics*, May, 1973.

———. "A Further Evaluation of the Effect of Diversification on Industrial Profits Performance." *Review of Economics and Statistics*, November, 1974.

Ripley, Charles M. *Life in a Large Manufacturing Plant*. Schenectady, N.Y.: General Electric Company, 1919.

Roosevelt, Frank. "Cambridge Economics as Commodity Fetishism." *Review of Radical Political Economics*, Winter, 1975.

Rosenberg, Samuel. *The Dual Labor Market: Its Existence and Consequences*. Unpublished Ph.D. thesis, University of California, Berkeley, 1975.

———. "Turnover and the Dual Labor Market." *Politics and Society*, Vol. 7, No. 2, 1977.

Rothbard, Murray N. "War Collectivism in World War I." In *A New History of Leviathan*, by Ronald Radosh and Murray Rothbard. New York: Dutton, 1972.

Ryan, Paul. *Job Training*. Unpublished Ph.D. thesis, Harvard University, 1977.

Shepherd, William. *Market Power and Economic Welfare*. New York: Random House, 1970.

Sheppard, Harold and Herrick, Neal. *Where Have All the Robots Gone?* New York: The Free Press, 1972.

Stekler, H. O. "The Variability of Profitability with Size of Firms, 1947–1958." *Journal of the American Statistical Association*, December, 1964.

Stigler, George. *Five Lectures on Economic Problems*. New York: Macmillan, 1949.

———. "The Statistics of Monopoly and Merger." *Journal of Political Economy*, February, 1965.

———. *Capital and Rates of Return in Manufacturing*. Princeton, N.J.: Princeton University Press, 1963.

Stone, Katherine. "The Origins of Job Structures in the Steel Industry." In *Labor Market Segmentation*, by Richard C. Edwards, Michael Reich, and David Gordon. Lexington, Mass.: D.C. Heath, 1975.

Studies by the Staff of the Cabinet Committee on Price Stability. Washington, D.C.: Government Printing Office, 1969.

Summers, H. B. "Control of Prices by the Trusts." In *The Trust and Economic Control*, by R. E. Curtis. New York: McGraw-Hill, 1931.

Sweezy, Paul. "Marx and the Proletariat." In *Modern Capitalism and Other Essays*, by P. Sweezy. New York: Monthly Review Press, 1972.

———. "Galbraith's Utopia." *The New York Review of Books*, November, 1973.

Tarbell, Ida. *The Life of Elbert H. Gary*. New York: Appleton, 1926.

Taylor, Frederick W. "Shop Management" in *Scientific Management*. New York: Harper and Row, 1947. [First published in 1903.]

———. "The Principles of Scientific Management" in *Scientific Management*. New York: Harper and Row, 1947. [First published in 1911.]

———. "Testimony Before the Special House Committee" in *Scientific Management*. New York: Harper and Row, 1947. [First published in 1912.]

———. *Scientific Management*. New York: Harper and Row, 1947.

Terkel, Studs. *Working*. New York: Random House, 1972.

Thompson, C. B. "Scientific Management in Practice." *Quarterly Journal of Economics*, February, 1915.

Thorp, W. L. *The Integration of Industrial Operation*. Washington, D.C.: U.S. Bureau of the Census Monograph III, Government Printing Office, 1924.

Trilateral Commission. *The Crisis of Democracy*. New York: New York University Press, 1975.

Urwick, Lyndall and Breck, E. F. L. *The Making of Scientific Management*. 3 vols. London: Management Publications Trust, 1945, 1946, 1948.

U.S. Bureau of Labor Statistics. *Welfare Work for Employees in Industrial Establishments in the United States*. Washington, D. C.: U.S. Government Printing Office, 1919.

———. *Handbook of Labor Statistics 1975*. Reference Edition. Washington, D.C.: U.S. Government Printing Office, 1975.

———. *Employment and Earnings*. Washington, D.C.: U.S. Government Printing Office, 1976.

U.S. Bureau of the Census. *Census of Manufactures: 1947*. Vol. II. Washington, D.C.: U.S. Government Printing Office, 1949.

———. *1950 Census of the United States*. "Special Reports: Occupation by Industry." Washington, D.C.: U.S. Government Printing Office, 1954.

———. *Historical Statistics of the United States: Colonial Times to 1957*. Washington, D.C.: U.S. Government Printing Office, 1959.

———. *1960 Census of the United States*. "Special Reports: Occupation by Industry." Washington, D.C.: U.S. Government Printing Office, 1963.

———. *Statistical Abstract of the United States, 1972*. Washington, D.C.: U.S. Government Printing Office, 1972.

———. *1970 Census of Population*. Subject Reports. "Occupational Characteristics." Washington, D.C.: U.S. Government Printing Office, 1973. [1973a].

———. *1970 Census of Population*. Subject Reports. "Low Income Areas in Large Cities." Washington, D.C.: U.S. Government Printing Office, 1973. [1973b].

———. *1970 Census of the United States*. "Special Reports: Occupation by Industry." Washington, D.C.: U.S. Government Printing Office, 1973. [1973c].

———. *Census of Manufactures, 1972, Concentration Ratios in Manufacturing*. Washington, D.C.: U.S. Government Printing Office, 1975. [1975a].

———. *Census of Manufactures, 1972, Subject Series, General Summary*. Washington, D.C.: U.S. Government Printing Office, 1975. [1975b].

———. *Current Population Reports*, Series P-60, No. 102, "Characteristics of the Population Below the Poverty Level: 1974." Washington, D.C.: U.S. Government Printing Office, 1976. [1976a].

———. *Statistical Abstract of the United States, 1975*. Washington, D.C.: U.S. Government Printing Office, 1976. [1976b].

———. *Current Population Reports*, Series P-60, "Money Income in 1975 of Families and Persons in the United States." Washington, D.C.: U.S. Government Printing Office, 1977.

———. *Enterprise Statistics*. Washington, D.C.: U.S. Government Printing Office, various years.

U.S. Census Office. *Twelfth Census of the United States*, Part I, "Manufactures." Washington, D.C.: U.S. Government Printing Office, 1902.

———. *Thirteenth Census of the United States* Vol. IV ("Occupations"). Washington, D.C.: U.S. Government Printing Office, 1912.

U. S. Department of Commerce. *Foreign Affiliate Financial Survey*. U. S. Government Printing Office, 1970.

U. S. Department of Labor. *Handbook of Labor Statistics, 1975 Reference Edition* (Bulletin 1865). Washington, D.C.: U.S. Government Printing Office, 1975. [1975a].

———. *1975 Handbook on Women Workers*. Washington, D.C.: U. S. Government Printing Office, 1975. [1975b].

U. S. Industrial Commission. *Final Report of the Industrial Commission*. Vol. XIX. Washington, D. C.: U. S. Government Printing Office, 1902.

U. S. Internal Revenue Service. *Source Book of Statistics of Income*. Washington, D. C.: U. S. Government Printing Office, various years.

U. S. President, *Employment and Training Report of the President*. Washington, D. C.: U. S. Government Printing Office, 1976.

———. *Economic Report of the President*. Washington, D. C.: U. S. Government Printing Office, 1977.

U. S. Senate, Committee on Labor and Education. *Investigation of the Strike in the Steel Industry*. 2 vols. 66th Congress, First session. Washington, D. C.: U. S. Government Printing Office, 1919.

———. Subcommittee on Antitrust and Monopoly. *Hearings on Economic Concentration*, Part 4. Washington, D. C.: U. S. Government Printing Office, 1965.

———. Subcommittee on Antitrust and Monopoly. *American Ground Transportation, A Proposal for Restructuring the Automobile, Truck, Bus, and Rail Industries* (by Bradford Snell). Washington, D. C.: U. S. Government Printing Office, 1974.

United States Steel Corporation. *Annual Report to the Stockholders*. Various dates.

———. Bureau of Safety, Relief, Sanitation, and Welfare. *Bulletin*. New York: various dates.

United States Strike Commission. *Report on the Chicago Strike of June-July, 1894*. Executive

Document of the U. S. Senate, 53rd Congress, Third session, No. 7. Washington, D. C.: U. S. Government Printing Office, 1895.

Vanderwicker, Peter. "What's Really Wrong at Chrysler." *Fortune,* May, 1975.

Vernon, Raymond. *Sovereignty at Bay: The Multinational Spread of United States Enterprises.* New York: Basic Books, 1971.

Wachtel, Howard. *The Inflationary Impact of Unemployment: Price Markups During Postwar Recessions, 1947–70.* Washington, D. C.: U. S. Congress, Joint Economic Committee, 1976.

Wachter, Michael. "Primary and Secondary Labor Markets: A Critique of the Dual Approach." *Brookings Papers on Economic Activity,* 1974.

Walker, Charles and Guest, Robert. *The Man on the Assembly Line.* Cambridge, Mass.: Harvard University Press, 1952.

———, and Turner, A. N. *The Foreman on the Assembly Line.* Cambridge, Mass.: Harvard University Press, 1956.

Ware, Caroline. *The Early New England Cotton Manufacture.* Boston: Houghton, Mifflin, Co., 1931.

Ware, Norman. *The Industrial Worker, 1840–1860.* Chicago: Quadrangle Books, 1964. (First published in 1924.)

Weber, Max. *From Max Weber: Essays in Sociology.* Translated and edited by H. H. Gerth and C. Wright Mills. New York: Oxford University Press, 1946.

Weinstein, James. *The Liberal Ideal in the Corporate State.* Boston: Beacon Press, 1968.

Weiss, L. W. "Econometric Studies of Industrial Organization." In *Frontiers of Quantitative Economics* by Michael D. Intriligator. Amsterdam: North-Holland Publishing House, 1971.

Weston, J. Fred and Mansinghka, Surenda. "Tests of Efficiency Performance of Conglomerate Firms." *Journal of Finance,* September, 1971.

White and Kemble. *Properties of the United States Steel Corporation.* New York: Dow, Jones & Company, 1903.

Wolf, Bernard. "Size and Profitability Among United States Manufacturing Firms: Multinational versus Primarily Domestic Firms." *Journal of Economics and Business,* Fall, 1975.

Work in America. Report of a Special Task Force to the Secretary of Health, Education, and Welfare. Cambridge, Mass.: MIT Press, 1972.

Wright, Erik. "Class Boundaries in Advanced Capitalist Societies." *New Left Review,* July-August, 1976.

Yanouzas, John. "A Comparative Study of Work Organization and Supervisory Behavior." *Human Organization,* Fall, 1964.

Zeitlin, Maurice. "Corporate Ownership and Control: The Large Corporation and the Capitalist Class." *American Journal of Sociology,* March, 1974.

Zwerdling, Daniel. *Democracy at Work.* Washington, D. C.: privately published, 1979.

INDEX